P9-CEY-977

RIGHT
FROM THE
START

RIGHT
FROM THE
START

Taking Charge in a New Leadership Role

Dan Ciampa
Michael Watkins

HARVARD BUSINESS SCHOOL PRESS
BOSTON, MASSACHUSETTS

Copyright © 1999 President and Fellows of Harvard College

All rights reserved

Printed in the United States of America
03 02   10 9 8 7 6

Library of Congress Cataloging-in-Publication Data
Ciampa, Dan.
Right from the start : taking charge in a new leadership role /
Dan Ciampa and Michael Watkins.
p.   cm.
Includes bibliographical references and index.
ISBN 0-87584-750-1 (alk. paper)
1. Management. 2. Leadership. 3. Executive ability.
I. Watkins, Michael, 1956- . II. Title.
HD57.7.C534   1999
658. 4'092—dc21   98-55292
CIP

The paper used in this publication meets the requirements of the
American National Standard for Permanence of Paper for Printed
Library Materials Z39.49-1984.

This book is dedicated by
Dan to Jim Richard
and by
Michael to Shawna and Aidan

Contents

Preface

Leadership is never easy. This is never truer than when a new leader enters an organization from the outside and must change its culture in fundamental ways. Regardless of how carefully one prepares for such a task, there are bound to be unexpected twists and turns in the road. The challenges are more formidable for those who have never led an organization but believe they are ready to make the move to the top. As confident as these new leaders may be, they (and those who hire them) cannot know in advance if they are ready to be the person of last resort. Tougher still are situations in which the new leader is hired as number two with the expectation of succeeding the incumbent CEO: here, the new leader must constantly balance the desire to prove herself and make the organization her own with the constraints of her position and the need to work with the leader she hopes to succeed. Transforming an organization, making a personal transition, and planning for succession are the core challenges of taking charge that we explore in this book.

That leadership is not easy is not news. The thriving industry built on studies of leadership has already produced many books and articles on the general leadership challenge of improving organizational performance and the organizational culture needed to sustain it. Before we began this project, we asked ourselves whether the world needed another book on leadership. After all, most books should be articles and most articles should be paragraphs. Readers of this book will be the ultimate judges of its usefulness. Even so, it might be useful to explain why we decided to write it.

First, we believe in the value of multiple perspectives on the complex task of improving a company's financial and operational performance to the point that its culture must change. While others have observed and studied this process, we came to believe that we have something unique to add: a rigorous, tested way to plan for such a transition—one that integrates strategic, tactical, political, and cultural approaches and that is grounded both in theory and in the practical experience of people who have faced this challenge.

Second, the stakes in top management transitions are very high for everyone concerned. For the new leader, failure could seriously derail a career. For the current CEO, failure could not only waste valuable time but also irreversibly damage his legacy; there is no greater satisfaction for a leader than to see the organization he has shaped and nurtured thrive after he leaves, and no more painful experience than to see it decline. For employees whose hopes and expectations are raised and whose livelihood and security hang in the balance, the effects of failure could be disastrous. This important phenomenon deserves to be analyzed from the point of view of the person who is tapped to change the way the organization works, referred to throughout this book as the "new leader."

Third, more and more new leaders will come into companies from the outside. Many will move directly into the number-one spot, but we believe there will be an increase in gradual, planned transitions in which new leaders hired by Boards of Directors and incumbent CEOs enter the number-two spot with the expectation of becoming the top leader. Not uncommon today, this pattern will become more common in the near future as leaders who grew up in the 1930s and 1940s continue to pass the baton to the generation who came of age in the 1960s and 1970s. In 1989, 18 percent of CEOs of the top 800 U.S. companies had come into their positions directly from the outside, and 12.8 percent had been with their companies five years or less before being named CEO. In 1997, these numbers had reached 24.1 percent and 14.8 percent respectively.[1] As we will see, many more new leaders accept the number-two position with the expectation of becoming CEO only to fail to reach that goal.

While readers in other leadership positions, and those who aspire to such positions, can benefit from the advice contained in this book, we have concentrated on senior executives who have made this particular transition. In writing this book, we drew on a combination of our own leadership experience, decades of consulting experience, and dozens of interviews. We have lived through leadership transitions and seen many people go through them. Some succeeded, some struggled more than they needed to, and some wish they could do it again and correct their mistakes. Through involvement, experience, and research, we have come to appreciate the difficulty of this sort of transition.

We interviewed and have worked directly with many senior executives who have been involved in leadership transitions and have drawn numerous illustrative quotes and stories directly from those interviews and experiences. As a condition of many of those interviews, however, we agreed not to identify the sources of quotes and not to use interviewees' real names. We believe that this approach permitted the leaders we interviewed to share their experiences, both successes and failures, with candor.

ACKNOWLEDGMENTS

Many people contributed to this book. First and foremost were the leaders who generously shared their insights in interviews: Kym Anthony (Executive Vice President/COO, First Marathon Securities), Jim Brown (President/CEO, Lincoln Institute of Land Policy), Nick Brown (President/COO, NAC Reinsurance Company), George Casey (President—South Florida Operations, Arvida/JMB

Partners), Frank Carlucci (Chairman, The Carlyle Group, and former U.S. Secretary of Defense), Dick Cavanaugh (President/CEO, The Conference Board), Toni Chayes (Board Member and Senior Advisor, Conflict Management Group), Andy Cross (CEO, Franklin Electronic Publishing Company), Jim Dagnon (Senior Vice President—People, The Boeing Company), Brian Dailey (Vice President for Strategic Development, Lockheed-Martin Corporation), Steve Gibson (President/CEO, The Colonial Group, Inc.), Daniel Goldin (Administrator, National Aeronautics and Space Administration), Brian Halla (Chairman/CEO, National Semiconductor Corporation), Steve Kaufman (Chairman and CEO, Arrow Electronics Corporation), Ed King (Deputy Chairman, McCarvill Corporation, and former Chairman, Western International Communications, Ltd.), Susan King (Leader in Residence, Sanford School of Public Policy, Duke University, and former President, Steuben Glass, Inc.), Greg Lee (Senior Vice President—Human Resources, Whirlpool Corporation), Ken Liebler (President/CEO, Liberty Financial Companies), Paul Liska (CFO, St. Paul Companies), Bob Martin (President, Institutional Products Division, Colgate-Palmolive), Tom Moore (President/CEO, Nelson Communications, Inc.), Joseph Nye (Dean, Kennedy School of Government), Roland Pample (former President, Apollo Computer, and former CEO, Bull HN), Andrall Pearson (Chairman/CEO, TriCon Global Restaurants, Inc.), Donella Rapier (Chief Financial Officer, Harvard Business School), Steve Reifenberg (Executive Director, Rockefeller Center for Latin American Studies, Harvard University), Ellen Richstone (former CFO, Augat, Inc.), Tom Ryan (President/CEO, CVS Corporation), Terry Scott, (Director, National Security Program, Kennedy School of Government), Fran Scricco (Executive Vice President/COO, Arrow Electronics Corporation), Henry Shelton (Chairman of the Joint Chiefs of Staff, U.S. Department of Defense), Lloyd Ward (President/COO, Maytag Corporation), John White (former Deputy Secretary of Defense), Robert Winters (former CEO, Prudential Life Insurance), and Frank Zarb (Chairman/CEO, National Association of Securities Dealers).

Then there are current and former colleagues and clients whose experiences have helped shape and test our ideas and whose stories are represented here: Joel Beck (Senior Vice President, EMC^2), Ed Bessey (former Vice Chairman, Pfizer Pharmaceuticals), Peter Daly (former Director, U.S. Bureau of Engraving and Printing), Robert Davis (Senior Vice President—Quality, NCR Corporation), Frank Faggiano (Vice President, Human Resources, Liberty Financial Companies), Hugh Farrington (Chairman/CEO, Hannaford Brothers), Ed Fogarty (former CEO, Tambrands), Wayne Fortune (President, Hutchinson Technology), Nigel Gray (President, Medical Technologies Group, Pfizer), Dave Harrington (CEO, Delta Rubber Company), Roger Howland (CEO, Eastern Tool & Stamping Company), Bob Joy (Senior Vice President, Human Resources, Colgate-Palmolive), Karen Katen (Executive Vice President, Pfizer Pharmaceuticals), Jim Kogan (President, Shure Brothers), Lou Lataif (Dean, Boston University School of Management, and former President, Ford Europe), Chris Letts (Executive Director, Hauser Center, Kennedy School of Government; former Vice President for Manufacturing, Cummins Engine; and Secretary of Transportation, State of Indiana), Mike Lorelli (former President, Pepsi East), Jerry Maurer (Senior Vice President, Human Resources, Seagate Technology), George Raymond (former CEO, Raymond Corporation), Doug Rock (President, Smith International), Harvey Rosenthal (former President, Melville Corporation), Gary Shultis (CEO, GDC International), Pete Simone (CEO, Xionics), and Tom Super (former Senior Vice President, Human Resources, Tambrands).

Others have served as sounding boards and provided invaluable encouragement and critique. For Dan, Bruce Henderson, Dave Berlew, Jeff Miller, Steve Rhinesmith, and Dick Beckhard stand out. His special thanks go to Alan Rush for constant intellectual companionship for almost thirty years, always available and always challenging. For Michael, Kim Clark, Peter Doeringer, Ron Heifetz, Marty Linsky, Mark Moore, Dan O'Brien, Howard Raiffa, Jim Sebenius, and Richard Walton helped to shape his thinking about leadership, negotiation, and organizational change. He would also like to express deep appreciation to Geri Augusto for many valuable conversations about organization culture.

We were fortunate to have the support of outstanding research assistants, including Charan Devereaux, Sarah Matthews, Usha

Thakrar, and Kim Winters, and the administrative support of Erin Murray. Valuable editorial guidance was provided by Theresa Pease. Working with our editor at HBS Press, Nikki Sabin, has been as pleasant as it has been rewarding. As copy editor, Ann Goodsell got everything right from the start.

The research for this book was supported by the Division of Research at the Harvard Business School. We very much appreciate the encouragement of Research Directors Teresa Amabile, Dwight Crane, and Mike Yoshino.

INTRODUCTION

Coming in from the outside poses unique challenges for new leaders. Consider the situation confronting Hugh, a newly hired President and Chief Operating Officer:

I got the call from Chet [the Chairman/CEO] at 3 o'clock on Saturday afternoon. He had been the most reticent during the interviews, but now he was excited. I got caught up in his enthusiasm, and we spent two hours talking about the possibilities [for dramatically improving company performance]. Saturday night at the cookout, all we talked about was my new job.

I woke up at 3:30 on Sunday morning anxious, but not knowing why. My heart was racing and I couldn't sleep. Not wanting to worry Elaine, I went downstairs, made coffee, and sat in the family room. After a walk around the block, I started to relax. By now it was 6:00. Sitting in the backyard, I began to understand what was going on. There was so much that I didn't know! Chet's call had just raised expectations. My selling job in the interview process was coming back to haunt me. There was so much that I didn't know, and it had nothing to do with the numbers or the history of how the company got to this spot. I didn't know how the place really worked, where the skeletons were, how deep the real problems were, who had influence. My past [successes] convinced the Board to give me the job . . . but what if they weren't enough to do what I needed to do to make it?

Hugh had good reason to be worried. He had committed himself to dramatically improving the performance of a large corporation with strong competitors. Because the company had been successful in the past and was not in a turnaround situation, most employees didn't recognize that profound changes were necessary to avoid a crisis. Hugh had the support of the CEO and the Board, but the hiring process had inflated their expectations. Because he was not the CEO, there were limits on the short-run changes he could make. But if he didn't make big changes that improved performance within two or three years, he probably would not succeed Chet. Aside from the Board and the CEO, no one had a personal stake in his success, and some powerful people might even have hoped he would fail. Hugh lacked the insider's detailed knowledge of the organization, its structure and systems, its politics and culture. He was unsure what was possible in his new company. When he had succeeded in the past, he had been thoroughly familiar with the organization and its problems, and able to rely on his functional marketing and sales expertise. Now he was one step from the top, with finance, operations, engineering, and a supplier division all reporting to him.

Hugh's situation was particularly complicated because, coming from the outside, he had to simultaneously manage a personal transition and lead an organizational transformation, in addition to managing his accession to the top job. Together, these elements of transition, transformation, and succession constitute a challenging scenario for a new corporate leader. Hugh might have had it easier if he had been an insider with a thorough knowledge of the organization, a power base, and a support system. His job might have been simpler if the organization had either been running perfectly or was recognizably in need of a turnaround. Finally, he would certainly have had more freedom to make early changes in strategy, structure, and key people if he were the CEO.

Another leader, recently appointed the new number two of a Fortune 500 company, put it this way:

> I've always been very fast on the trigger . . . but that wouldn't work here. I've done turnarounds before, but this is much more challenging. In other situations there was lots of low-hanging fruit, and everyone knew there wasn't any other option but to change. But here the problems are not that blatant. The situation is much more subtle. It requires walking a fine line. You have to figure out what's important and what's not, who the opinion-makers are, and whose support you need. You have to get people on your side and get them to want to change. Then you've got the Board and the investors on the other side, breathing down your neck, expecting results yesterday. I've had to keep my powder dry, and that's not been easy.

The mandate to these new leaders is to improve performance and then sustain the improvement, and doing so always requires changing the culture of the company. Further, these new leaders have come on board with the understanding that success will lead to their ascension to the number-one spot when the CEO retires within a few years. Leaders in this situation face a higher risk of failure than those who ascend through the ranks or those who arrive as likely successors but without the mandate of making fundamental changes.

The potential to fail is very high. A significant number of new leaders like Hugh fail by not being named CEO after all. Forty-seven percent of executives who were appointed president but not CEO of publicly traded U.S. corporations in 1993 had left their companies within the next four years without being named CEO. When we looked closely at the fates of those promoted from within and those hired from the outside, the differences

	Left the company	Promoted to a higher position	In the same position
Promoted from within	38%	46%	16%
Hired from the outside	64%	24%	12%
Total	47%	39%	14%

were revealing: insiders have a much better chance of being promoted to CEO.[1]

Leaving the company is not synonymous with failure, but the fact that nearly two-thirds of new presidents hired from the outside had left their companies within four years signals that it is important to investigate the dynamics of succession processes.[2]

New leaders coming in from the outside can significantly increase the likelihood of meeting these challenges by managing their transitions in an integrated and systematic way. In fact, doing so has a direct impact on whether they succeed in their new jobs. We will focus exclusively on how new leaders can manage the period between the onset of recruiting and the end of the first six months on the job, which we call the *transition period*. Gabarro (1987) found that new general managers tend to implement significant changes in three distinct waves over a two- to three-year period.[3] Based on this observation, he posed a model of the overall change process consisting of four stages:

1. *Taking Hold:* a period lasting up to six months that begins when the new manager enters the job and culminates in the initiation of the first major wave of change.

2. *Immersion:* a period lasting from five to eleven months during which the new leader continues to implement the first wave of changes, observes their impact, learns more deeply, and plans for the next wave.

3. *Reshaping:* a period lasting from three to six months when the second major wave of change takes place.

4. *Consolidation:* a period lasting from three to nine months when the new manager and his team observe the results and make the necessary adjustments in a third wave of change.

We examine the period that corresponds to Gabarro's taking-hold stage, but have broadened our scope to include the period between the commencement of recruiting and formal entry into the organization. This is precious time that the new leader can use to begin to learn about the organization, shape expectations, build relationships, and think about what must happen in the first few months following entry.

We chose to concentrate on the transition period because we have found that the actions experienced leaders take then have a disproportionate impact on their overall success or failure in the subsequent two or three years. Transitions are pivotal periods: organizational patterns can more easily be unfrozen and reshaped then, in part because change is expected to take place. New leaders are also most vulnerable during their transitions because they lack detailed knowledge of the organization and have no preexisting base of relationships to rely upon. Both the leader and other employees of the company are forming early impressions that powerfully shape subsequent expectations and actions, either expanding or constraining the new leader's scope for action.

Our intent is to offer prescriptive advice to new leaders in corporations (and to the CEOs and Boards who hire them) about how to take hold of their new organizations and surmount the challenges posed by transition, transformation, and succession. Helpful research has examined each of these areas, but little work has been done on managing the intertwined processes of taking charge and introducing large-scale change in a compressed time frame.[4] Nor has enough attention been paid to the challenge of political management, a necessary skill when the new leader lacks free rein to make early changes in strategy, structure, and key people, and must earn the right to transform the organization by building supportive coalitions.[5] When offering prescriptive advice, our intent is to articulate some basic principles that individual new leaders can then elaborate and shape to fit their own styles and circumstances.

This book offers several specific take-aways:

- A set of common traps new leaders fall into and ways to avoid them

- A framework for orienting oneself to a new situation by mapping the organization's strategy and assessing its technical capabilities, culture, and politics

- An integrated approach to creating momentum by securing early wins while building personal credibility and laying a foundation for deeper change

- Strategies for learning, developing a personal vision, and building political coalitions in support of change

- Guidelines on managing oneself, given the tensions that inevitably arise when transition, transformation, and succession are intertwined

This framework for taking charge was developed by working with new leaders and by synthesizing the insights of other leaders who had weathered such transitions in the past or were doing so when we spoke with them. It was also informed by the literature on organizational change, negotiation, leadership transition, and succession.

SOME GENERAL ADVICE

Several pieces of advice came up so consistently in our conversations with leaders that they merit presentation up front:

First, *take advantage of the transition period.* Having the chance to shape the company in your image means you are in it for the long haul. Use the precious time before and just after entry to learn about the organization and to think through how to create momentum. Most of the new leaders we studied believed themselves ready to lead their organizations from the day they arrived. Their confidence was one reason they were hired. But they all admitted wishing, once they were on board and some time had gone by, that they had been better prepared prior to joining. The transition period is a precious opportunity to ready yourself for what is to follow.

Second, *don't underestimate the importance of advice and counsel.* The complexity of the situation the new leader faces calls for finding the right balance of help. Hubris—the conviction that you have things in control and know what needs to be done—is one sure way to fail. Good advice and counsel help new leaders avoid pitfalls. The right network of advisors and counselors will take time to construct. If you are already in a senior position without a solid network, get to it! Make sure that those providing help are the best available, that they complement and balance each other, that their help will adapt to your changing needs over time, and that the appropriate effort is devoted to helping them help you.

Third, *show some empathy for the person you are succeeding.* We have approached this study of leadership from the point of view of the new leader. An equally legitimate point of view is that of the CEO who is letting go—which is as much an art as is taking charge. Many of those who are soon to retire face the painful reality of passing on to someone else a place they have put their mark upon. Letting go of such a substantial part of one's life can be far more emotionally intense than taking charge. Like seeing one's child marry or go off to war, leaving is a necessary part of life but it can also be among the most difficult.

Finally, *become a student of leadership.* Learn to look at the world with inquisitive eyes and from a leadership perspective. We are all leaders in some settings and followers in others. Our experiences as followers can help us become better leaders. Embedded in every newspaper article about the actions of managers, legislators, or heads of state is a story about leadership or its absence. Every sporting event is an opportunity to analyze a coach's performance. How effectively—or badly—do leaders communicate their messages? How do they try to influence? Do the leaders whose performance you observe have well-developed visions of where they want to take the city, the company, the nation? How could you do it better in their situations? Taking charge is an art. It is mastered by those who have prepared themselves through the hard work of constant observation, practice, experimentation, and refinement.

1

THE
CHALLENGE

Andy arrived at his office earlier than usual that fateful Monday morning. He had been president of his company for six months, but recently he had become increasingly frustrated. Eight months earlier the Board and the CEO/Chairman had chosen him to give their company a boost, and to take over when the CEO retired in three years. The company had stagnated, unable to keep up with more nimble competitors who had reduced prices while improving service. The company remained profitable, but it was losing share in a growing market.

The Board had considered inside candidates, but ultimately decided that new blood was essential. As the chairman of the Compensation Committee had put it to Andy, "We have to have someone in here who is going to shake this place up. It's gotten complacent, too satisfied. The people here have started to believe their own press and stopped being innovative. They're good people; they just need a leader. Ted [the Chairman and CEO] is a real good guy, and he knows the industry and everyone in it. He's very well respected in this company. He's all for this move, by the way. He wants to see these last few years of his career with his successor in place and the business growing again—that's what we need, Andy: growth!" He emphasized his point by slamming his hand on the dinner table so hard that the glasses teetered. "We have always been a company that pays dividends religiously. Every quarter. Our stockholders depend on it. Well, it looks like we're going to have trouble keeping that record going over the next year unless we get some growth and get it fast. That's your mandate, Andy: get this place growing again. We've done a lot of due diligence on you, and we've interviewed a few pretty good people, but we on the Board believe you're our man."

Then he went for the sale. "Andy, this situation is tailor-made for your skills. Strength in Sales and Marketing is what we need, and it's not an area we've excelled in. In your company now, there's some great Sales and Marketing talent you have to compete with . . . and a lot of them aren't that much older than you. It could be ten years before you become CEO. Now, you're probably wondering whether Ted will really give up control. Let me put it this way, Andy: what Ted really cares about is leaving behind a company that's growing. He wants the stock price up. He understands that the only way to do that is to grow the top line, and he knows he can't do it himself. Ted came up through Manufacturing and Engineering, and he knows that side of the business very well, but he doesn't have the skills to reposition this company in the marketplace. We need to get this place growing again. That's what we need and everyone on the Board knows it, including Ted."

Andy enjoyed the fast track. After business school, he had been a consultant before joining his former company, where he had quickly rotated through various departments and spent a year as an assistant to the CEO. After a few years in finance, he had moved to marketing. In his mid-forties, he had become senior vice president for Marketing, Business Development and Sales—the youngest senior vice president in the history of the company. It seemed that nothing could stop Andy from eventually becoming CEO. But that was the problem—eventually. The other SVPs in his company were in their early fifties and the CEO was in his late fifties. It could be years before Andy had a shot at the top. When it became clear that moving would enable him to be a president now and a CEO in three years, he knew he would take the job.

Andy wanted to be fresh and relaxed when he started work. He and his wife quickly found a house and got the kids enrolled in a new school. Andy spent plenty of time with them, knowing that he wouldn't be able to once he began his new job. The family even chartered a boat in the Caribbean while their new house was being remodeled. When Andy got back, he was ready to go.

Andy's first days on the job confirmed his initial impressions. The company was slow but basically solid, with good procedures, a strong financial system, and reasonably competent manufacturing and engineering people. Because the company had traditionally been strong in product development and manufacturing, he was surprised that the plants he toured seemed slower and had more inventory than he was used to. But he believed these problems would be solved by pumping up demand and getting product moving again.

Andy's strategy for growth was a classic one-two punch. First, he would reduce prices on the company's flagship product. He would energize the sales force by changing incentives, reorganizing to take out a layer of the structure, beefing up the sales information systems, and improving communications between Sales and Marketing. By pumping up demand, he would quickly win back some market share and grow the top line; but because of pricing and mix problems, he would have to sacrifice margin. Second, he would concentrate on the bottom line by accelerating the introduction of high-margin new products already in the pipeline. As these new products started to flow through the plant, costs would come down. In order for that to happen, of course, Engineering and Manufacturing would have to do their jobs.

Andy was pleased that he could lead with his strengths. The Board wanted a leader, and he had to get out in front of the troops and get them excited. Because he could concentrate on things he knew well, he anticipated that he could rapidly build momentum. Andy was convinced that the demand side was the place to start fulfilling his growth mandate, and that problems on the supply side would not be difficult to solve.

Ted offered to fill Andy in on the company's history and help him get to know key people in Manufacturing and Product Development. Andy was courteous, but he had his agenda. He really didn't care that some guy in Engineering had been around a long time: he was part of the old guard anyway. Andy knew what had to happen, and he just wanted Ted to be supportive. This was a once-great company that had to look forward, not back, and with the right leadership it would be dominant again. He had prepared his whole life for this chance, and now it was within his grasp.

Andy was gratified when his changes in the sales force quickly took hold. Orders steadily increased, and his decision to cut prices on the flagship product caught competitors flat-footed. But as demand increased, unexpected problems began to show up in Manufacturing. Work-in-process inventory built up at bottlenecks as the plants and distribution system strained to keep up. Engineering fell behind on the schedules for new product introductions. Andy had to go back over ground he had already covered on how Manufacturing should be operating and the importance of streamlining the product-development process. He believed he had explained the first time around in a way any reasonable, motivated person could understand.

Andy was working as hard as he could, and he sometimes thought he was the only person who really wanted the company to excel. Stress was building, and for the first time in his life Andy had trouble sleeping. He was often short-tempered.

Over the next two months, Andy became increasingly frustrated as manufacturing costs increased, shipments were late, and engineering schedules fell further behind. It became obvious that the Vice President of Manufacturing did not have what it took and had to be replaced. Andy spoke to the head of Manufacturing at his old company and knew he could get him to come. He asked the head of Human Resources to prepare an early-retirement package for the VP of Manufacturing and to begin the recruiting process. He also suggested a similar package for the head of Engineering.

A week later, the head of HR told Andy that Ted had blocked replacement of the VP of Manufacturing. Andy was shocked. He and Ted had spent little time together, but Ted had not objected to any other moves Andy had made. When Andy asked why he had balked at the change, Ted responded coolly that Andy should have consulted him and that the company's problems were complex and had to be handled carefully. When Andy countered that the head of HR supported his changes, Ted said he was not in favor and had told Ted that Andy had never asked for his opinion.

Now Andy was as angry as he was frustrated. The problems weren't that difficult to understand: the company was foundering because Ted had been too slow to move and more concerned about how people felt than about growing the business. Slowing down now, just because Ted wanted to be gentle, put Andy's plan in jeopardy.

After his meeting with Ted, Andy's anger turned to concern. What was going on here? Why did this happen? If Ted blocked a change like this, would he block others? Maybe he wasn't going to give up the reins after all. If Ted was going to second-guess Andy's decisions, the growth plan would be slowed and Andy would take the blame for lack of growth. If that happened, he would not win the support of the Board to become CEO. Andy could not waste time; he needed to make some decisive moves now. He arranged to meet with the chairman of the Compensation Committee, the second most powerful person on the Board next to Ted and the outside director with the most influence on him. Andy did not want a conflict with Ted, just someone to get Ted to back off so he could implement his plan.

Andy was reading his notes for the meeting when the phone rang. It was the chairman of the Compensation Committee. After saying good morning, Andy started to lay the groundwork. The Board member cut him off and said flatly, "Andy, we are not going to meet." Andy could feel himself flush. The chairman went on, "We've decided that this probably isn't the place for your skills, and that you should leave the company. Now we understand that we uprooted you, and of course we'll treat you fairly. You've worked very hard . . ." The receiver was still glued to Andy's ear, but the voice was drowned out by the pounding in his head.

ANATOMY OF FAILED POTENTIAL

So what happened here? Andy lost his job because he did not understand how to manage a leadership transition. He is a smart and talented guy who is accustomed to excelling. On paper, he was the perfect candidate for the job. His strategy was probably the correct one for this company. But being right did not lead to success. Why? We asked many of the leaders we interviewed to pinpoint the root causes of Andy's failure. Their answers can be summarized as follows:

First, Andy did not learn enough about the organization. He failed to use the time before entry to jump-start his transition. Once aboard, he did not learn enough about the politics and culture of the company. When he did focus on learning, he concentrated on areas he already knew well and assumed problems elsewhere could be resolved easily.

Second, he overemphasized action at the expense of understanding what it would take to make changes. He moved ahead with his agenda rather than combining what he believed to be important with what was important to Ted. In the process, he forgot who was the boss.

Third, Andy failed to motivate others, especially the senior managers in Manufacturing and Engineering, to abandon their comfortable habits and work patterns. He had a mission and a strategy, but not a compelling vision. Because he had not learned enough, he could not envision what the organization would look like once it was performing at a higher level. Without a personal vision, he had no hope of creating a shared one.

Fourth, he became isolated. Andy never built coalitions to support his efforts to transform the organization. He also misread existing coalitions, overvaluing his initial mandate from a key Board member and failing to build a constructive working relationship with Ted. Andy never recognized that he had more to gain from the relationship than did Ted. Most fatally, he misread what Ted cared most about. In the final analysis, treating respectfully those who had been loyal to him was more important to Ted than growing quickly—or Andy's success.

Finally, Andy did not manage himself well. His overconfident personality and lack of maturity caused him to make several bad judgments. A need to be seen as competent and in control blocked learning and prevented him from building supportive coalitions. His failure to manage stress, combined with his belief that his plan was correct, led him to blame others and kept him from recognizing warning signs or seeking advice.

THE CHALLENGES FACING A NEW LEADER

The challenges that Andy faced confront every new leader who arrives from the outside with a change mandate.

Whether successful or not, all the experienced leaders we spoke to agreed that their transitions into new companies as SVPs, EVPs, presidents, or chief operating officers were more difficult than anything they had experienced in their careers.

What are the key challenges they faced? The leaders we interviewed named five primary challenges.[1]

Acquiring needed knowledge quickly

A common refrain was "There was so much I didn't know." Even the best-prepared new leader cannot possibly know all she needs to in order to function effectively in a new organization. As one leader put it:

> You may think you know an area, and you've got people working for you who have been doing it for years and who really know it. But there's a level of detail below what you know, and a level of detail below that, and a level of detail below that. You're not going to be able to master all that all at once. So carefully picking some priority issues and mastering them, so you can go down at least a couple of levels fairly quickly, is important.

The new leader may lack critical knowledge in any or all of three domains—technical, cultural, or political.[2] As one leader said:

The company is never what you thought it was. It doesn't matter how many questions you've asked, doesn't matter whom you've talked to before you got there. It's just going to be different, just by the process of living there versus talking to people. The important thing is to be as open-minded as you can be when you get there and feed yourself as much information as you possibly can. You just get out and meet as many people as possible, spend time with them. You immerse yourself in information, and at the same time you're creating building blocks with people that you're going to need in order to deal with them over the next few years.

In the technical domain, the new leader may have to grapple with unfamiliar markets, technologies, processes, and systems. In the cultural domain, the company's norms, values, and behavioral expectations almost certainly differ from those of the new leader. Politically, the new leader must understand the "shadow organization"—the informal processes and alliances that exist in the shadow of the organization's formal structure and strongly influence how work actually gets done.[3] For the new leader, this political domain is both important and difficult to grasp, because it isn't visible to those who have not spent time in the company and because political land mines can easily cripple one's efforts to establish a solid base of support. Here's how one observer described the political reasons for a new leader's failure:

I knew someone who became the COO of a software company. He came from the Air Force, where he understood the hierarchy—who was above and who was below. But he didn't understand that there was this close relationship between the CEO and someone who had been the very close friend of his son who had died. And that person wanted to be COO but was not very capable. And this guy began to realize that that person was in cahoots with the chief financial officer, who also was close to the CEO. He was caught in a total squeeze and he had to leave within a year.

The learning curve must be climbed quickly. Expectations are high when a new leader arrives, especially one with a change mandate. This overlay of time pressure increases the likelihood of missing something and makes it more important to establish good working relationships.

Establishing new working relationships

New leaders typically leave well-established working and mentoring relationships to enter situations where they have neither. The impossibility of functioning effectively without this crucial "wiring" makes it important to establish productive working relationships and build credibility as soon as possible. These working relationships are essential for getting things done; they provide support as well as predictability. As one leader put it:

> The biggest problem in a transition is that you're from the outside and you don't have the relationships you need, especially at the middle level. You can't pick up the phone and talk to Charlie, who worked on a project [with you] ten years ago, and say, "Charlie, what the hell is really going on down there?"

When relationships with the CEO, key subordinates, and other members of the top team have to be built from scratch, early interactions are fraught with risks and opportunities. Even under the best of circumstances, it takes time to establish productive working relationships. The new leader will have met few of his peers and subordinates, and his knowledge of their expectations, hopes, and concerns will be based largely on the opinions of others. New leaders cannot fully control how they are perceived by the people who in large part will determine their success.

Juggling organizational and personal transitions

New leaders are brought in from the outside because a Board or CEO has concluded that change is needed quickly and that no one inside is able to do the job. Employees typically become aware of the change mandate shortly before or after the new leader's entry. Such timing raises expectations as well as anxieties. Those who respond "It's about time!" will look for the new leader to address quickly what they believe should be changed. Others who respond with a more cautious "We've seen these guys before. Let's wait to see if he's for real" will withhold support until the new leader wins it. Still others will be threatened by the arrival of an unknown person in such a powerful position ("No way!").

The new leader is likely to evoke all of these reactions, and is unlikely to know at first who is reacting how. Little if anything can be done to avoid this. The new leader may end up reacting to expectations during the first few months, rather than firmly establishing the prevailing tone and pace.

Nor is the new leader entirely in control of her own transition. If she is entering the number-two spot, the CEO can determine the schedule of her entry. Moreover, employees will not allow the leader to enter unobtrusively even if she wants to. New leaders were often disturbed by their lack of control. Here's how one new leader put it:

> You've got the uncertainty of your arrival and all that might mean for the governance of the organization. Then there's the uncertainty of your own impact on an interpersonal basis. There's also the uncertainty of never having been in a spot like this before. And so the challenge is to talk directly to those realities.

Managing expectations

The expectation-setting and expectation-managing processes begin when the search person first calls. Executive-search people are initially cautious because they do not want to waste time on an unpromising candidate. The candidate is also cautious, to avoid becoming distracted from current duties and appearing too eager. If both parties sense there is something to be gained by continuing, expectations inevitably rise. As each becomes more intrigued, determination also rises. The people conducting the search and eventually the Board and CEO want to hire a person who is right for the company. The candidate wants to be offered the position and to negotiate an attractive financial package. The result is growing expectations on both sides.

Employees' expectations are inevitably raised by informal scuttlebutt and by official announcements. The new leader has little control over either. All he can do, typically, is to try to comprehend the prevailing expectations and to deflate—carefully—those that are dangerously high while taking advantage of those that are useful.

Maintaining personal equilibrium

Some version of the first four challenges confronts all new leaders during their transitions. Handling them successfully often depends on maintaining emotional balance and exercising clear-headed judgment.

What does the new leader feel just after joining a new company? The people with whom we spoke described a rich mix of emotions, ranging from anticipation and excitement to disorientation. The physical demands of the transition are high. The new leader logs many hectic hours traveling to field sites and attending meetings, only to face a bulging briefcase when she returns home at night. The emotional demands are also extreme: alongside the challenges at work, the usual rhythms of home life are disrupted, and spouses, friends, and children are coping with their own transitions. As one leader put it:

> The first time, I felt like the proverbial person who was thrown into the swimming pool and told "Swim or drown." In those days I used to work extraordinary hours. I'd come into the office at 6:30 or 7:00 in the morning and go home at 11:00 at night, and I was still barely coping. But I just had an enormous amount to learn, since it was totally new. Nobody ever sat down and taught me how to make a transition. My approach was [derived] from experience: the first time was the time I learned how to do it. So going into a senior leadership position was a lot easier the second time around. I knew what to look for and how to do it.

A clear head can provide a substantial edge, given the amount of knowledge most leaders need to amass about new products, technical skills, distribution practices, and customer-service capabilities. Likewise, emotional balance maximizes one's capacity to assess the culture, recognize existing coalitions, and develop productive working relationships.

New leaders should explicitly prepare for the emotional impact of transition and develop mechanisms for preserving equanimity:

> You need to think through what the demands will be personally as well as on your family. You need to make sure you're willing to step up to that. No one wants a leader who feels like "I'd rather be somewhere else." And so you think, "What will I have to do? What will be the impact of all that on my lifestyle, on our marriage, on the children, on the quality of time we can spend together?"

Another leader described her practical preparations:

> I focused on putting other parts of my life on automatic, knowing I was going to have to send messages about discipline and work ethic and everything else. I found a laundry service. I did a lot of personal things. Even paid bills in advance. It was like I was going away to war.

COMMON TRAPS FOR THE NEW LEADER

One important step in self-management is recognizing, rather than denying, the strong and potentially disruptive emotions involved in transition. A second aspect of self-management is watching for and controlling certain personal traits, such as a high need for control or a low tolerance for ambiguity, that can increase one's susceptibility to falling into some common traps.

All of our experienced leaders described having gotten caught up in negative feedback loops—vicious circles—in which seemingly sensible actions triggered negative reactions, resulting in downward spirals that sapped their energy and wasted valuable time.

Falling behind the learning curve

Not using the time before entry effectively can undermine one's ability to learn and to get on top of the job right away.[4] One leader pointed out: "There is a strong tendency to put off getting to the job until the last minute, because you're trying to organize personal affairs or trying to tidy up at the old location." It is tempting to use the interval between leaving an old job and starting a new one to take some time off or to get one's family settled in a new location. But the time prior to entry is a priceless period when the new leader can absorb information about the organization and begin to plan. Upon formally entering the new organization, the new leader inevitably gets swept up in day-to-day demands and has little time to do background research.

Using the time prior to entry to begin identifying and analyzing the issues increases the probability of getting a running start on learning what must be learned, developing a compelling vision, and ensuring the political support necessary to realize it. Never again will the leader have such ample uninterrupted time to focus and prepare, as one explains:

> A lot of people I've seen moving up want to start the job as soon as possible. My attitude is always that I want to start the job as late as possible, because that maximizes my chance to get ready. Talking with people [before formal entry] sends a signal about commitment and interest. You're not yet in the chair, and people open up tremendously because somehow they think, "He's not my boss yet, so I can talk."

Becoming isolated

It's easy for new leaders to isolate themselves, which is dangerous because important relationships and sources of information about what is really going on don't get developed. As one leader noted:

> The number-one trap is to be invisible. When someone new comes in who's running the organization, people say, "I want to see him. I want to touch him." And if the person instead goes into a corner office and closes the door, then people react with a very immediate sense of disappointment—and then skepticism that they have any understanding of what the organization stands for and is really trying to do.

Another leader highlighted the danger of having a small group of close associates that excludes other points of view:

> New leaders get in trouble by isolating themselves, creating a little coterie of advisors that nobody can penetrate—not relating down sufficiently, just totally operating in a vacuum.

New leaders typically fall into this trap when they focus too narrowly on financial and other quantitative measures to assess the organization. Annual reports and analysts' assessments are often the only sources of information available during the recruiting process, and candidates understandably plumb them for insight into the state of the organization. After entry, more detailed operating reports are an obvious place to focus attention. Such reports do reveal a lot, but overreliance on them can lead to an incomplete picture of what makes the company tick. For a new arrival from the outside, these reports are most valuable as pointers to the people with a more nuanced understanding of the story behind them. Impressions, ideas, or strong feelings about how to deal with the issues are often more important in making crucial early decisions than are financial analyses. As one leader said:

> There's lots of data to be absorbed. There's lots of paper to look at. And there's a pressing urgency to come up with a plan, so there can be a tendency to say, "Well, I'll lock myself in the room and I'll come up with the plan." That is important, but you're not going to lay the groundwork to be able to execute, to speak with authority and execute with authority, until people feel like they know you.

Coming in with the answer

Another common trap is to show up with a single answer—to assume that a universal fix can address complex and varied organizational problems. Some new leaders rely too much on technical solutions, such as new technologies, changes to organizational structure, or manipulation of the measurement and reward systems. Others rely on motivating employees, either through one-on-

one contact or in large group sessions. The point of both approaches is to change the organization's culture in ways that will support higher performance. But cultural change requires altering power balances, norms, and habits that people will cling to stubbornly. There are no quick-fix solutions, and for a new leader to suggest that there are will only undermine the potential for building support:

> I've seen a lot of people get in trouble by coming in and saying, "I've got the answer. I've looked at it, I've studied it, I figured it out." But you really don't know how it works, and resistance builds. I think it's a huge cause of either suboptimal performance or derailment. There's a strong relationship between the amount of time you invest in orientation and assimilation and your long-term success.

New leaders fall into this trap out of arrogance or insecurity, or because they believe they must appear decisive and establish a directive tone. If the new leader is seen as dealing superficially with deep problems, the resulting cynicism makes it difficult to rally support for change. Showing up with the answer also blocks the new leader's learning, because employees may hesitate to share information if they believe the new leader already has a made-up mind.

Sticking with the existing team too long

New leaders, especially those with a collegial style, often believe the subordinates they inherit deserve a chance to prove themselves. For some, this is a matter of fairness; others are motivated by arrogance ("I can make these people change better than my predecessor did") or hubris ("All it takes is hard work, listening, giving them support, and just plain leadership"). Whatever the rationale, keeping team members with a history of mediocre performance seldom works. As one leader said: "A classic mistake is simply to not make any personnel changes at all during the honeymoon period, to keep the same people, not develop your own team, let things go on as they are." The new leader has been brought in to improve performance by importing new ideas, making tough decisions, and instilling a can-do spirit of achievement. What she usually finds is a group of direct reports who are not sufficiently able or flexible to embrace change.

The new leader will not be held responsible for an inherited team's performance during the transition period, but after that its performance is very much her problem. Aside from accountability, sticking with direct reports who are not up to the task will squander precious time and energy. She need not be unfair, expect miracles, or fire people precipitously. The point is that the new leader must set a time limit for deciding who should be on the playing field. Most leaders suggested a limit of six to twelve months, depending on the company's financial condition.

Attempting too much

Some new leaders try too many things at once. One rationale appears to be faith in the law of averages: "If I get enough things going, something is bound to click." They also are trying to convey that winners are active, quick, and able to handle diverse challenges simultaneously. The trap, however, is that the organization is confused and overwhelmed, rather than spurred into action. Priorities can become unclear, and the leader may appear to have attention-deficit disorder. One leader observed: "Some [new leaders] want to change everything, perhaps because they want to put their stamp on the organization. And so they try to do too much and throw out the baby with the bathwater."

It is important for the new leader to experiment with different approaches, to discover what works and what doesn't. But too much experimentation can mean that promising change initiatives receive insufficient resources or lack the attention they need to reach fruition. The roots of this trap sometimes lie in poor prioritizing or up-front planning, allowing the leader to be diverted by peripheral issues.

Being captured by the wrong people

It is inevitable that those who have exerted influence in the old regime will jockey for position in the new. Because many people seek to influence him, it is all too easy for the new leader to devote

time to people who cannot help because they are incapable, outdated, or actually wish to mislead. As one of our leaders pointed
out: "A lot of people want to try to influence the new guy, and they
express opinions or ideas or thoughts. And people are watching.
So you have to be very careful." Another noted that new leaders
are particularly at risk if they have come from a different industry:
"A classic trap is to get captured by the bureaucracy. Because when
you come into a new environment, especially in an industry where
you may not be used to the language and the discipline, you have
to rely on the people who are in place—but the bureaucracy in
place was most likely a big part of the problem."

The new leader must make careful decisions about whom to listen to and how much to listen. If one's internal advisors represent a
narrow constituency, have skewed or limited information, or use
their proximity to the leader to advance partisan agendas, other
people who should be listened to may inadvertently be alienated.
Or their input may simply be overlooked. One leader recalled:

> I found things I agreed to in the first three to six weeks were things
> I always regretted later on. Folks came in to try to score some quick
> points on other folks . . . and that's the normal game-playing. You
> know: "Let's get him to kill this cow before he realizes it's a sacred
> one." You've got to watch out that you aren't fiddling with the vital
> organs of the organization.

Just as one is known by the company one keeps, so, too, are judgments made about new leaders based on perceptions of who influences them.

Leaders promoted from within often find that continued reliance on their previous advisors risks signaling that others' input
is less valued and that loyalty counts more than balanced information. Similarly, a leader coming in from the outside should take
pains to keep lines of communication open and to balance internal
influences carefully.

Falling prey to successor syndrome

Many leaders we spoke to had struggled with "successor syndrome." At greatest risk is the new leader hired as second-in-com-

mand with the expectation that success will lead to promotion to the top position. Successor syndrome goes something like this: The new leader enters the organization believing that the CEO wants significant change. This point has been emphasized by the Board and the executive-search consultants who did the recruiting, and in conversations with the CEO. As the new leader begins to press for change, however, the CEO begins to withhold support, or appears to. Because the relationship is not fully developed, neither acknowledges the growing problem. Initially cordial relationships become progressively more strained. The CEO voices concern to trusted aides and then becomes critical of the new leader. Eventually factions form, to the point that the new leader and the CEO are competing for loyalty. The new leader's ability to implement needed change and meet the expectations of the Board is compromised, and the whole company loses. Here are two leaders' observations about successor syndrome:

> It can create serious problems if the new person arrives and gives the impression he was sent there to fix a lot of things that were wrong, and—as soon as this old guy is out of the way—he is going to make some big changes. It gets communicated in body language and what he says or does during the transition period. That can be very, very dysfunctional. I think that is best described as jumping the gun in some way. It's more a matter of perception than it is an actuality. In other words, you can come in with a list of things you have been told must be done. The Board of Directors has given you some orders, but how you approach that during the transition is very important. Because I think you can put the organization through some real trauma.

> You can't regard [the CEO] as a guy that you get together with every few months and tell him something brief about what you're doing. You've got to have him involved if he's going to be an ongoing factor. That's a big lesson for people, I think: not to take your predecessor for granted.

The CEO may experience the new leader's efforts as implicit criticism or a threat to his legacy. He may also find it unexpectedly difficult to let go of the reins of power. Alternatively, he may simply be exhibiting caution or fostering a slower pace, rather than withholding support. Whatever the cause, the successor is in a difficult position. On the one hand, he must push hard for substantial change or things will not improve in the time frame he has been given. On the other hand, the harder he presses, the more difficult it will be to build a healthy relationship with the CEO.

MEETING THE CHALLENGE: SEVEN FUNDAMENTAL PROPOSITIONS

We have distilled seven key principles for managing leadership transitions from the experiences of people who have personally come in from the outside to successfully transform organizations. These fundamental propositions, and the three core tasks we will explore in later chapters, constitute the pillars of our framework for effectively managing a transition.

1. *A new leader has two to three years to make measurable progress in changing the culture and improving financial performance.*

New leaders tend to plan and execute organizational change in two- to three-year time frames, which we call *eras*. The transition period (from the onset of recruiting through the end of the first six months) marks the beginning of the new leader's first era in the organization. The length of the first era ranged from 24 to 36 months for the new leaders with whom we spoke. The CEOs and Board members we talked to cited the need to judge the new leader's capabilities carefully because of the importance of the decision. One explained: "When we [on the Board] make a choice like this, it has to be the right one. There isn't any margin for error here." Another concurred: "It would be pretty embarrassing for us and bad for the company if we blew [this decision]." If the new leader didn't make substantial progress within two years, the Board and investors, as well as some employees, began to lose patience.

At the other extreme, roughly 36 months was the maximum time that new leaders would wait before moving into the top job. A representative comment was: "I couldn't leave behind what I had [at my former company] without a time deadline. The Board and [CEO] had already decided he was going to retire thirty months after I joined. We all had that end point in mind. If it had been much longer, I don't think I would have come."

While this two- to three-year time frame was dictated by the situations our new leaders faced, it also took them at least that long to understand the capabilities of their new companies, see substantive changes in performance, and make inroads into the organization's culture. As one leader put it: "I think you can get real change in a culture in two to three years but not before that, because most of the cultural changes you have to make require changes in people. It takes you a while to learn what needs to be changed and then to get new people, even if they're people already in the organization."

To accomplish substantial change in two to three years, the new leader must start moving quickly. This means that the interval before entry, as well as the first months after officially joining, must be used well. By not managing the transition period wisely, the new leader could be disadvantaged and, like Andy, fail.

2. On arrival, the new leader should already understand the organization's current strategy and associated goals and challenges, and should have formed hypotheses about its operating priorities. During the first six months, these hypotheses must be tested and either validated or changed.

As we have suggested, it is costly to waste time prior to entry. The transition begins the minute the search person calls, not when the new leader formally joins the organization. Anticipating the day-to-day demands of the job, the wise new leader jump-starts the learning process. This pre-entry period provides precious uninterrupted time to assess the organization and begin to formulate hypotheses about what needs to be done. When the new leader first sits in the chair, he should already understand as much as possible about the organization's strategy and its strengths and weaknesses and should have formulated some hypotheses to begin testing. One leader asserted:

> You need to understand the organization you're going into—how it's laid out, what the vision of the current leader is, and what [your predecessor] was trying to accomplish. What are the goals and tasks that already have been laid out for the organization? How do they tie in with what you think are your boss's priorities? You start to form a mental picture before you go in—an understanding of how they're operating, and, in many cases, why they're operating the way they are. I think it's important to know if there are any really tough issues you're going to have to deal with early on.

We refer to the interval from initial recruiting contact to the first day on the job as the *fuzzy front end*, a term borrowed from new-product development in high-tech manufacturing.[5] For purposes of defining a project and tracking its costs, the starting point is typically the naming of a product-development team. But much has already taken place, including thinking time, conversations, experimenting, creating prototypes, and writing proposals. This front-end period is "fuzzy" in the sense that it is not measured, but it is a step that must be taken into account to understand what it takes to develop new products successfully. Just as a successful product-development process is built on what occurs during the fuzzy front end, so is the new leader's successful transition founded on the ability to leverage the important period before entry.

3. New leaders must balance an intense, single-minded focus on a few vital priorities with flexibility about when and how they are implemented.

During the transition period, the new leader ought to select the vital few priorities—what we call *A-items*—for the remainder of the era. As one leader recalled: "I wanted to come on fairly strong and impart a lot of energy. The great danger was of flying off in all directions and not setting priorities. One key thing I had to do was ask myself what my strategic priorities were." A-items are key objectives that serve as the basis for a road map tailored to the situation and the leader. They also generate milestones to track progress.

Focus must be carefully balanced, however, with flexibility. New leaders capable enough to be hired as future CEOs are justifiably confident about their abilities to define objectives and establish priorities. But they must often master two essential supporting tasks they are less good at. The first is to understand the technical and cultural capacity of the organization to grasp and act on the priority objectives. This capacity is almost always more limited than the new leader expects. If people in the organization were good at reading warning signs and changing quickly when necessary, a new leader would probably not have been brought in from the outside. It is unrealistic to expect people to "get it" just because the new leader declares that change is necessary or presents a logical analysis. An effective new leader must be prepared to postpone actions that at first seem urgent until employees grasp the need for them.

The new leader must also be prepared to modify A-item priorities as circumstances warrant, the second supporting task. One leader described the importance of being flexible:

> If you are a running back and you see a hole in the line, run through it. If the play says you're supposed to go off-tackle, and there is no place to go off-tackle, you just say, "I'll get three yards between the guard and the center." But if you suddenly see that there is a wide-open hole over by the end, you don't say, "That's not in the play book." If you have a mechanical sense of priorities, you fail to take into account that the world may change or opportunities may open up. Then you're missing something.

Adjustment may take the form of elaborating priority objectives or of rethinking the relative urgency of priorities. Doing so often increases the clarity of the issues and what to do about them. As one leader put it:

> My [A-item priorities] were on target, and they were clear in my own mind, but it wasn't until I got to see all of our customers and all of our suppliers that I could really express them forcefully. They came alive for me, and I think had more credibility to the folks here.

4. *Within the first six months, the new leader must make key decisions about the "organizational architecture" of people, structure, and systems. Most crucially, the new leader must decide whether the composition of the inherited team is appropriate, and whether the organizational structure must change.*

To extend the product-development analogy, the relationship between the new leader's first six months on the job and the rest of the two- to three-year era is analogous to the relationship between investment in early design work on the product and the number of problems that emerge when the product is put into production. Getting the new-product architecture (marketing plans and infrastructure, suppliers, production space, inventory targets, sales training, and so forth) correct early on reduces the number of problems, and therefore costs, encountered later—a multiplier effect.[6]

For a new leader, the key architectural elements are the top team, the organizational structure, and core management processes. If these elements are not quickly brought into alignment with each other and made to fit the leader's style, making progress will be an uphill battle. Specifically, after six months, the people a new leader has inherited become her team to a much greater degree. As one leader explained: "You inherit what you got from day one, but after about six months you have bought into everything that's still going on. Regardless of whether it's good, bad, or ugly, you have now bought in."

The new leaders we interviewed universally agreed that it is best to decide who should be replaced, and prepare to replace them, within the first six months. If a change of top managers should be made, it is much easier to do so in the first year before close relationships develop. During the same interval, the new leader also needs to decide whether the organizational structure and key management processes are appropriate for what must be accomplished.

5. *By the end of the first six months, the new leader must also have built some personal credibility and momentum. Early wins are crucial, as is beginning to lay a foundation for sustained improvements in performance.*

Getting the architecture right is necessary but not sufficient for success. By the end of the transition period, the new leader must also have built personal credibility and begun to create some momentum—promoting the perception that the organization is moving in promising directions.[7] To build personal credibility, the new leader must begin to establish productive working relationships with the CEO, with subordinates, and with other direct reports to the CEO, while making a positive impression on the broader base of employees.

Early wins energize people and focus attention on needed change. Momentum will not get created without one or two dramatic improvements in areas important to the company. At the same time, the new leader must figure out how to lay the foundation for sustained momentum beyond the transition period. One leader said:

> [A new leader] has got to do something in the first six months to build momentum, because people just can't see it's going to take five to seven years. They've got to see results every step of the way, and I think the first six months is about the right time frame. If you can't get some things moving in six months, you're a dead duck.

To do otherwise is to risk achieving some temporary success only to watch the organization return to its old ways of operating. The objective is to create a portfolio of change initiatives with short-term payoffs to provide initial boost and longer-term payoffs to provide sustained thrust.

6. *The new leader must earn the right to transform the organization. The initial mandate from the Board and CEO is never sufficient, nor will it remain static. It must be diligently and regularly reassessed. The new leader must also work actively to build coalitions supportive of change.*

As one leader commented: "When I read about executives who come in with a mandate to turn the company around, and nine months later they are gone, my own reaction to that is: I wonder if those guys understood what the real problems were when they came in, and I wonder if they took what they came in with and verified that was what was really going on."

The problem with initial mandates is usually not that people are being dishonest during the hiring process. Essentially, it is that recruiting is a selling-and-influencing process, an intricate mating dance. The person performing the executive search, the Board, and the CEO are all trying to influence the favored candidate to say yes; a candidate who wants the job is in turn trying to impress them enough to be offered an attractive financial package.

There is also much that the parties simply don't know. The Board's outside members are bound to be influential in choosing a probable successor, but—however close they may be to the CEO, the stockholders, and the investors—they are observers of the organization and therefore not expert in what it takes to change it. Second, the CEO who is preparing to retire is about to experience unfamiliar emotions. He may unexpectedly experience difficulty letting go. Watching someone else change an organization one has created, or at least called home for years, can be a wrenching emotional experience. His reaction cannot be predicted while a successor is being recruited months or years before retirement.

Third, the new leader's mandate must be carried out in part by employees who were not involved in its definition. The right to lead the organization must be earned from key subordinates and from the broader organization. When the new leader is in the number-two position, gaining acceptance for big changes can be an even more formidable challenge. Some skepticism is inevitable as the new leader enters the spotlight, where every move will be analyzed and judged. The main qualities necessary for the new leader to win loyalty are clarity about where she intends to take the organization, and credibility and consistency over time while leading it in those directions.

7. There is no single best way to manage a leadership transition. New leaders' approaches will inevitably be shaped by the situations they face, their prior experience, and their leadership styles.

Nothing in our research leads us to believe that there is a single best way to manage leadership transitions while transforming the organization. New leaders' approaches vary because of differences in their situations and differences in their experiences and leader-ship styles. Said one leader: "I think there are a lot of different ways of doing these kinds of jobs, and people should do them in their own natural ways. If [your natural way] doesn't work, then you're not the right leader for the job. But changing your style won't do it. By the time we get to these positions, we've learned too much—be it good or bad—to change what we are."

While changing one's leadership style may not be appropriate, new leaders must understand their own styles and their own strengths and weaknesses. Self-understanding allows the new leader to build a personal support system that helps augment the strengths and compensate for the weaknesses. As another leader cautioned: "It's important to understand who you are and what you do. And also it's very important to understand what you don't do well and where you need help and what your weaknesses are."

CORE TASKS

The seven propositions we have just examined are primary guide-lines for new leaders that emerged from our interviews. Success in putting these principles into action during the transition requires, in turn, that the new leader concentrate on three core tasks:

1. **Creating momentum:** rapidly getting employees moving so that their energy is targeted in the most profitable ways and they be-come confident that they can succeed

2. **Mastering the enabling technologies of learning, visioning, and coalition building:** learning in order to engage in informed vi-sioning, which promotes supportive coalitions, in turn leading to more and better learning

3. **Managing oneself:** exercising clear-headed judgment, staying on the "rested edge," and avoiding the "ragged edge"

Task one: creating momentum

By the end of the first six months on the job, new leaders must have begun to create momentum. Generating enthusiasm for change will help propel the organization through the remainder of the era. Failure could leave the leader, like Sisyphus, rolling a boulder uphill.

Over and above using the time before entry and the first six months to create momentum, leaders who succeed at building an early base for sustained improvement pay close attention to at least three interlocking elements: (1) finding a way to solve certain vexing problems that have hindered the company's progress; (2) laying a foundation for deeper cultural change; and (3) building credibility with bosses, subordinates, employees, and the Board.

Task two: mastering the enabling technologies of learning, visioning, and coalition building

Success in creating momentum rests on effectiveness in learning, visioning, and coalition building. Learning is important because so much is unknown when the leader first arrives. Visioning is important because forming a clear image of the transformed organization will greatly increase the likelihood of its being realized. Coalition building is important because of the need to build a base of support rapidly.

Task three: managing oneself

Finally, the new leader must exercise clear-headed judgment, stay focused, and maintain emotional evenness. Knowing and managing oneself is as important as knowing and managing the organization. The new leader must understand the strengths and limitations of her own style and work to build a personal support system.

Figure 1-1 depicts schematically the tasks, challenges, resources, and personal qualities that feed into the process of taking charge, to be explored in the rest of the book. Part I will examine momentum-creating processes. Part II will look at what we call the enabling technologies, which equip the leader to build a foundation for sustained improvement: learning, visioning, and coalition building. Part III explores self-analysis and the creation of effective networks of advice and counsel.

FIGURE 1-1 FRAMEWORK FOR TAKING CHARGE

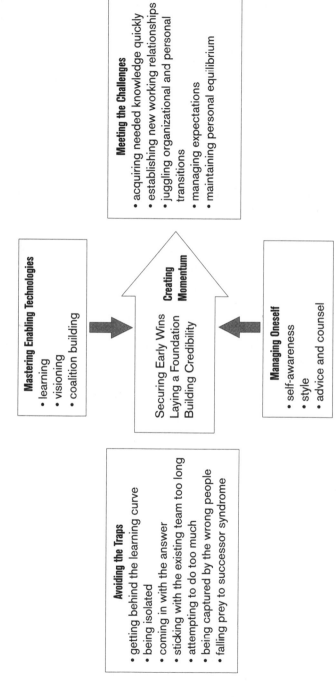

Meeting the Challenges
- acquiring needed knowledge quickly
- establishing new working relationships
- juggling organizational and personal transitions
- managing expectations
- maintaining personal equilibrium

Mastering Enabling Technologies
- learning
- visioning
- coalition building

Creating Momentum

Securing Early Wins
Laying a Foundation
Building Credibility

Managing Oneself
- self-awareness
- style
- advice and counsel

Avoiding the Traps
- getting behind the learning curve
- being isolated
- coming in with the answer
- sticking with the existing team too long
- attempting to do too much
- being captured by the wrong people
- falling prey to successor syndrome

Part I

CREATING MOMENTUM

A new leader invariably arrives at her new position as an accomplished manager. She and those who hired her are confident of success, but she has been chosen for a task that she has never faced before. If, as was the case with the company Andy joined, the business had a history of financial success, few employees have recognized the need for change. But those who selected the new leader realize that, unless something is done, the company will enter a period of decline. The level of performance required calls for fundamental changes, not merely new skills or more sophisticated information technology. The new leader has to implement better models for running the business to achieve breakthrough improvements in speed, quality, and costs. These sorts of changes in turn require new processes and ways of operating. More fundamentally, they require changes in the culture of the organization—the norms, habits, beliefs, and rules that govern how people approach their jobs.

The most important initial task facing the new leader is to create momentum during the transition period. She typically has a window of two or three years to achieve substantial improvements in performance. If she can establish herself and move the organization in promising directions by the end of her first six months, she will have created a base that will make it much more likely that the remainder of her era in the organization will be a success. If she fails to create enough momentum by the end of the transition period, she will face an uphill battle.

To establish oneself and create momentum in a new organization in just six or so months is a substantial challenge. The new leader has experience and the Board on her side, but she is just one person with relatively little knowledge of the culture of the company and no established power base. She must rapidly find ways to leverage her own skills and to concentrate employees' talents on the most important changes that must take place. Doing so requires capturing and channeling their energies. In other words, the new leader must create momentum despite significant constraints. Because she is not the CEO, she will not be able in the short run to change the strategy, structure, or key players in fundamental ways. She must work in an unfamiliar culture and political milieu. At the same time, she must proceed in ways that are consistent with her personal leadership style, leveraging its strengths and compensating for its weaknesses.

When the leaders we interviewed were asked what it takes to create momentum during the transition period, they consistently emphasized three strategies. The first is to secure early wins by addressing vexing problems the organization has not been able to solve. The second is to lay a foundation for deeper change by beginning to establish political and cultural bases necessary beyond the transition period. The third is to build credibility with employees and the CEO. Our own observations suggest a fourth strategy: that new leaders must orient themselves effectively by mapping the organization's existing strategy and assessing its technical capabilities, culture, and politics.

Chapters 2 through 5 examine these four undertakings separately, but in practice they are intertwined in the overarching process of creating momentum during the transition period. Early efforts to map the landscape, for instance, contribute both to securing early wins and to laying a foundation for sustained improvement. Similarly, the process of building personal credibility enhances efforts to learn and plan and is in turn fed by them.

2

SECURING
EARLY
WINS

In the first six months, the new leader must energize people and focus them on solving the most important problems of the business. It's crucial that employees perceive momentum building during the transition. Seeing tangible improvements in how work is performed boosts motivation and encourages further experimentation. As one leader explained:

> You have to get some victories so people will feel good about themselves. The initial goals you set are short-terms goals. If you achieve them, make a big deal of them. It feeds on itself. Then you make more goals. As time goes by, the goals begin to broaden, but by then it's not so damaging. And so people begin to think of themselves as winners. It's extraordinarily important.

Early wins call for identifying substantial problems that can be tackled quickly, and whose solutions will result in tangible operational and financial (not just behavioral/attitudinal) improvements in performance. Examples include bottlenecks that limit productivity and incentive systems that undermine performance by creating internal conflict. By contrast, team-building or improving the effectiveness of meetings may contribute to the business, but do not qualify as early wins.

How early wins are achieved is also important. Beyond producing tangible results, early wins should create models of behavior consistent with the new leader's vision of how the organization should function. This means carefully designing and overseeing the processes used to secure early wins: involving the right people, defining stretch goals, marshaling resources, setting deadlines, pushing for results, and then rewarding success. The ultimate goal is a virtuous circle that progresses from modest initial improvements to more fundamental change in a rising tide that reinforces desired behaviors.

Early on, new leaders must target a *center of gravity* for their change efforts, a pivotal decision about where they are going to take their initial shots.[1] But figuring out where to focus is not easy for a couple of reasons. First, choices about where to seek early wins have to be consistent with the new leader's broader priorities and with what he hopes to achieve in his first era. This means that identifying the center of gravity must be part of a larger process of era planning. And the new leader's ability to identify the right center of gravity and create a good era management plan rests on his ability to learn about the organization rapidly yet thoroughly. Learning, planning, and action are inextricably linked during the transition.

EARLY WINS AND ERA PLANNING

A well-executed era plan helps a new leader to identify opportunities for early wins and to lay a foundation for more fundamental change. In other words, the era planning process helps the new leader launch the rocket while laying the groundwork for a later second-stage boost into orbit.

Characteristics of effective era planning

Experienced new leaders manage their transitions and transform their organizations in remarkably similar ways. Four shared elements stand out: prioritization, leverage, measurement, and specificity.

Prioritization. The new leaders we interviewed were relentless in prioritizing and focusing their efforts. They quickly developed a compact set of objectives, which they used to focus attention—their own and that of their organizations. The special difficulties that new leaders face in setting priorities were a constant refrain. One leader likened the challenge of staying focused to being eaten by the alligators while you're trying to drain the swamp. "Without a solid transition plan," another said, "you run the risk of being captured by the flow of events. Suddenly you're concentrating on what's a crisis, not what's really important. You haven't thought through where you want to go, and so it becomes very difficult."
Another leader cautioned:

> Some people think the answer is to read everything that is put in their in-box—and that's a trap because that's the way you lose your priorities. How are you going to keep your own priorities and not be a captive of your in-box? That's not easy to do, because the pace is so quick and there are so many demands on your time. It's very hard to maintain your priorities.

Leverage. Effective new leaders avoided early challenges that carried the risk of failure. Instead, they concentrated on areas—centers of gravity—where they were likely to make progress and to leverage their scarce time and knowledge. They sought out broad operational areas and processes where early effort could result in quick and substantial improvement in performance.

Measurement. They also established frameworks for measuring progress. Some leaders used the formal measurement system in their new companies to judge progress, while others created more informal and personal baselines. Some were careful to document progress regularly—one even carried around a chart of indicators for six months and insisted his top team do the same—while others preferred more visceral assessments. But regardless of their methods, these leaders used markers and milestones to track how far they had come.

Specificity. Finally, new leaders demanded from themselves and their subordinates a high level of specificity about the steps to be taken and the sequence in which they would occur. Some, preferring to set out with a map that they could modify as they gained experience, constructed fairly detailed plans within the first four to six weeks. Others chose an overall direction, but postponed specificity. Later on, typically after three or four months, they drove for specificity and precision in defining steps and sequence. Said one:

> Without a doubt, the thing that surprised me most was that the ways [necessary] to get things done evolved over the first six months or so. I came in here pretty clear on the key things [that had to be done] because the Board and [the CEO] were very clear with me . . . They had done their homework and they knew what they wanted. I'm a pretty confident person, and I was hired here because of what I had accomplished at [two other corporations]. But I came to realize that at this level [in the company] and with the culture here, what worked before and how I got things done were not necessarily the answers here. I had to work hard to learn what would work here and what would not work. I guess every place is different even though the problems are often the same.

A framework for era planning

People who are chosen to run businesses are usually capable planners and often accomplished strategic thinkers as well. They have their own methods of planning that have worked well in the past. So why spend time here on a framework for planning the new leader's first era?

Most senior executives are adept at forming plans to grow market share or reduce operating costs, but few have experience planning to change the culture of an organization. The transition period is the best time to construct a plan for improving performance, but it is also when the new leader has the most to learn. While managing a personal transition, the new leader must also assume control of an ongoing enterprise and begin to change its culture. As one leader put it: "I am very confident in my planning and strategizing abilities. These have always been strengths for me. But when I came in here, it was like I was in a maze for a while, because there were some very big things I had to have a plan for . . . and most of them had to be done simultaneously." Although certain useful principles and frameworks apply to any sort of plan, changing the culture of an organization requires a particular kind of diagnosis and the ability to dislodge deeply ingrained habits and norms.

By the time a new leader is settled in a new job, has a routine, and can rely on staff aides and a structure of groups, information, and management, he will have pieced together a support system that enhances his strengths and compensates for his weaknesses. But at the beginning of his first era such complementary support has yet to be built, and the new leader is largely alone in thinking through the initial plan. A planning framework geared specifically to the needs of the new leader can thus provide useful guidelines to support what is essentially a solitary undertaking.

Although by no means the only way to go about era planning, the framework that follows has proven useful to many new leaders. Like any framework, it is only a starting point—a tool to help the new leader move forward in potentially fruitful ways. As such, it must be adapted to each individual's unique circumstances and personal style. This planning framework consists of four interconnected activities: (1) identifying a center of gravity, (2) establishing A-item priorities, (3) initiating pilot projects to secure early wins, and (4) forming a personal vision.

These activities do not represent a linear series; instead, they overlap in an evolving process of learning and planning. Identification of a center of gravity helps the new leader to articulate his priorities. Similarly, the learning that occurs in pilot projects helps him to secure early wins as well as to clarify a personal vision.

Taken as a whole, the process systematizes the new leader's efforts to prioritize, leverage scarce time and knowledge, measure progress, and drive for specificity. The planning process lays the groundwork for creating a vision. Until that vision can be articulated, the era-planning framework provides a map and compass with which to navigate through the transition and beyond.

Identifying a center of gravity. Selecting an explicit center of gravity, or COG, helps the new leader articulate priorities. To identify a suitable center of gravity, the new leader should concentrate on major operational areas or processes—such as the new product-development process or the distribution system—whose improvement can have a disproportionate impact on overall operational or financial performance. COGs can be equated with the major systems of the human body (such as the central nervous system, the cardiovascular system, and the muscular-skeletal system), in which a problem results in generalized underperformance and improvement substantially enhances overall well-being.

By identifying an appropriate center of gravity and initiating changes within it, a new leader can minimize the time and energy necessary to achieve tangible results that benefit the larger organization. Substantial and noticeable improvement in a COG helps the new leader earn the right to pursue more extensive change. As one leader put it, "It has to be something that's relevant, it has to be something that would be seen as important, and it has to be something that symbolizes what you're trying to do."

It is usually unwise to attempt to bring about changes in more than one COG during the transition period. The potential for getting more early wins is more than outweighed by the risk of spreading oneself too thin. The act of committing oneself to making things happen in one center of gravity also has a wonderful way of focusing the mind. Concentrating on a particular operational area and mastering it not only contributes to early wins, but also provides a knowledge base that can be drawn upon throughout the era. In the words of one new leader:

> I wasn't an engineering or manufacturing expert in any sense of the
> word when I came here, but because of [our early programs] I be-

came identified with Operations and learned a lot about it. I brought marketing and leadership points of view to it rather than a technical one, and we made changes through the years that have made us number one. There are probably a lot of people who believe I came out of that area.

Establishing A-item priorities. Leaders are more likely to succeed if they define, articulate, and progressively elaborate overarching objectives for their eras. Defining the new leader's major objectives for the first two- or three-year period helps clarify the goals of the transition period by putting them in the context of the era as a whole. Near-term actions thus serve double duty by helping the new leader secure early wins while advancing longer-term objectives. Many of the people we spoke with stressed the importance of identifying and communicating a few overarching priorities for their first eras. One leader said: "The most important thing [to create momentum] is being clear early on as to your goals, and why they are your goals, and articulating them over and over again."

In addition to communicating her own priorities, well-chosen A-items crystallize the new leader's understanding of what it will take to meet the performance expectations of the Board and the CEO and to realize the company's strategy. A-item priorities should be neither too general nor too specific, offering clear direction but allowing flexibility as the new leader learns. As one leader put it:

What I found was that if I stayed in the middle [between general themes and specific goals], I could best manage the short term and also keep one eye on where I wanted to end up. At least for me, it's important to do this for two reasons. One is motivational: it has always worked for me to get people excited by laying out objectives for two to three years rather than only pushing on short-term, here-and-now goals or always talking about something that is so far away it's hard to visualize it. The other reason is that this sort of thing [changing the fortunes of a company] is best done by moving in phases you're able to handle and control, where the conditions the business operates under stay more or less the same.

A-items tend to address several levels of specificity. Some define performance objectives in the selected center of gravity, both by the end of the transition period and by the end of the era. An example might be halving the time it takes to get new products from concept to customer. Others, necessarily less explicit, will concern establishment of a solid political base and a foundation for changes in strategy, structure, people, and culture. Defining A-items is by nature somewhat iterative; it is a process of stating, testing, refining, and restating. The new leader may arrive with a good idea of what his priorities will be, but they will almost certainly be modified and clarified as he learns more.

Initiating pilot projects. Pilot projects are specific initiatives within the center of gravity aimed at securing early wins. If, for example, the center of gravity is the new product-development process, an A-item priority might be halving the time from concept to customer by the era's end. If the process of launching new products has customarily created waste and bottlenecks in the plants, the new leader might launch a pilot project to improve the handoff from R&D to Operations.

One new leader concentrated on reducing manufacturing set-up times (the time it takes to reset or prepare production equipment to make a new model or part). Dramatic reductions in set-up times would eliminate a major bottleneck for an important product backordered by several large (and unhappy) customers. He had also discovered during his first month that the same problem plagued many other product lines at the company's main plant, and that response times were problematic across the company. His stints at a Japanese manufacturing company and at a U.S.–based pioneer in flexible manufacturing techniques convinced him that set-up times in this particular operation could be reduced by at least 75 percent without any capital expenditure. He also believed that, with the right people working at the right intensity, a reduction of this magnitude was possible within ninety days. Success would in turn enable him to launch similar efforts elsewhere in the plant.

Within four months the team assigned to this initiative had exceeded the target, achieving almost a 90-percent reduction in downtime. The positive outcomes reverberated:

First, it showed people that they could get dramatic results by operating in a different way, and could do it fast. Second, it set a tone that created a buzz throughout the plant. I made a big deal of celebrating the win, and the people in the team got a lot of good press. Other people on other [production] lines wanted to try it out and get their share of the limelight. The third thing, which was more important in the longer run, was that it got people to understand that time could be a powerful weapon, and it got us started on the road to speed and flexibility in all we do.

Pilot projects' implementation plans should define the standards to be applied, the resources needed, and the methodology to be employed. They should specify short-term tangible goals (such as reduction in time or costs) and less tangible ones (improving cooperation and communication, for example). In addition, they can play a more strategic role if structured to encourage the sort of behavior that should become common throughout the organization. Improvement will be measured both by early wins and by the models of behavior that are created for the future. To be successful, a new leader's pilot projects must meet the following criteria:

☐ They must be perceived as *important*. Issues of customer service, quality, and efficiency are good candidates. For instance, they could target problems that have caused tension with customers, such as a slow, unpredictable logistics process, or an administrative system at headquarters that delays approval for needed new equipment.

☐ They must have the potential to make *dramatic operational improvements* by attacking old problems with new techniques. Slight gains will not be substantial enough to grab people's attention. The improvement must also address operational and financial performance. Merely toning up some skills is not dramatic enough.

☐ The target has to be *achievable* with available resources within a brief time. A dramatic, attention-getting gain that takes more than a few months is not an early win.

☐ Pilot projects should serve as a *model* of the kind of behavior that will be the norm when the organization runs as it should. Early wins can thus provide concrete illustrations of the new leader's vision for the organization. Such a model also permits employees to try out new behaviors in a safe, experimental way.

☐ The pilots' success should *enhance the standing* of the new leader. He need not be front and center, but those who are in the spotlight should acknowledge the new leader as the primary visionary and catalyst. Comments such as "He never took credit, but it wouldn't have happened if he hadn't gotten it started, provided us with air cover, and stuck with us when the going got tough" generate respect, trust, and high expectations for the new leader.

Forming a personal vision. The new leader's efforts to identify a center of gravity, establish A-item priorities, and initiate pilot projects contribute to her ongoing efforts to form a personal vision of what the company will become. They allow her to better define how the organization will work once problems have been solved. A personal vision is a compelling image of what the new leader will see when the organization is working as it should, and it serves as the guiding star for the leader to follow throughout her era. The process of creating a personal vision and preparing to make it a shared one is part of laying a foundation for deeper change. It is discussed in more detail in Chapters 3 and 7.

LEARNING AND PLANNING

Era planning can't be pursued in a vacuum: new leaders have to plan in order to learn and learn in order to plan.[2] An effective plan for transforming the organization calls for assessing the strategy and capabilities of the organization the new leader seeks to transform. A frame of reference is necessary to develop an era plan, which means understanding what others before him have sought to achieve, the strategies and plans they put into place, and why they did so. He must also understand the capabilities of the company's people and their capacity for change. One leader noted that to come in from outside calls for becoming something of a historian:

> Where did this place come from? Why is it what it is? Who did what to make it what it is? Is it a high-cost organization that is used to being that? Why? Who did that? It didn't just happen—someone caused that attitude. How long ago? Are his people still here, and are they acting the same way? What about the people? Where did we get them? Are they the best in the industry or just like everyone else? Where did the stars come from? What happened to the ones who used to be the stars who aren't here anymore? Why did they leave?

Another leader recommended canvassing the organization to gain different perspectives:

> In the assimilation phase, I spend an awful lot of time learning the business. I focus on learning the long-term strategy, the immediate business plans, the business issues and challenges that we're faced with, the competitive set, the whole financial structure from the balance sheet to the income statement. I spend a lot of time with Finance people, understanding just essentially how we account for things.

The link between learning and planning endows the process of preparing an era plan with as much importance as the contents of the plan itself. Quick mastery of the environment speeds the ability to prioritize and be specific, which in turn helps the new leader achieve substantial early successes. To paraphrase Dwight D. Eisenhower, plans are nothing but planning is everything.[3] The learning process begins during the fuzzy front end with a broad assessment of the company's strategy and performance. Early in the post-entry phase, this learning should enable the new leader to identify a center of gravity that is crucial to overall performance and in need of improvement. Having identified the COG, the new leader must assess the capabilities of the organization in order to determine where in the COG to focus, who should be enlisted, and how to engage them. Simultaneously, he can begin to outline

A-item priorities—the broad objectives that will be his targets of effort over the next two to three years.

Learning continues as the new leader further pinpoints areas in the COG where pilot projects will result in early wins and models of desired behavior. Settling on these areas allows the new leader to begin to develop and disseminate measures and improvement goals that will jump-start the change process. Meanwhile, the learning and planning undertaken to define pilot projects helps the new leader begin shaping a personal vision for the organization.

The resulting process, illustrated in Figure 2-1, consists of overlapping steps: learning leads to planning, which in turn requires further learning to equip the new leader to develop more detailed plans. The net effect is that the new leader is better able to prioritize, measure, and specify a pathway to a successful first era.

Pete's Experience

The overlapping processes of learning and planning that help secure early wins usually begin early in the recruitment process. They pick up speed during the fuzzy front end as the new leader becomes more familiar with the company and come into full flower immediately following entry. This progression is well il-

FIGURE 2-1 LEARNING AND PLANNING

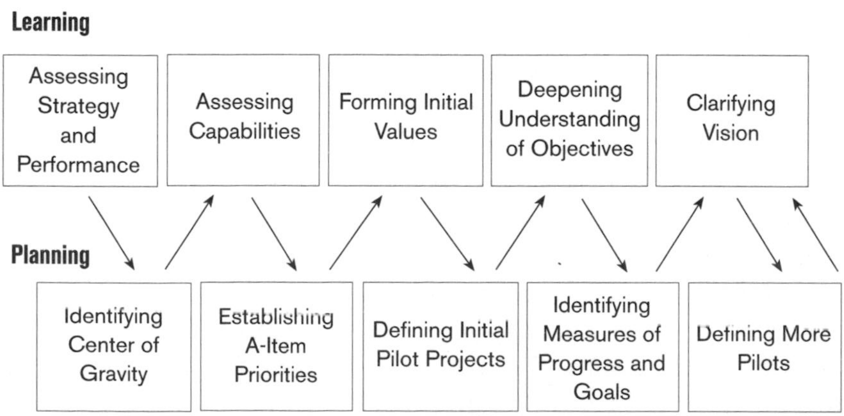

Learning

Assessing Strategy and Performance	Assessing Capabilities	Forming Initial Values	Deepening Understanding of Objectives	Clarifying Vision

Planning

Identifying Center of Gravity	Establishing A-Item Priorities	Defining Initial Pilot Projects	Identifying Measures of Progress and Goals	Defining More Pilots

lustrated in the experience of Pete, the new president of a consumer products company:

> During my interviews the same couple of things kept coming up from the Board, [the CEO], and the headhunter. Even though they put it in different ways, they all said that we had to figure out how to deal with a rapidly changing distribution system. Our customers were consolidating in this country for their own economic reasons, and our business in Europe [40% of the company's volume] was changing because of movement to a common [European] currency and more [pan-European] regulations that affected how we made our products as well as how we shipped them.
>
> With all this, what I kept thinking about was efficiency and speed. Our distribution costs were much higher than the best-in-class, and that said to me that we weren't efficient. And if that was the case, there were bound to be a lot of non–value-added steps that slowed things down. Distribution costs had to come down and we had to get a lot faster and streamlined. There wasn't, according to what I heard, very much awareness [in this company] of these changes—or at least of how they were going to impact us.
>
> The second big thing that seemed to come out was that, with all this change in our markets, we had to learn how to deal with our customers in a very different way. Take the U.S. There were the signs of major realignment as customers we had had for years were being bought or were merging. That created a handful of larger customers where there [had been] many. And it meant that we had to be prepared to not only sell to different people but also come up with a different way to price our products, because these fewer, bigger customers were going to squeeze us on price. With all this, there was also the [emergence of] buying groups of the smaller customers, who were trying to stay independent but get some leverage at the same time. What all this said to me was that we were entering a new chapter where we had to look at and deal with our customers differently. I wasn't quite sure how, at the time, but the evidence mounted pretty quickly the more I learned.

Based on his assessment during the fuzzy front end, Pete hypothesized that he had to work on the separate but related issues of streamlining distribution and dealing differently with customers. There were other problems, but he suspected that these two challenges were by far the most important. If other problems were solved but these two weren't, sustainable and profitable growth—as well as success for Pete himself—would be much more difficult to achieve. He concluded that he had to verify these hypotheses as soon as possible after officially joining the new company. During his first three months, he studied the industry, talked to the employees most knowledgeable about customers and the marketplace in general, and, in particular, visited customers. By the end of his first ninety days, he had decided that the center of gravity was the distribution system and that the A-items related to it should head his priority list. Pete then began to formulate more specific objectives. Here's how he described it:

> I had a general plan for making progress on these two things, but that was in the abstract, before I really got to know this place and knew enough to be sure they were the things I should focus on. I set out to see what [the capacity] of this company was, and because I didn't have the luxury of a lot of time, I had to do that at the same time that I was verifying that [my A-items] were the right ones. I sort of bounced back and forth from answering whether or not it was right to focus on distribution and customers and, at the same time, what had to be changed here so that we could improve in both areas. I found myself always having two agendas as I was trying to judge [our] ability to change . . . What I mean by that is that it was common for me to be in a meeting of [my staff], or even speaking at a sales meeting or a product launch, thinking on the one hand about what I had to get done there, but at the same time asking myself if these were the people that could pull off some sort of step-level improvement, or if this report we were going over about our market share or back orders was the right one [and contained the right information] for the market that we were up against.

I also kept going back to the strategic plan that had been done. It was pretty good at first blush. But the more I probed, the more suspicious I got. [For example], when I traced the broad objectives from the strategic plan to what specific plans were in the annual operating budgets, I discovered there wasn't much of a connection. Then I went over the notes from management committee meetings [held] over the past year and found that . . . the top people had done [no work] on what the strategy said. Everything seemed to be reacting to what was important at the time. The plan was okay on paper, but it evidently had never been translated to the day-to day actions and numbers of the business. I finally decided that the strategic plan didn't really highlight any one part of the business to take the lead over the next few years. Every [part] was supposed to get better, but it seemed that there just wasn't an area that you could really get your arms around that could provide an overriding purpose.

Well, after a few months I had to get off the fence, and I figured I had seen enough to start making some choices. There was no question that they were the most important ones for our success over the next few years, and that the strategic plan had some good ideas, but it wasn't a document that was alive and that guided day to-day decisions. I decided that if I could make real progress in the way we got our products into the field and to the customer's receiving dock, a lot of the problems we faced in other areas could be solved too. Getting the customer more in our face could force product development to speed up—and manufacturing bottlenecks would stand out too. Maybe, by focusing us on this part of our business, improvements in other parts could be easier.

It also became clear, the more I delved into it, that [some of] the people here just were not up to the challenge. The perspective of the people I had inherited was just not broad enough, or up-to-date. Our customers had changed their thinking about suppliers, but we hadn't changed our ideas about how to work for them. I decided that there were four things that had to change. First, I had to change some senior people. We had a couple of senior Sales people who were nearing retirement, and one guy who ran Distribution who just hadn't performed well. But we had no early-retirement package, and the performance reviews done on this head of Distribution were not very complete, and there just wasn't the documentation I needed. It was also clear that there wasn't enough teamwork between the parts of the company. Each function head was king of his area, and most people had moved up inside the function, so there wasn't much awareness of the other areas. So I knew that I had to make some changes. And once I had made them, and replaced these people [with others better equipped for the task], I knew I would have to find a way for the top group to operate more as a team and less like a collection of people each running their own silos.

Another priority was our information systems. I was very frustrated that our systems could never get me the level of detail I needed or that I was used to. When I came here, there were different opinions about our exact market share by product and by region, and each was backed up by some report. There were too many opinions because there was too much data and not enough information. We also had not gone as far as we should have at automating the sales force. I found out from my customer visits that [our major competitor's] salesmen could find out the buying history of customers and were linked into their warehouses to get up-to-the-minute [information on] inventories, while some of our people didn't even have laptops and the ones who did weren't on any central database. This lack of leadership in IT really put us at a disadvantage in the marketplace. But the IT people we had were good—it wasn't really their fault. We were just underresourced there. I knew that fixing this would take a long time and be very expensive, so I had to decide fast which way to go.

The third priority turned out to be getting everyone here lined up behind the customer. There was no evidence that our manufacturing people were aware of our customers, and if some were, it sure didn't translate back to fast, flexible production. Our IT people weren't focused on our customers. Even Human Resources didn't know what our customers were demanding . . . [That showed up] when I saw the way they were recruiting mid-level people. The criteria they were using for making a judgment of who to bring in for interviews, and the advice they were giving about the ones to make an offer to, didn't make much sense when you put them up against what our customers were demanding from us. This was a big internal marketing challenge, and it was probably the most difficult one to pull off, looking back on it, because our culture here was so strong. And we hadn't made a practice of bringing in people from the outside, so new ideas from the outside were limited too. If that didn't change, we were always going to be behind our competitors.

The [fourth] priority was of course the distribution system itself. The other things [the first three priorities] were necessary to make something new work in getting the product to our customer . . . What I had to do was find a way to come up with that new system that actually got it there.

After deciding that the center of gravity was the distribution system, Pete defined his A-items on two levels: efficiency and speed in getting products to customers, and learning how to deal with customers who were changing the rules for their suppliers. At the next level, he decided to build a new top management team, revamp information technology and the systems it provided the business, promote a company-wide focus on the customer, and design and implement a new distribution system. Then he made decisions about how to measure success in each area. Having worked hard over the years on his visioning capabilities, Pete approached this task by asking himself what he would see and hear and what would be tangibly different if each area of the company were functioning optimally. He imagined that he could wave a wand and have the perfect situation for each A-item, and then tried to describe what perfection would look like and how people would behave:

I took a whole weekend and sat down and just wrote on each priority. I listed the characteristics of the ideal people I'd hire if I could find them—what sort of backgrounds they would have and what they'd bring to us. I even thought through what top-team meetings would be like with the right people there. I also listed the things that the ideal IT system would give us, and how it would make our decisions better and faster. On the customer side, I tried to imagine what evidence I'd see if we were really customer-focused: what would happen differently in management meetings, how our new product development projects would change, and what would happen differently when I'd go out into the field. The distribution system design priority was a bit easier, because I knew we had too many warehouses and that the product traveled too long a way to get to the customer. The best distribution system was more direct and much less complicated. I had a better idea of what the new distribution system should look like than I did about how to create it.

I went as far as I could this one weekend, and it wasn't complete, but I was on the way to figuring out how, specifically, these four areas would look if each were humming along at a world-class level.

Pete spent the next several weeks verifying his assessments by talking to the CEO, a few outside advisors, and his CFO, who was quickly becoming a trusted advisor. He also talked to the presidents of two of his largest customers about how they had transformed their own organizations. Both offered help with core capabilities they had upgraded in their own companies: one would provide IT help, and the other would help reduce time in the distribution system. These conversations enabled Pete to add a partnering element to the measure of his customer-focus A-item. He also looked into outsourcing some IT, and found three companies where his IT manager could conduct benchmark visits.

The lesson of Pete's story is that he systematically moved down an analytical funnel of learning and planning in order to secure some early wins and define priorities for his era. He developed hypotheses early and then tested them, using what he learned to form his plan. Within his first six months, Pete had largely clarified the steps he had to take. His planning was influenced by his discussions with the Board and the CEO about their perceptions of major threats and by his assessments of company strategy, the adequacy of company systems, and the capability of the people to change. These discussions were also the steps that most influenced his eventual vision of what the company had to become.

GUIDELINES FOR EARLY WINS

As we have seen, a good era-management plan should not only establish broad priorities to be achieved by the end of a 24- to 36-month era but also highlight an area of the business where concentrated action will have a substantial positive impact by the end of the first six months. Success in leading this effort should help the new leader become firmly established and recognized as offering unique value to the company. Success should also help create a virtuous circle leading to additional successes that move the company forward toward its strategic objectives and realization of the new leader's vision.

We have also seen the importance of learning in order to plan and planning in order to learn. The new leader should focus early learning efforts on mapping the organization's strategy and assessing its technical, cultural, and political capabilities in order to identify locations for early wins. The remainder of this chapter offers guidelines for moving further down this path.

Maintain your own style

The way Pete managed his transition to leadership mirrors his style. Pete is careful, systematic, and logical, and he prefers to reach his own conclusions before involving others. But there are additional ways to get early wins. Another leader, John, provides one example.

John's Experience

The company that John joined had launched an extensive information system makeover several months before. The project had been initiated with great fanfare and high expectations (unrealistic expectations, in John's opinion), and one group of consultants had been replaced for not driving the project assertively enough. John believed the line managers should have been responsible. As he learned more about this initiative, it became a case study of the organization's strengths and weaknesses.

John found that most of the people involved considered the budget inadequate; some predicted that the actual cost of completing the system would be two or three times the highest official estimate. He also began to worry that the new technical consulting experts brought in to manage the system transition were unskilled at preparing the company culture for such a change. Although concerned, he was reluctant to sound an alarm until he knew more.

John decided to learn more by taking advantage of his new company's practice of designating senior managers as project sponsors. Each project's steering committee could designate two or three senior executives as sponsors. A sponsor is not the senior person in charge of the project, nor is the sponsor accountable for its success. Instead, the sponsor's role is to act as a guide and sounding board, and to ensure the involvement of leaders whose departments would be internal customers or primary stakeholders and who could offer advice on project strategy and budget requests.

By taking advantage of this practice, John learned about the company's technical shortcomings in a safer and quicker way that he otherwise could have—safer because his role was supportive and not evaluative, and quicker because his role as a sponsor gave him more open access to both managers and technical staff. The insights John gained from conversations and sponsor meetings, and in particular from informal discussions, would not have been possible had he not chosen to be a sponsor. As John reported:

[Being a sponsor] gave me some benefits I didn't realize at first that went beyond just being able to influence this project. For one thing, I found out more about our technical capability from sponsor meetings and informal discussions that would not have happened if I wasn't a sponsor . . . [For example], it was very interesting to me that, in a project team review with the steering committee, people would agree on something—but then the same people would decide something very different on the same question the next week, when they had their functional hat on in one of my staff meetings. The net effect of this was that I got a snapshot of this place [that pinpointed some areas] I had to figure out how to upgrade later on when I knew more.

In addition to grist for future action when his knowledge and political bases became firmer, this project enabled John to have immediate impact:

The consultants that [had been] hired were very good technically, but they really didn't have a clue when it came to getting people involved or coaching them. We were behind in our IT capability and we didn't have a good infrastructure at all. . . [The consultants] were very helpful there, but the problem was that their style caused our people to get so ticked off at them that they were not benefiting from the knowledge [the consultants] had. Meetings weren't set up very well, training materials weren't very polished, there were lectures when there should have been discussions, and the worst part was that they really didn't understand our culture and how we did things here, so something they'd say or how they'd operate might have worked fine in some companies but here it was causing problems on the style side of things that really jeopardized this [project]. And because this was the second group of consultants we'd had in, if this didn't go well it could have really set us back.

John, unlike Pete, is an outgoing person who readily expresses what he is thinking and enjoys involvement with people. He is also a skilled manager of meetings and a gifted presenter and lecturer.

I decided I had to get involved in this. I mean, really, I couldn't hold myself back. I'm not an IT expert, but I had to do something to help on the process side. I didn't want to show up the people on the steering committee or the other sponsors, so I went to each of them and said I'd like to help and needed their support. A couple of them didn't know what I was talking about, so I spent more time explaining [my concerns]. And then I got them all together, steering committee people and sponsors, and we spent a whole day going through an analysis of what was going well and what wasn't. I got everyone talking, and at one point we broke up into a couple of teams so that some of the people who were not participating as much could have their chance. Then I laid out a way we could do better at this by taking on the management-process/cultural stuff ourselves and focusing the consultants on the things that they knew how to do. This [approach was going to require us] to change how we had organized this project, but people didn't seem to mind.

The CFO reported that John's expertise at organizing projects became obvious to everyone and his personality just won people over: "He was enthusiastic, but even more he wasn't threatening. You just got the sense he was a guy just like us, who had some experience we didn't have, but he knew how to make a project like this successful. It was probably the single most important thing that got people to fall behind John. They could just see this guy was a leader and they followed him."

Both John and Pete succeeded at creating momentum during their transitions by means of early wins. Both did so in ways that were consistent with their very different leadership styles.

Use an approach that suits the culture

What constitutes a win will vary from company to company. The new leader must understand the culture of the organization well enough to recognize what is a win and what isn't. Wins must also be achieved in ways that are perceived as legitimate. In some organizations, for example, the best wins are achieved through low-key collaboration, while others reward high-profile, individually-driven successes. One leader recounted the following experience of confronting a new culture:

The people here needed leadership. They were good people who worked hard and have pride in their company. They are willing to do what is needed, but they have to be directed. I started to schedule meetings to get them pumped up. I worked hard at it and [performed in a way that] would have gotten rave reviews at [my former company] . . . I was really on. But I noticed that people were more subdued than they should have been. You know, you can tell sometimes how effective you are by the chatter you hear as people leave—if they're animated and if there's a buzz. But there wasn't. So I started to ask a few of the people I'd gotten to know, and I got some feedback that people were reacting in a sort of a wait-and-see way—not exactly what we needed. As it turned out, the problem was not my message, or that they weren't ready, but it was my style and some of the terms I was using. I was used to a rough-and-tumble company, and talking to a sales force about winning against all odds, gutting it out, pushing the ball over the goal line, and guerrilla tactics—a lot of war and sports [metaphors]—but here the people responded to different things. Nothing wrong with that at all, and once I understood it I adjusted. It seemed like such a small thing, but it was important to them. They didn't want to hear me do a half-time locker-room talk. The next time, I started out the meeting but then had a few mid-managers who had been around a long time and had great credibility come in to talk . . . Then we broke people up into small groups to discuss what had to happen on their own. And, you know, that helped me in a lot of ways, because it gave me an appreciation that a different approach can work just as well as the one I was comfortable with.

Efforts to achieve high-profile early wins can easily backfire and damage the new leader's credibility. This is especially true if the organization is (or believes it is) functioning reasonably well. As one leader put it:

It didn't take me very long to figure out the culture is not oriented to stars. You are not going to succeed here if you have much "I" factor: "I did this, I'm going to do this, I'm that, I'm this." What I have done here is quietly work through others. But I also have to not appear so detached that I don't know what's going on. A big mistake in this company would have been for me to try to prove my credibility by having eight big successes they could tag to me. That would be a recipe for failure here. Now if I were in [another company], which I know pretty well, it would be entirely different. There you have to be a bit of a grandstander. You have to market yourself. You have to say, "These are the things, and look what I have accomplished," to get noticed in that highly competitive environment. There, you are out the door in three months if you haven't produced a list of real success stories. Here that would be fatal. The key is to read the tea leaves of the environment and say, "How do I get the job done in this environment? How can I be successful?"

Leaders uniformly reported that they had to tailor their plans to the cultures of the organizations they had joined before they could hope to change the culture. As one leader explained:

As long as we get to the end objective and don't do anything illegal or immoral, I don't much care how it happens. I'll give people a lot of leeway and let them carry the ball and decide the best way. That way, I know they're committed. But the thing is that, when you gain that commitment, you can't also have control over exactly how they do it. You become more of a coach, to make sure the movement is always toward the end goal.

Similarly, U.S. diplomat Richard Holbrooke described his goals at the 1996 Bosnian peace talks in Dayton, Ohio, as "firm on goals, flexible on means."[4]

The leaders we interviewed worked hard to understand the cultures of the organizations they joined. Those who were unaccustomed to moving from one company to another found this task more difficult, but they all had to work at it.

I believed I was really ready for this [challenge] because of the headhunter and how open and accessible the CEO was. I had an idea of what had to be done that turned out to be more or less on target. But knowing what you have to do and pulling it off are two different things. I had to get my feet on the ground here first to understand what would work . . . and I couldn't depend on how I had done something somewhere else.

Anticipate uneven progress

Planning and creating momentum would be easier if all the parts of the organization could be made to move in unison. The pace would be consistent on every front and the pieces would interlock smoothly. Changes would spread horizontally among the staff and line departments and vertically among executives, managers, front-line supervisors, and hourly workers. Marketing's new understanding of emerging markets would mesh with Manufacturing's mastery of new technologies and Product Development's smooth merger of the two into outstanding new products.

While the new leader should aspire to such consistency, the likelihood of achieving it is remote. Different departments are incented and measured differently, and staffed by people with different needs who have progressed up the ranks in silo-like fashion, making their loyalties more local than organizational. As one leader put it, "Getting this place to move in the same direction and building momentum was like herding cats." Because of these inevitable differences, the task facing the new leader is both demanding and unpredictable.

Entering a longstanding social system made up of groups and individuals with different needs and drives, the new leader should expect uneven progress even after momentum begins to build. There are at least two ways for new leaders to create momentum in such situations. One is to launch a frontal assault on the culture of the organization—by issuing edicts, for instance, and hiring people from outside who are loyal to him. This may be an appropriate strategy for an organization in such dire straits that the new leader is under pressure to save it from extinction. It also might be successful if he has been hired as the CEO. For the people we are focusing on, though (neither coming into a crisis nor entering as CEO), we believe this way of operating would be quite dangerous.

The second option is to watch and listen attentively during the initial months, to figure out what momentum-creating actions are likely to be most successful, and to pick initial shots deliberately. By doing this well, the new leader becomes identified with what is important strategically, gains a platform to display his strengths, and is seen as able to lead the company toward important early wins.

Be relentlessly efficient with your time

All the leaders we interviewed invoked effective time management as a prerequisite for success. Said one:

> I laid out a game plan [for the first] 100 days. The first ten days I planned to assess my own team. [During the rest of the first month I planned] to identify where the fires were . . . and which ones were going to burn most brightly . . . and then to get an assessment of the state of the business and where we were on our business plan. In other words, we have a commitment that we've made to the corporation for hitting some numbers . . . Is there risk [of not reaching] that goal? If there is, to get that up on the table with [the CEO] real quick and then to find out the things that exist [that can get us there] and [whether people understand what "there" means]. Then to find out whether this company has a vision, a mission, and then a strategy. If it does [have those elements], how do people feel about them? I use the [rest of the first] ninety days to analyze the environment where I compete and get to know the competitors, the needs of the end users, and the needs of [distributors]. Also, I look at what technology I have and whether or not people know how to use it. Then I look at the trends in the marketplace and then look at the marketing programs that we've had historically—what's worked and what hasn't worked. Then at the whole regulatory environment—what are any hot issues with that [and how do they] affect our business? Pricing trends, new product activities—learning [what are] the key drivers of consumption in this business are all things I look at around that time. I wanted by the end of ninety days to have a vision of where we were going to be in five years and a strategy. It needed to be a home-run strategy if we were going to get big—and we needed to know how we were going to get big, in terms of our product line, technology, knowing who our competitors out there are, which ones might be worth buying, which ones are worth attacking, and which ones we wanted to stay away from.

Another gave the following account:

> I wanted to make sure I was being aggressive enough to make some real changes and achieve some real results, but I also knew that I

was not going to triple earnings all at once. I did a 100-day plan that I developed with my boss. I broke things into phases. The objective for the first thirty days was to meet [as many people as possible] in the organization and form some initial impressions, and then tell them what I wanted to accomplish. In the second thirty days I focused on the business plan and [figuring out how to get it] in good shape for the next year. I also tried to understand some of the departmental issues . . . and [what it would take] to get them to work together. In the third thirty days, I wanted to start to show a real ability to drive results to make a difference in performance.

Many leaders also talked about the premium on available time. They were generally proficient time managers and some ranked time management among their primary abilities. But all described themselves as less proficient than they needed to be given their new roles. As one leader put it: "I think that's the toughest thing you face, because you get all kinds of external demands you just don't expect and really can't control. The only thing that helps is to be real good about prioritizing, and at the same time not to be surprised when you can't spend your time on your priorities. You have to be extra-structured, but at the same time you have to be flexible."

Early wins are critical, but they represent only part of what the new leader needs to accomplish in order to build momentum. Next we'll look at how to lay a foundation for more fundamental change.

3

LAYING A
FOUNDATION

Early wins can help get the new
leader off to a good start, but they are not enough. To meet the
Board's expectations (and her own), the new leader must also lay a
foundation for sustainable improvement in the company's performance. Are there steps she can take to do so during the transition
period? Leaders point to three such steps: developing a clear vision
of how the organization will eventually work, extending and
strengthening the political base necessary to support change, and
beginning to modify the culture by introducing new operating
norms.

The new leader's actions in these three areas during the transition period should be included in her era plan. Besides planning for
early wins, effective era planning involves envisioning a desirable

future state for the organization and working backward to spell out how to realize it. New leaders have to be like Janus, the Roman god of beginnings who had two faces, one looking forward and the other backward. This double perspective anchors the new leader in the present while pulling her toward the future.

It may be useful to underline the obvious: there are definite limits to what the new leader can do to change the fundamentals during the transition period. Barring unique circumstances, key people will not be let go, the corporate strategy will not be changed, plants will not be closed or relocated, new products in progress will not be scrapped, acquisitions will not be consummated . . . or at least none of these moves will be decided solely by the new leader. The new leader's efforts to lay a foundation for longer-term improvement during the first six months will focus more on the cultural and political dimensions of the organization.

This chapter explores the three foundation building blocks—creating a personal vision, assembling a political base, and pinpointing ways to change the culture—and some tools that the new leader can use to promote cultural change.

VISIONING

By the end of the first six months, the new leader should have come up with a rough mental image of what the organization will look like at the end of his first era. As this working model grows clearer by being tested, it will eventually become a powerful guiding star. At some point following the transition period, he will share his personal vision and from it will mold a shared one.

How does a vision form? How is it used? Sometimes the image begins to form during the fuzzy front end or immediately after joining the company. One leader described his experience this way:

> I knew quite a bit about [the company] because I'd done a lot of homework before joining. But of course it was about what existed at the time—the products, its history, where the key people had come from during their careers, the patterns of their marketing pro-

grams and how they attracted and kept customers, their success rate on new product introductions—that sort of thing. But I really didn't think about what I wanted the place to become. Maybe that was because I just didn't know enough, or maybe it was that I was so busy trying to get up to speed. Once I saw firsthand how people made decisions, and the [slow] pace of how things happened, the picture [of what should be happening] formed in my mind pretty clearly. I guess I needed to see concretely how things worked to be able to get clear in my mind how they ought to work. The key for me, I think, was to make this image as [graphic] as possible.

I found myself in meetings with people who were really trying hard but who just didn't have it. I'd take over the meeting and drive for a decision, and we'd walk out having a direction set about what to do next. But I was frustrated that I had to be the one to do that all the time. My HR guy gave me some feedback that some of the people at these meetings weren't too happy either. He said that they appreciated me taking the leadership and moving things [forward], but that they felt [inadequate] each time I did it. Well, at first I got ticked off— but when I calmed down a little, I realized that we weren't going to win [if people felt] that way. I thought I was making good stuff happen when I really was making these people more dependent. The more I drove for decisions myself, the more was getting done—but the less powerful people felt to do things on their own, and the more frustrated I was getting.

I had scheduled an off-site with my staff and their key people, and as part of it I wanted to get this issue out on the table. My HR guy interviewed me with everyone looking on, and [by responding to his questions] I was able to describe the sort of meetings I wanted and be very specific, because he pushed me. I'd say, "I want people who take responsibility," and he'd say, "Okay, now what does that mean exactly? . . . How will you know that someone is taking responsibility?"

Well, as a result of this session, I made some real progress in understanding exactly what I wanted and in [conveying] it. Two of the things that happened were that one senior guy who was struggling [with doing things in a new way] came to me to say he was going to take an early-retirement package because he just wasn't going to be able to do what I had described, and the other was that a few of the people who were at this meeting got together [with the HR manager] to talk about how to help people do what I tried to describe . . . And that led to us doing some training in decision-making.

This leader found that the people in his company were more likely to understand what he meant if he described very specifically the behavior he expected. The more he was called on to talk publicly about what he had in mind, furthermore, the clearer he himself became about what he wanted.

I knew generally what I expected, and I'd recognize it if I saw it, but it needed to be explained to the people here so that they could envision it. I was talking about some pretty new things, as far as their world went, and if I talked in generalities like, "I want people to be more innovative," they'd nod but think, "Hey, I'm innovative now"—but not in the way I meant it.

He used every opportunity during his transition period to specify the behavior he wanted to see, and he worked at describing it in positive terms.

In a job like this, it's all about getting people to understand that they have to act differently . . . and [doing so] in a nonthreatening way. At least here, I found that the clearer I was myself, the clearer I could be with [my people] and the quicker they understood. [Describing the behavior to aim for] was much more effective than pointing out that the way they were acting wasn't good enough.

A personal vision can coalesce in different ways, depending on the new leader's learning style and the conditions he encounters. The task of clarifying a vision is often largely a matter of taking advantage of serendipitous events, as it was for the leader just discussed, and of familiarizing oneself thoroughly with the characteristics of the organization. Chapter 7 offers a detailed discussion of how to form a personal vision and how to develop and communicate a common vision.

BUILDING A POLITICAL BASE

Early wins help attract the political support necessary to make changes in organizational culture. But the new leader must also begin to think through likely support for and resistance to change initiatives, and decide how to build a supportive coalition capable of overcoming resistance.

Many leaders followed the same sequence of steps in pursuit of political support. First, they won the loyalty and respect of the key people below them. Then they worked at establishing a solid relationship with the CEO, and, at the same time, with peers—corporate senior managers, other division heads, and the like.

It's important for the new leader to solidify the support of subordinates early on, because they understand the organization and hold the keys to making change happen quickly. Also, they need to feel that the new leader is, at least to some degree, representing their interests in discussions with the CEO. Success in gaining the support of subordinates, some of whom are likely to be advisors to the CEO, makes it easier for the new leader to build credibility with her boss.

Concentrating on the boss, rather than subordinates, backfired in several cases, as the following story illustrates. Walter was hired as a division manager and likely successor by the CEO, who simultaneously hired someone else to run another division. Of the two, Walter was more highly regarded and more accomplished, and was given the largest and most important unit. Eighteen months later, he resigned under pressure and the other general manager was elevated to the number-two spot. The CEO explained why:

> [Walter] spent more time managing up than he did paying attention to his business. I never felt he really understood our company very well . . . He understood the industry, and he brought some very good things here. He's a very talented guy—don't get me wrong— and he accomplished a lot. But, at the end of the day, I had to decide who was going to take over from me, and [Walter] just didn't have enough support from the people under him.

It started in the first few months, where he chewed out a junior product manager in front of everyone . . . That sort of stuff just doesn't happen here. I talked with him about it, and things were okay for a while. Then he started to show signs of being more concerned with . . . the trappings of power. He made a big play to move up here [to the corporate executive offices] instead of being with his troops. And when I said no, he got some expensive furniture for his office and put up framed diplomas and things like that. We've got some well-educated people here—some who reported to [Walter] come from better schools than he did—and, believe me, there isn't any office in this company with diplomas and top-of-the-line furniture . . . It just isn't our way.

He spent a lot of time on things that were important to me. But when he made presentations, he wouldn't bring his people, just him . . . and that always surprised me a little. He never gave his people a chance to shine. I never saw him not treat his people well, but after he left I heard stories of him being too demanding and not very respectful of secretaries and analysts. The thing was, as good as [Walter] is and as much talent as he has, he just didn't gain the respect and loyalty of his people. If someone can't do that, he's not going to be CEO, at least not here.

Walter didn't understand what it took to build a base of support in his new company. His failure to get subordinates behind him undermined his efforts to build credibility with his boss. It's easy for new leaders to fall into this kind of political trap. Analyzing potential sources of resistance to change and building supportive coalitions to overcome it will be discussed in more detail in Chapter 9.

CHANGING THE CULTURE

Changing the culture begins with identifying patterns of behavior that stand in the way of improved performance. Diagnosing the culture is a key aspect of learning during the transition and of the formation of a compelling personal vision. At the same time, the new leader must make sure that early wins also serve as models of behavior that advance her vision.

Thinking through the impact of early initiatives beyond the transition period will raise a number of strategic questions. What options will early projects create or foreclose? Can they be expanded or replicated elsewhere to leverage change efforts? Do they have natural extensions? What can be done to disseminate the models of behavior established in these early efforts? These considerations should then be embodied in the design of early change initiatives.

The process of diagnosis, and how it contributes to the development of a vision and of promising change initiatives, is well illustrated by Alex's experience.

Alex's Experience

Recruited as president of a large hard-goods manufacturer that had until recently been the leading firm in its industry, Alex was the first senior executive in the company's 100-plus-year history to come from outside the industry. Trained in manufacturing engineering, he had spent his career in consumer packaged goods, moving from Operations to Marketing. Alex was accustomed to an ever-quickening pace of new-product development, short product life cycles, and changing distribution systems.

Alex was chosen because the Board and the CEO were convinced that the company needed to revive its innovative practices to compete in a changing marketplace. They believed the company would soon face conditions requiring a new approach—one geared to speed in responding to competitive threats and new customer demands, and to the distribution complexities of a global technology-supported marketplace. Even though competitors had already innovated more and faster, invested in new systems and technologies, and gained an edge in some areas, they believed they still had time to revitalize the company.

In his first month on the job, Alex spent maximum time learning as much as possible about the process of innovation. While talking with engineers and marketing managers and reviewing product-development projects, he was guided by two questions: "What enabled us to be innovative in the past and why did we stop?" and "What has to happen for us to regain our former dominance in an industry that has gotten tougher and more complex?" Over the years, he knew, the company had successfully introduced new products and ways of manufacturing and distributing them that had dramatically changed the industry. More recently, though, competitors had begun to outstrip the company's rate of innovation. Unless something was done soon, Alex feared, the competitive distance would be too great to make up.

Alex split his learning efforts between inside and outside. Inside, he reached down into the organization to put together a team of high-potential mid-level managers. Their mission was to map the new-product development process, identifying sources of new ideas, outlining key steps and measuring how long it took to complete them, and evaluating the efficiency of the development process. Alex had the team investigate recent product introductions as well as track products currently being developed in two of the company's major categories. He also instructed them to gather data on the product-development processes of world-class manufacturing organizations. To underline the importance of this effort, he relocated the team to corporate headquarters for ninety days and had it report directly to him.

Outside the company, Alex sought to learn why competitors were better at innovation. He used his planned visits to customers and suppliers to learn how they viewed his company's capacity to innovate and how they compared it to its toughest competitors. From the research he had done before joining, Alex knew the structure of the industry was changing because of new economies of scale, technological advances, and changes in distribution channels. It appeared that two competitors had recognized new opportunities and driven down costs by aggressively adopting new manufacturing techniques and streamlining distribution pipelines. Alex concentrated on testing his hypotheses and on gathering a rich set of impressions about the company and the industry.

Alex learned that a key competitor had recently introduced a low-priced model whose design was more sleek, contemporary, and attractive than anything else on the market. His top managers insisted that the competing product was "all fluff" and that the quality and customer loyalty of their product could not be threatened by a mere new design. Several weeks later, after the team took the same posture, Alex pointed out that the competitive product had gained more market share faster than any product of its kind ever had. The reaction was silence; Alex realized that his people had not been tracking this threat. He knew then that he had to change how people in the company thought about competing, and he did not have a lot of time.

Two months after Alex launched the team, he began to pull together what had been learned and grew more concerned than ever: the development work on one of the two new products, code-named Phoenix, had fallen behind a schedule that had already been revised, suggesting not only that the pace was too slow but also that the process might not be under control. He convened the team and asked for a summary the following day of what it had learned so far. Here's his description of the meeting:

> Because I asked them to give me a report before they had pulled together all their data, and about three weeks before they were to give a final report, it flustered them. But in a sense that turned out to be good, because they gave a more spontaneous and frank report. I'd found that people here spent more time on the formats and bells and whistles of a presentation than they did on its substance. And even though I didn't do it for that reason, I was able to avoid a pretty presentation and get right to the heart of it. I went to their project war room, rather than having them come to my conference room, and they walked me through the process map they had done. They were not completely finished yet, but were far enough along for us all to get a handle on the extent of the problem. Seeing it laid out on a wall like they had it, it became very obvious why Phoenix was behind schedule: there were too many people involved, too many approvals, and too many controls. It was a very convoluted sequence, where decisions at every major juncture had to be okayed or verified.

What was I thinking as I looked at it? Two things. First, it was like looking at a project plan to fix the Shuttle after the Challenger disaster—everything was fail-safed. But we weren't NASA after a disaster—we were more like a fighter squadron that had to prepare for dogfights. The second thought I had was that now I knew what all the people we had did all day. They checked on something that should have been done right in the first place, but probably wasn't because the person doing it knew it was going to be checked.

The team's report made it clear that the company developed new products in a way that hadn't kept pace with the new competitive realities of simultaneous speed, quality, and low costs. It was not a case of resistance to change, but of failure to understand that it was necessary to change. If there was resistance, it was to finding out what was going on outside the boundaries of the company and experimenting with new ways of doing things.

Alex launched a communication campaign, personally feeding back the team's analysis and highlighting the convoluted and wasteful character of the existing new-product-development process. He laid out this analysis not just to his staff but also to those below them, in the belief that pressure for change from below would reinforce his own pressure from above. He then directed the middle management team's attention to fashioning a new development process and identifying a couple of promising pilot development initiatives. Meanwhile, he set up a second team to look at how the company gathered and disseminated information on customers, product quality, and competition.

Dysfunctional cultural patterns

Like Alex, other new leaders pointed to lack of innovation as the primary cultural problem they faced. All spoke of struggling to instill a new creative spirit in the organizations they inherited. Symptoms and specifics varied, but three classic dysfunctional patterns eroded the capacity for innovation: inward focus, diffuse responsibility and accountability, and complacency.

Inward focus. The people in Alex's company focused on internally defined reference points and paid little attention to changes in the market and among competitors. Companies like Alex's fall prey to this problem either because of arrogance, which too often accompanies a long history of success, or because the company has become balkanized and caught up in internal conflicts. One leader described the syndrome this way: "I found we had internal processes and they had nothing to do with anything external—no competitive activity, no customer analysis, only our own internal look. We would put together internal forecasts of our revenue every month, and then at the end of the period, when we didn't make it, we would rationalize."

Diffuse responsibility and accountability. Alex found that no one was ultimately responsible and accountable for results. Every key decision on new products or processes could require dozens of signatures, severely diffusing responsibility and accountability. Another leader reported:

> I took a look at [the organization] and I saw that there was no accountability. There was no accountability because there was no designated responsibility, and I'm not overstating the fact. Eighty-five people had to sign off [on a product] before it got launched. I said, "Who is responsible?" Nothing. I said, "This program is over budget. Where is the baseline?" We have none.

Complacency. Alex's people lacked the necessary sense of urgency. Efforts to develop new products and processes were incremental, signaling a belief in the inherent superiority of the company's way of doing things. This syndrome too may be a consequence of a long history of success, or it may reflect insufficient contact with external realities.

Getting started on culture change

Sometimes boosting innovation takes the form of introducing leading-edge products. At other times it demands a new market strategy for profitable growth. In some cases it means creating enthusiasm and a can-do attitude, while other circumstances call for convincing employees to change comfortable, time-honored ways of doing things. Whatever the particular cultural change needed, the new leader has to get people to think differently and consider new ways of operating. What can new leaders do in the short term to initiate culture change without having to alter strategy, reinvent structure, or replace key people? These six approaches were identified by the leaders with whom we spoke:

- **Setting up pilot projects:** initiating experiments that allow employees to try out new tools and new behavior

- **Changing the way performance is measured:** changing the metrics by which success is judged, and aligning the objectives of managers and employees with those new standards of measurement

- **Educating and involving:** exposing people to new ways of operating and thinking about the business, especially by helping them to develop new perspectives on customers and competitors

- **Building on islands of excellence:** identifying sites of outstanding performance within the organization, encouraging them, and utilizing them as examples for others to emulate

- **Collectively envisioning new ways to operate:** bringing people together to envision a new approach to doing business

- **Importing someone from outside to stimulate creativity:** bringing in an outsider who can help make the most of opportunities to think creatively

Technique one: launch pilots. As we saw in Chapter 2, pilot projects can dramatically improve operational results. They must be selected with care, staffed with the right leaders and contributors, provided with the necessary resources (including time, training, and budget), and then nurtured.

The best pilots generate early successes that also have a cultural impact, by demonstrating the sort of company the new leader wishes to create. Most new leaders we spoke with launched pilot experiments during their transition periods; the purposes of the projects varied depending on the specific business needs and cultural changes they were intended to address. Designed appropriately, pilot projects help sustain momentum beyond the transition period by modeling behavior that should become routine when the vision is realized, and by supplying the means, including political support and trained people, to undertake more and more far-reaching initiatives.

Tom's Experience

As the new leader of a manufacturing company, Tom found his three facilities unable to deliver products at the rate required to catch up to more nimble competitors. He identified bottlenecks at each plant, but the more he understood the problems, the more difficult they seemed to fix. He had inherited an outdated production system and an operating plan he had not had a hand in creating.

Tom had very little time to speed up production if year-end goals were to be met. He brought together the manufacturing vice president and his staff to ask why shipping dates were constantly missed. They explained that the on-schedule performance of the three factories had never been much better than it was currently. If this was true, Tom asked, why did the operating plan call for much higher volumes than had ever been produced? Receiving unsatisfactory answers, he probed more deeply. What emerged was the picture of a planning process in which the CEO, Tom's boss, had pushed aggressively for higher target numbers, and the manufacturing staff had acquiesced to the targets even though it believed there was very little chance of reaching them. The plant managers and their staffs, feeling powerless to affect the goals that had been set, proceeded to operate as they had in the past.

Tom had a demoralized production staff operating in ways that would not achieve the volume goals he wanted to reach. They were working for manufacturing leaders who were passive and had been intimidated into agreeing to what they considered unrealistic goals by the person to whom Tom was now reporting. But, in Tom's words, "it turned into an opportunity because we got some projects going, to get rid of some of those bottlenecks, and we came very close to those numbers. People in the plants saw they could get some remarkable results by operating in a different way."

After finding the bottlenecks, Tom told the management group at each plant that he was not going to give up on the targets. Instead, he intended to launch pilot projects in the areas where bottlenecks were slowing production. The cost of the projects would come out of his headquarters budget and not be charged to the plants, but any benefits would accrue to the factories in higher volumes and cost savings. Over the next few weeks, Tom worked closely with the plant management teams to shape the projects and arranged for targeted consulting help and training. He required supervisors to manage the pilots in their areas and insisted on staff sizes sufficient to attain quick results. Because he was not well-acquainted with the people in manufacturing, Tom was not in a position to staff the teams himself. He exerted control, however, by approving project selection and goals as well as establishing the selection criteria of people for each team. He also met with each project team weekly.

Of the seven pilot projects Tom approved, four met the stretch goals, two exceeded them, and one failed. The division came closer to reaching the operating plan than anyone would have imagined when Tom joined. Reflecting on the experience, Tom observed:

> This was really much more than your proverbial moral victory, because at the start of the year no one thought we'd come close to the numbers. But we came within 80 percent of the volume figures and 90 percent of the net income targets. When you realize that was better than anyone thought was possible without the pilot projects, it has to be seen as a success.

As for the impact of this effort on sustaining momentum, Tom concluded:

> It had a huge impact. Because of their success in the pilot efforts, these people proved to themselves that they could get dramatic results by operating in new ways. They needed to know that the leaders here believed in them, and they needed to have a win and prove to themselves that they could make things happen. The pilots did that.

The pilot projects had a galvanizing effect, bringing people together to achieve a common goal. When they exceeded their own expectations, they became willing to try more:

> What happened the following year is that the manufacturing people were more willing to take on new challenges and look at new ways of operating. We began a benchmarking program to get our people out of here so they could look at new ways of manufacturing, new pay systems, new ways to deal with unions . . . the sorts of things we have to do more of here. These things wouldn't have happened if it weren't for the pilots.

Technique two: change performance measurements. Many leaders changed how their organizations measured performance or introduced supplementary performance measures.[1] Convinced that measurement systems exert a powerful influence on behavior, they sought to align rewards with the behaviors they wanted to encourage. New leaders who believed deeply in teamwork sometimes confronted measurement systems geared to a hierarchical command-and-control philosophy. Others who believed in the primacy of customers joined organizations focused on internal financial metrics rather than external customer-oriented yardsticks. Such mismatches represent opportunities to begin to reshape the culture by revising performance measurement and the incentives that flow from it.

The new leader rarely has enough knowledge or sufficient influence to change the company's entire measurement system. Even so, she can take steps during the transition period to spotlight its importance and lay the groundwork for a new system. For example, the new leader can use her position's bully pulpit to argue for aligning measurement with the organization's mission and values. A new leader who finds a measurement system that does not appropriately reinforce the company's mission and values must address this inconsistency early on. Here's how one leader described the experience of doing so:

> I was appalled, when I first came, at the way the measurement system was seen here. It was secretive and controlling, and no one trusted it. I remember talking to my merchandising managers when I first came, and I asked them how they measured [the effectiveness of the] merchandising programs—you know, what the metrics were. They paused and glanced at each other, and I knew I asked something that made them uncomfortable. I finally got them to admit that the CFO and the Chief Merchant used the measurement system as a club on these people. They were so afraid that if they were off just a couple of basis points they'd get hammered. They always had two sets of goals—the official ones, that were ultraconservative, and the ones that they kept to themselves and that they operated on. Well, what bothered me about this was that we had this list of company values on plaques all over the place that talked about empowered people and openness and all-in-it-togetherness.
>
> I thought about this overnight and I called those people into my office and I basically said, "Look, let me be real clear about something. I believe a measurement system should be a way to learn more and be a tool to motivate people, not to scare them. It sounds like we have a system—or maybe just the way it's implemented—that demotivates, and it's made people afraid of it enough so that they sandbag it and we have this shadow system. Well, I don't know how we're going to do it, but I'll tell you something—we're going to change that . . . We're going to have a system that people use and that they learn from!" Well, I didn't quite realize how hard it was going to be to do that—it took a few years because the control mentality was pretty strong here . . . but we did it eventually.

This leader used performance measurement as an opportunity to communicate and to learn. She held her people accountable to their de facto targets. When she became corporate president, and shortly thereafter CEO, one of her first initiatives was to replace the CFO and introduce a new measurement system based on a balanced-scorecard methodology.[2]

An alternative approach is to create a few new metrics and then focus intense attention on them. Some leaders deliberately introduced new performance metrics that raised the profile of aspects of performance they wanted to emphasize. One leader described the new metrics he implemented as

> a simple way that I could put together a report card that I can look at and help others see as well. It's much like what a pilot has in flying an airplane. When you're flying an airplane, you don't need to know everything that is going on in that airplane, or even how that airplane works. But you need to know the direction you're going in, you need to know the height that you are above the ground. I called the new system Scan the Gauges.

The metrics new leaders chose typically involved customers and/or suppliers. The former tracked indicators such as customer satisfaction, revenue from new customers, customer turnover, profitability of different classes of customers, and the rate and cost of signing up new customers. Supplier-based indicators supplemented existing cost measurements with on-time delivery, supplier certification by standards groups such as the International Standards Organization, and zero defects of delivered subassemblies or raw material. One new leader justified his expenditures on a supplier quality program by tracking cost savings and balance-sheet benefits in an area the existing system had no way of recognizing— elimination of incoming inspection systems and reduction of spare parts and work-in-process inventory—as suppliers were certified to be more reliable.

Marketing and Sales administration departments were typically assigned responsibility for implementing new customer measures; the procurement or purchasing function was given responsibility for supplier metrics. Results were typically made available either monthly or quarterly. At first, new leaders sometimes called these metrics "operational measures" to distinguish them from "financial measures," but over time they were incorporated into the formal financial system and linked to the reward system.

Technique three: educate and involve people. Most of the leaders we interviewed sought opportunities to educate people in their new companies about competition and different ways of operating. They recognized the limitations of personally attacking problems, and the unlikelihood that they could sustain momentum while operating alone: the people under them had to do their share. As one leader put it: "There's not enough of me to go around. You quickly find out you can't fish for other people; you have to teach them to fish."

The question is how. One approach might be to fill key management positions with new people who could shoulder some of the load. But the leaders we interviewed believed that the transition period was too early to take such a step, given the need to establish a strong political base. Another approach might be to restructure the organization with a focus on the key issues and to place in more powerful positions current employees capable of sustaining momentum. Here again, most leaders considered such sweeping action premature because they lacked the knowledge to make correct choices or had not yet built up sufficient support.

How then can the new leader ensure that managers and other employees learn what they must? Several leaders employed consultants to oversee the transfer of skills to selected employees. Some consultants delivered simple written guidelines or manuals, while others trained employees to transfer knowledge to their co-workers.

Another way to stimulate learning during the transition period is through best-practice benchmarking.[3] A number of leaders led or sent employees to other companies to find out how they handled problems comparable to those facing the new leader's company. The results were mixed. As one leader reported: "I made a big deal of getting my people out of here and visiting other companies, but it didn't work all that well because I sent the wrong people and they had the wrong attitude." He had required his top managers, who were highly skeptical about the need to change, to visit a few companies he knew to be world-class performers. The top managers—invested in maintaining the status quo and not yet committed to the new leader's ideas—believed that they already *were* world-class and visited the other companies with the belief that they had little to learn.

Other new leaders had more success educating through best-practice benchmarking. Their experiences suggest that this approach works best when the following conditions are put in place:

☐ The learning goals should be specific: it should be clear what information is to be gathered, what is to be learned and why, and how it is to be used. Unfocused visits do little to create momentum.

☐ Benchmarking should be an ongoing project that people believe is important. Often, the best results occur when a team that has worked on a successful pilot then visits other companies where they observe even better performance of the same type.

☐ The benchmarking group should prepare thoroughly, gathering background on the organizations it is to visit and deciding on specific questions to be answered. Each person should take responsibility for seeking to answer a particular question. Advance arrangements should be made with a high-level person at the host company who can serve as a point of contact.

☐ Upon returning, the group should be required to educate peers. By doing so, they will not only share what they learned, but will also internalize more and take the task more seriously. A written report imposes on the benchmarking group the discipline of recording its key findings and explaining the rationale for its recommendations.

☐ The new leader should demonstrate particular interest in the benchmarking process, treating it as a special undertaking both before and after benchmarking visits. She should make it a demonstration of how the business should operate and use it to communicate what she believes is important.

☐ Employee participation is much more effective than using outside consultants to conduct benchmarking. A consultant should be used only to identify the best places to visit and help prepare the people who are assigned the task.

Technique four: build on islands of excellence. Identifying and building on islands of excellence in organizations can have a powerful impact on their cultures. Such islands may be innovative people or groups that haven't been given enough scope, technologies that have been underutilized, or projects that have languished for lack of funding. All the leaders we spoke with found examples of creativity and excellence and tried to build on them. As one leader said:

> The third week I was here, I told the employees, "This company feels like I'm standing at the edge of a field, and somebody comes up to me and says, 'There's a million dollars in pennies out there. All you've got to do is go find them and stack them up and you're a millionaire.' " To this day I keep finding pockets of technology that I didn't know existed, that somebody had cranked out because they could, but it either got undermarketed or underresourced—it was languishing. So that was a pleasant surprise.

Having identified these pockets of excellence, the new leader can shape their objectives, channel resources toward them, and elevate their visibility. Another leader described the process this way:

> I knew that in this company, like every company I'd been in, there were a handful of people who were going to make all the difference. They were going to be superstars that would make contributions by their example; they would motivate and influence others. And so I stood up at my first employee communication meeting and I said that I would go out of my way to find who those people were. And I would work to remove roadblocks so they could be successful. And so, through a process of asking the management and looking at whose name popped up time and time again, I got to know as many of these [people] as I possibly could, and then I just started having very frequent one-on-ones with them: "What do you think? What are the obstacles? What do you need that you're not getting? What do you think about our chances in this technology? Where have you failed in the past that surprised you?" And you get a pretty good view of the corporation from that standpoint and it makes everything fairly straightforward.

A more in-depth and formalized version of this process was adopted by a leader who concluded that the company he joined had to become more cost-conscious. Because it had no tradition of cost containment, Roger found few examples of low-cost successes. During his first few months, devoted to an orientation program arranged for him by the CEO, he was unimpressed with employees' ability to be creative in the face of complex, competitive problems, and to do so with the cost-consciousness he believed necessary for the company to be a winner.

Roger's former company had adopted a total-quality (TQ) and just-in-time (JIT) manufacturing philosophy in the early days of the TQ movement, and had successfully spread those principles throughout the organization over a dozen-year period. His new company exhibited less drive for excellence, and lacked the years of training his former company had invested in to create the skills and attitudes necessary for continuous improvement. Complicating factors were his still-superficial understanding of the core technologies of his new company and his dependence on others to analyze the impact of his decisions. The more he learned, the more convinced Roger became that he had to rely on the people who understood the technology. "I began looking for the people who had been working in the trenches and might have been the unsung heroes, in the sense that they were getting outstanding results and doing it by keeping their costs down, something [their peers] were not doing."

He discovered some people working in ways that were encouraging. "I was looking for things that were vital to us . . . I wanted to point to examples of people who were operating in the way that everyone should." In his fifth month as president, Roger inaugurated the President's Unsung Hero Award, announcing that it would be given annually to groups or individuals who had achieved remarkable results in a cost-conscious way. He asked employees to appoint a group to establish criteria and judge nominations from other employees. "It was only one step toward getting people to focus [their attention] on this, but it helped. People liked the idea of nominations, and [of] employees making the selection rather than me doing it. And it got people to think that they could do something special and be efficient at the same time."

Technique five: visualize collectively. When new leaders are not ready to push for change on their own, they can sometimes use group processes to create impetus. One example involves Jim, who was hired by an industrial products company that supplies whole-sale distributors and mass merchandisers. The CEO had decided to retire early because of illness; the overlap period was expected to be a year. The CEO was highly regarded by his employees, and his illness reinforced their loyalty to him. Jim was horrified by "a 1960s-vintage organization style with too many silos, each with its own Sales, Finance, HR, and Distribution." But he was reluctant to make substantial changes quickly because "the people didn't know me, and I didn't want to come across as a hired gun and start taking apart everything [the CEO] had under him." Out of respect and to avoid a backlash of negative feelings, he waited until the CEO left the company ten months later to make important organizational changes.

How did he lay the groundwork for eventual change and encourage innovative thinking?

> I got some good advice early from a few people who knew me well and who understood the company [culture and business]. I had decided pretty quickly that there were big-time changes I had to make . . . but the advice I got made sense to me. It was basically that I'd be opening up a Pandora's box if I moved too quickly. Even if [employees were likely to agree that] they were the right things to change, there was a chance that they'd resent me doing it, and if that happened it would cause some real resistance [because these steps] were going to be painful. I couldn't risk that.

The circumstances were unusual, but the dilemma Jim faced was one often confronted by someone hired as a number-two. Jim could not make dramatic changes even after he had decided what they should be. As his reference to Pandora's box underscores, employees may react unpredictably even to correct actions. Unwilling to take that risk, he opted for a collective approach to change.

It appeared to Jim that most of the upper- and mid-level managers were open to a new strategy. He also found that the newer employees in that group tended to be frustrated because there was no identifiable business strategy and no forum in which they could have input into the strategy and related issues.

Jim formed a strategy council composed of fifteen people he considered able to embrace a new vision of how the company could operate. When Jim announced the council's formation, he explained that its mission would be to begin the process of updating the strategy for the business and to make sure people had a chance to participate. To avoid threatening the vice presidents who reported to him (and to whom the members of the council reported), he emphasized that it would be purely advisory and that policy-setting authority would remain with the top-management group. The two vice presidents he considered the most creative and open to change were also appointed to the strategy council.

Jim asked the four most creative thinkers to coordinate the meetings and establish an agenda for subsequent months. These four had impressed him as being driven to see the company do better and eager for change. He told them he wanted the council's first event to be an off-site workshop to discuss a new vision for the company; he would run the meeting, and the results would be presented to the top-management group.

The off-site session accomplished several goals: (1) Jim had an opportunity to assess which members of this management group he might eventually promote; (2) the participants agreed in general terms on a mission statement and five-year growth targets; (3) Jim tested his emerging ideas of what the company must become to achieve such targets; (4) the group agreed on the general profile of what sort of company would capture their commitment and enthusiasm. He explained: "I didn't want to go too far on this [because] we weren't ready for specific things like how the organization structure might be and the kind of people we needed. We stayed on the emotional level [and] got into what would make us proud and really pump us up and get us excited to come to work."

Technique six: import creative inspiration. Outside people can sometimes stimulate creativity. Jon joined a successful company, with experienced and capable managers, which remained an innovator in its industry. But Jon, hired as head of its largest division, believed that continued success called for new ways of marketing and distributing products. The CEO was not opposed to trying new approaches: "I had a great deal of faith in Jon and I wanted to support him; what he said made sense. We needed to find some new markets, and if we had to make some changes to get that done, well, we'd just do it."

Jon realized, however, that he had joined a company whose people would try something new only if it had been thoroughly tested and was backed up with hard research. The products required highly technical expertise, and power thus tended to reside in scientists responsive to established expertise or hard facts. But what Jon believed to be best for this company had never been done before. How was an untested approach going to gain the support of the people he would eventually lead? Jon explained his thinking this way:

> Even though Ray [the CEO] was behind this, I wanted to avoid having him be the reason the others would be supportive. After all, that's how most creative things had been done in the past [with a push from Ray]. I wanted this to have his backing, but I also wanted it to be mine, not his. I couldn't pull out scientific evidence saying great companies in the past had done this before, because we were trying to create something new. So I did the next best thing.

Jon's solution was to convince his former boss and mentor, Howard, now retired, to work for him. Well known in the industry as a tough and creative manager, persuasive and very thorough, Howard had impressive academic credentials and several patents to his credit. He joined as a vice president for special projects, reporting to Jon. His mission, Jon said

> was to help me figure out how to get support for preparing to get our products into new markets. He took it on and I backed off. He put together a series of programs that were very focused and very well thought through. He brought a few young, bright, high-potential people in to help him and pieced together a plan you just couldn't argue with. But he laid the groundwork by the way he influenced the top people around here. He'd wander into their offices

and have a conversation about what they were doing and not try to sell them on anything. He was building relationships with them.

Jon's mentor built a case for launching experiments to take three products into new markets. One was a product whose patent protection had expired, and that the company expected competitors to copy. Its customary approach was to allow such off-patent products to decline, in the expectation of fueling growth with new products. The other two products he chose were derivatives, outgrowths of laboratory work on existing products few people were paying attention to. The plan was thus a threat to no one because it involved products outside the mainstream, and its conceptual quality and logic were so solid that even the most skeptical people were impressed.

These six techniques are all potentially useful ways to begin laying a foundation for culture change. Note, however, that we did not see an example of a new leader who tried to use all these techniques. Those we talked with attempted at most to use two or three as building blocks. Which ones they employed and the way they employed them were functions of the unique situation each new leader faced, and of personal strengths and shortcomings. Is it conceivable that a new leader might use all six? Yes. Is it likely? No. We recommend using them as a checklist to help decide how to move forward.

A FINAL CAUTION

The new leader's efforts to lay a foundation may cause trouble with the CEO and, if not managed carefully, can contribute to successor syndrome. What the new leader sees as a performance-undermining overreliance on top management, for instance, may be a direct consequence of the current leader's style and part of his legacy. Efforts to lay a new foundation must thus be approached with great care, especially if they involve key people or core technical elements such as strategy, structure, and systems. The new leader must either build political support for such change or accept that some needed change will have to be deferred. As one leader we interviewed put it:

The problem that I had coming in is that the company had some very distinct and significant operating problems that developed because there were not a lot of formal business controls and things were forgiven. But the one situation I didn't want to be in was where I decided to make a change or put a control in, and they [subordinates who were long-time associates of the CEO] went around me to [the CEO], and he comes to me and says, "Don't do it." It's a credibility-buster. So you have to sort of pick your shots, and decide where you think you can make some impact on the organization. And I think what I decided to do was to leave certain areas alone because I just didn't feel that I could fix them in the near term.

One of the reasons you're coming in from the outside is because they want someone who is not burdened by the history. And they believe that, until it gets to the point where there are some hard actions that need to be taken. Then it's kind of, "Well, I didn't mean you should go that far." It took me a while to really understand what the legacy issues were and where the deeper emotional commitments were and where they weren't.

While working to secure early wins, the new leader must begin to lay a foundation for deeper change by developing a vision consistent with A-item priorities and pursuing some change initiatives that contribute to longer-term objectives. Given time constraints and limited authority to change the structure, people, and systems, new leaders should concentrate on: (1) developing a compelling personal vision and beginning to think about how to make it a shared vision; (2) developing a political base; and (3) beginning to take actions to change the culture. But in order for any of these initiatives to be successful, the new leader must build personal credibility.

4

BUILDING
CREDIBILITY

The new leader cannot hope to see his efforts bear fruit without building personal credibility and productive working relationships.[1] Key constituencies must come to believe that the new leader can lead the company to a desirable future before giving him their loyalty. This means that the leader must inspire confidence, embody an attractive set of values, and bring energy to the organization.

People's early assessments of the new leader can determine whether he builds (or loses) credibility. Does he have the insight and steadiness to make the tough decisions about where the organization should go? Does he represent an attractive set of personal values that people relate to, admire, and seek to emulate? Does he bring the right kind of energy to the organization, demanding high levels of performance from himself and others? If the people with influence come to see the new leader as having good judgment, attractive values, and energy, he will probably pass this credibility test. If not, the best possible planning to secure early wins and lay a foundation for change won't help. One leader spoke to this point and emphasized the need for gusto in describing General Electric's Jack Welch: "I've asked several people that work for GE: what is Welch's biggest contribution? Along with high standards and demanding questions, it clearly is that he is the energizer of the organization. His energy is just driven through that business."

Unlike the tasks of securing early wins and laying a foundation for sustained improvement, which call for the new leader to manage something outside himself, building credibility requires significant emotional involvement. Personal credibility emerges from myriad decisions, actions, and interactions, both subtle and obvious. It is the result of a slow process of accretion (or erosion) as the leader's patterns of conduct become evident.

The transition period is a crucial time for building credibility because early impressions can be difficult to reverse. Early in the new leader's tenure, people understandably strain to take his measure. Initial impressions can easily become self-fulfilling prophecies that block out contrary evidence: some onlookers will tend to judge the new leader's behavior selectively so as to confirm their own early appraisals. Once such impressions have hardened, there is virtually nothing the new leader can do in the short term to alter them. As one leader expressed it:

> If you're there for a few months and no one's really sure what you've done, that's probably bad. I think you probably have sealed your fate. You may not get fired but I think people do get thumbprinted early on whether they're rockets or average performers. I think you get a good night's sleep, eat a high-protein breakfast, and come in charging all the time, every day. Just show the high energy. You can relax a little once you get the lay of the land. It's like Kennedy, that first 100 days. I think he understood that.

The power of first impressions makes it important to move deliberately and carefully. At no other time will the new leader be under such intense scrutiny and have such limited influence on employee perceptions. Because he lacks close relationships with people who can proffer unflagging support, and is unfamiliar with the nuances of the culture, the first impressions he creates are not entirely within his control. The transition period is a time when impressions carry more weight than deeds and when interpersonal skills and maturity matter greatly. In the early months, an inadvertent slight or an off-the-cuff comment about a predecessor may take on disproportionate importance. As one leader remarked: "I've been on Boards that have removed CEOs, and in every case it has not been for lack of strategic vision, lack of knowledge of the organization, or lack of marketing skills. It's been for lack of interpersonal skills."

This chapter explores how new leaders build productive working relationships with subordinates, bosses, and peers. We will examine the process of becoming "of" an organization without falling captive to the past or to others' agendas, and will look at how a new leader's pattern of conduct sends signals to the organization about judgment, values, and energy.

ESTABLISHING CREDIBILITY WITH EMPLOYEES

How should the new leader seek to be perceived by subordinates and, more broadly, by the organization? How can he influence their perceptions? This is an issue for all new managers. But the new leader's circumstances—that he comes from outside the organization, that many of his subordinates will have preexisting relationships with the CEO, and that some may have been internal competitors for his job—make this an especially delicate process. As one leader described it: "It's very hard for number twos to come in [from the outside] because they either are eaten up by the next level, [some of whom] think they should have been the number-two person, or they can never quite . . . sort it out with the number-one person, the CEO, as to what they're supposed to do and not supposed to do."

The leaders we talked to all emphasized some common themes. One was that setting expectations and shaping the behavior of subordinates and employees are among the new leader's most important tasks. As one person put it: "You have to make clear [what are] the behavioral limits . . . Sit down with each of [your direct reports] and say, 'Here's the way I do things and how I understand things and how we'll get on well as we work together. Here are the things that will drive me crazy and I'll be very angry at.' "

Another was that the key behavior-shaping tools at the leader's disposal—beyond the formal authority conveyed by her position in the hierarchy—are the vision she creates, the model she establishes through her own behavior, the feedback she offers, and her selective use of incentives and disincentives. A tangible and compelling vision of a desirable future engages people. The new leader's own behavior, and its consistency (or inconsistency) with what she espouses, reveals her real values and motivations. Clear and constructive feedback defines expectations for behavioral change. And positive and negative incentives provide necessary reinforcement.

The styles of the new leaders we questioned differed markedly, but there was surprising consistency in how they wished to be viewed by employees. In essence, they wanted to be seen as:

- ☐ demanding but able to be satisfied

- ☐ accessible but not too familiar

- ☐ decisive but judicious

- ☐ focused but flexible

- ☐ active without causing commotion

- ☐ willing to make the tough calls but humane

We have come to see that these are the fundamental tensions that new leaders must reconcile as they seek to build credibility. None of them is necessarily easy to negotiate, and all involve balancing contradictory objectives and making difficult judgments.

Being demanding but able to be satisfied

It is essential to establish high but reachable standards for subordinates and for the organization. One leader described a device he used to communicate his standards in a memorable way:

When I first arrived, I had a set of points on a [overhead projector] slide that I brought with me to about twenty meetings. It was my M.O. [modus operandi]. It was written in a folksy style, but it was pretty clear what I wanted. It said things like: we will deliver the numbers we promise; there's a time for input and a time for execution; I will always seek your input on major decisions, but once we decide where we're going we're all going to execute it 100 percent.

An effective new leader presses his people to make realistic commitments, and then holds their feet to the fire. His very low tolerance for failure to meet commitments encourages people to be more realistic in what they promise. One leader described how he went about instilling the importance of making and meeting realistic commitments:

At first, people would come in and make commitments to me and then not keep them. So I started wagering silver dollars with them each time they made a commitment. At company status meetings, I started to give a summary of how many dollars I'd won. I was trying to get these people to recognize they were making commitments but not meeting them. At one meeting I told them: "So far I've won ten silver dollars," and I showed them the silver dollars. I said, "Any time somebody's made a commitment to me or to the company that I thought was an important one, I've wagered a silver dollar. I've won ten so far. And I'm going to be a wealthy person by the time I leave here." Everybody laughed. So I went to another meeting, and there were three managers working together in a team, and they had a commitment to me and they really missed their date. So they owed me three silver dollars. And I said to them, "When the hell are you guys going to make a commitment to me that you're going to meet?" And there was a young manager, God love him. He said to me, "I'm willing to make a commitment that we will fix this problem." And I said, "Well, what's your commitment?" And he said, "My commitment to you is: we will have this done, fully qualified, by a certain date." And I said, "OK, if you do that, you will get the three silver dollars that these guys owe me plus a silver dollar from me." This guy and his team, I want to tell you what they did. It became symbolic. Beat me out of the silver dollars. They killed themselves. They worked overtime. It was extraordinary what they did. At one point I tried to get them to assign some people to work on something that really was more important. They said to me, "We can't detract from the commitment." When they actually beat the date, they invited me over to the building. They had all employees there to tell me. This young guy was walking on cloud nine, and in the next meeting I had this fellow stand up. And I said, "He made his commitment." I said, "This should not be an unusual feat. It's the way we should operate in general. He made his commitment and he got four dollars." Well, what happened is people started to change.

While it is essential to demand superior performance, it is equally important not to acquire a demoralizing reputation for being impossible to satisfy. Equally damaging can be failure to celebrate successes adequately when they occur. The new leader should never forget the motivational power of recognition and other nonmonetary rewards.

Being accessible but not too familiar

The need to get out and meet people rapidly was a common refrain among the leaders we interviewed. Many also stressed the importance of being personally accessible to employees. Accessibility doesn't mean making yourself available for indiscriminate contact with anyone who wants it; it means being approachable. One leader explained:

I don't spend much time behind the desk. I'm usually out. I have meetings in the different areas. You give people a chance to tell you what they are doing. What's their job? And it takes an extraordinary amount of time the first three months. But by the time you're through, you should have touched a lot of the employees. They get to see you as a human. They get to see you as a person that's interested in what they're doing.

Many leaders warned that failure to encourage an open flow of information impedes the leader's ability to learn about important problems and build supportive coalitions. Here are two accounts of very different styles and their consequences:

> I worked for a CEO who was a screamer. His version of dealing with a problem was that whoever brought him the problem, he took a big stick and hit them over the head. But at the same time, he wanted the information as soon as possible. So if you didn't bring it to him immediately, he'd beat you over the head; but if you brought it to him, he'd beat you over the head, then turn around and beat someone else over the head. At the same time, we would get into staff meetings and he'd talk about teamwork. What he did was drive everyone into shells. Nobody wanted to tell him anything. It ended up dividing everyone. You'd think everyone would come together, but, because he was so divisive in the way he attacked people, and because he flipped back and forth so badly, no alliances were ever formed.

> What I most value is candor. Tell me the bad news and I won't bite your head off. Tell me the bad news and I won't start looking for someone to blame, because the biggest risk you run as the CEO of any organization is that you'll never hear the truth again. You can't let that happen. So what I tell folks is, "I want you to be candid and honest with me. And I recognize that puts a tremendous obligation on me—because if I ever make you regret you were candid with me, you will never be honest with me again. So start out being candid and honest, and give me your bad news. You'll decide when to stop being honest based on how I deal with it."

Accessibility should go hand in hand with maintaining some psychological distance from employees. Many leaders stressed the importance of making connections at a personal level, but in such a way that one's authority is not undermined. Said one leader:

> I think a lot of it is about developing rapport. I'm going to work very closely with these people. And I want to develop a personal link

because we'll be working together. At the same time, you have to be very careful because you have to be respected. It's a fine line.

Another added:

I think it's always dangerous to get too close in a friendship way to the people in your organization, because sometimes you've got to do things people don't like.

Being decisive but judicious

A new leader wants to establish a reputation as being able to take charge. But it's easy to get in trouble by appearing impulsive and making moves before other people are ready for them. The resulting tension is particularly difficult to manage early in the transition, when a new leader who knows what she wants to do still has to defer key decisions until she learns more and gets other people up to speed.

Fortunately, there is usually a grace period during which the new leader is not expected to make big decisions unless they are truly pressing. Here are two descriptions of this honeymoon stage:

During my first sixty days, I did a lot more listening than talking. I would make only decisions I had to make, give direction only where I had to give it. This [watch-and-listen] period was very important. I wanted to learn enough about the culture so that when I had to start putting some stakes in the ground I knew what I was going to run into. I also was careful not to make any big, irreversible choices too early on.

I think there are three phases when someone joins an organization. In the first phase, if you do it right, you create an open environment where you get a lot of input and people feel it's a relatively low-risk time to express opinions—sometimes about other people, often about what the organization is doing and what the organization needs. That period lasts maybe two to three months. Then there's a period where you have maximum influence in the organization, because they feel they've given you some input and now they're going to see what you do with it. Usually, the instinct is to say, "Gee, I need a little more time to sort it out." But in point of fact, you don't have all that much time. You need to think fast and move fast. After that, it's follow-up. That's where people decide whether or not you mean what you say, whether or not you have the personal discipline to actually execute the changes, programs, or promises that were made in phase two.

While there is a risk in postponing all "decisive decisions" early on, it is often possible to project decisiveness while putting off the really crucial decisions. One leader described this stance as being decisive, but deciding not to decide yet. He described his approach this way:

> I try to pick certain kinds of decisions that can be made quickly to set a tone. Somebody comes in to me and says, "I agreed to hold off on my salary increase because we're going to see how this business is developing. Now it looks like we're going to come in at 50 percent over our objectives. I would like to see if I could get my salary increase." That's where I make a snap judgment and say, "Reinstate it, retroactive back to January 1." They say, "Wow, he's precise and he's decisive." But if someone else comes in and says, "I want to take a giant chunk out of this business operation, and these are the reasons," I say, "Well, that's your prerogative, but let's think about this a little bit further." You try to communicate the right message about your attitude, to communicate a proactivity even while you're holding off on the giant decisions. For the first three months, the objective is to have people say, "Wow. He's a decisive person . . . but he hasn't made up his mind yet." You can do that for the first three months, but after that you had just better get consistently decisive.

A related issue is involving subordinates in decision making. The new leader has to establish authority while at the same time encouraging input and consultation. This can be a difficult balance to achieve:

> It's hard to build consensus about some of these very difficult decisions. It's a dilemma. If your objective is to build consensus and you

can't make a decision until you have consensus—I've seen that kind of leader—you're in deep trouble because it's paralytic. The buck has to stop here. The alternative is to get a lot of input, to make people understand that their thoughts and their views are being solicited, but that the leader is a decisive person. And you want the right balance, not like "He doesn't listen to anything that I say, he doesn't even understand the organization and he's making all these decisions," but rather "He really listened to me. I didn't persuade him this time, but he asked me a lot of good questions."

Another important skill is the ability to convert consultation into commitment to the leader's decisions. One leader described his approach:

When I arrived, there was some whining about how they never got asked for input and would go to meetings and kind of smile, nod their heads, and walk out saying, "Boy, was that stupid." So I got them together and said, "You guys have told me you didn't think our plans are rooted in what the customers need. So here's your chance. I want you guys to give constructive criticism here." And they did, and we really had a good session. The turning point came three or four weeks later when we were going to present the plans to all their people. I grabbed them before the meeting and I said, "Look, you guys have had input. I want you in front of your people to show public support for these plans now. You had your chance to change the plans. Now I want you guys to step up and lead your people, not just sit there like one more member of the audience." That was a little bit of a defining moment for how we were going to work around here.

Being focused but flexible

Another difficult balancing act pits focus against flexibility. Most new leaders are achievement-oriented and driven. They are able to concentrate on the end objective to the exclusion of almost everything else: it's the price of admission. But a vicious circle can result if the new leader comes across as inflexible and unwilling to consider more than one way to solve a problem. Stubbornly maintaining one's course is dangerous. Some leaders we interviewed warned against appearing too dogmatic and directive:

> Some people tend to think there's only one answer to a problem, maybe because they were successful [applying it elsewhere]. I think there are multiple ways to solve problems. It's very important [to recognize this]. I may feel very strongly about something, but if somebody comes up with something that's really contrary, I will give them a shot if it is well thought-out. [The key is not to] get caught up in the ego thing.

> You get into trouble if you come in and tell people, "This is wrong." Now I believe there are ten different ways to solve the same problem. It doesn't matter which one [we end up using]; you get to the same result. So I think it's very, very important when you go into a company to signal that you trust people and are open to their ideas.

Being active without causing commotion

There can be a fine line between getting things moving and overwhelming the organization. Leaders must be active without being perceived as going off in all directions or pressing people to the point of burnout. As one leader admitted: "I came perilously close to pushing people beyond their limits of what they could tolerate in terms of change." This typically happens because the new leader feels he has to make big changes to be recognized: "Some people take over a business and practically dismantle the whole damn thing. That produces a lot of disruption and hurts the business. You pay a price for that. If you don't know what you're reorganizing to do better, all you do is destroy continuity without achieving any particular goal."

Another hazard is overestimating employees' ability to absorb change. One leader expressed it this way:

> I think the people who are most successful at transitioning into new places really are change agents. The ones that are really successful

follow the basic tenets of a good change-management discipline. They are strong leaders to begin with, and understand all the old principles—you know, "We're only as good as the weakest link," and "You've got to bring everybody along." You have to recognize that everybody comes along at different speeds. It means readjusting your expectations sometimes, understanding what's important and what's not important at a particular point.

The successful leaders we interviewed carefully calibrated the number of initiatives they pressed the organization to undertake, in response to tension levels in the organization. They know when to turn up the heat a bit and when to pull back.

Being willing to make the tough calls but humane

Most leaders inherited at least one subordinate who needed to be replaced, requiring an early tough call involving a person's career and livelihood. In the words of one leader:

> You have to have the fortitude to step up to the fact that you have to make people changes. Nobody likes to tell somebody that they didn't make the team or that their services are no longer required. But if you don't do that, and people see that the same people are kept around forever, it sends a real bad message throughout the whole organization. I'll be honest: when we let certain people go, I got a ton of e-mail congratulating me. If I kept those people on, others would have said, "Oh, here we go again. More of the same."

When the new leader decides that someone must leave, it's important to move quickly and not prolong the inevitable. Said one leader:

> It's important that it be done [as positively as possible], but also done decisively. The approach I've taken is to sit down with someone and explain the situation, explain the challenge it's been for me to reach the conclusion I've reached, but say, "Hey, the right thing

for you to do is to move on, and here's a generous financial package to do that." Then I treat it as a decision made [and try to move on].

At the same time, our leaders recognized that these changes must be managed in ways that will be perceived as fair and that will preserve to the greatest extent possible the dignity of the people involved. One leader pointed out the risks of perceived callousness: "You have to find who you don't want and then you have to deal with them fairly, because people are watching." Even if other employees agree that a particular individual is not performing well and should be replaced, the new leader's credibility will suffer if the deed is perceived to have been handled unfairly. Peoples' opinions often hinge on whether the leader has offered other options to an employee who is well regarded but ill suited to a particular job.

ESTABLISHING CREDIBILITY WITH BOSSES

Experienced leaders point to some keys to success in building a productive working relationship with the boss.[2]

Clarifying mutual expectations early

Goal discussions with the CEO and the Board during the recruiting process represent the first opportunity to begin to shape a clear set of shared expectations. As one executive reported:

> I'd say, "Tell me how you would define in one year and in five years whether or not the person who takes this job is successful? What are the must-do's?" And what didn't they want? And then I'd say, "Tell me what constraints you have in mind." You can't just [expect them to] turn over the keys. What is it that is essential in this job, and what are the things that there's local option on? What are my areas of latitude with respect to people who work there? What do you want done and what are the limits?

A straightforward focus on defining achievable expectations can convey that the candidate is careful about committing only to what she believes she can accomplish.

The wise new leader is also careful to learn enough about her new organization and its capacity for change before making iron-clad commitments to a new boss. Early commitments can be double-edged swords, and many experienced leaders adhere to the same wise rule for dealing with new bosses and with industry analysts: underpromise and overdeliver.

Getting quick results in areas important to the CEO

Whatever one's own sense of the priorities, it is important to identify what the CEO cares about and to pursue results in these areas. One person we interviewed put it this way: "There was an issue I didn't think was a priority but he did. I thought, 'Well, if it's that important to him, let's get it done. If this is going to be one of his priorities, it's going to be one of my priorities.' That's the way it works."

As Andy's experience illustrates (see Chapter 1), ignoring what is important to the CEO can have serious consequences. According to one of several new leaders who commented on this need to balance their own and their bosses' agendas:

> He [the CEO] kept talking about inventory. He never said, "Fix it," or even "Come back to me with a plan," but just sort of mentioned it a lot. I didn't pay much attention to it . . . It wasn't really on my screen. Then [the CFO], who I'd gotten to know pretty well, said one day that [the CEO] had been in his office ranting and raving about inventories growing and lower [inventory] turns, and complained that I wasn't paying attention. He [the CFO] explained some history to me, when we'd gotten into real trouble in the past. I hadn't heard the story before. It was a near-death sort of experience, and [the CEO] steered the company through the tough times. Since then he had used inventory levels as a prime indicator of our [operational] health and as a predictor of problems. I never talked to [the CEO] about it, but the next week I started regular inventory

and asset-management reviews. From then on, I paid a lot more attention to it.

Getting good marks from those who influence the CEO

The new leader parachutes into a terrain bristling with preexisting relationships between the CEO and key advisors. Some may be direct subordinates of the new leader, others peers; still others will be several layers down. Sometimes the CEO's closest advisors are on the Board. Regardless of their formal status, the CEO will look to these tried-and-true advisors to confirm or refute his own impressions of the new leader.

The new leader must therefore work to understand those relationships. As in other areas we have looked at, becoming something of a historian can help. Who has grown up professionally with the CEO? Who worked with him in the best and worst of times? Who moved in tandem with the CEO and who did he keep promoting?

Never forgetting who's boss

A new leader who is hired to improve performance with the expectation of advancing to the top spot naturally wants to produce tangible results quickly, and for others to see those results as having arisen from his efforts. New leaders are chosen because they bring different ways of operating to their new companies and because of their abilities as change agents. If, like Andy, they formulate a plan without the buy-in of the CEO, the risk of failure is high whether or not it is the correct path for the organization. New leaders who get caught in this trap are victims, in part, of expectations raised by the Board and the CEO. After failing in his new position, Andy insisted: "I was only doing what they [had] told me they wanted . . . I know I was right." While it is true that the Board and the CEO had encouraged Andy to act in a way that led to his failure, he overlooked the CEO's alarm at his approach, which ultimately led the CEO to convince the Board that Andy should not succeed him. Addressing this issue, one leader said:

Sometimes [subordinates] get the idea that they can go around you and skip a link in the chain. Or they'll inform you lightly enough so that you can't complain that they went around you and didn't inform you. And you have to alert them to the fact that you know about things like this, [and yet] not do it in a way that is hostile or keeps them from [providing adequate feedback]. I remember calling in one of my people after he did this once, and I said, "You do this again and I'll fire you." And he said, "I'm sorry, it was just the circumstances, and I promise I'll never do it again." And that person kept the bargain.

In another case, a new COO recognized warning signs and adjusted before a problem developed with his boss:

It [inconsistent behavior by the CEO] got to be so bad that my people were starting to notice . . . That's what got my attention. I didn't go to confront him, because I wasn't sure how he'd react. So I just tried to figure out the [cause-and-effect] relationship between when he'd acted that way and things that might have triggered it. Once I did that, I began to see that some things had happened that put me more in the spotlight. Maybe it was analysts who paid a lot [more] attention to me than to him, or a call for an interview that came to me rather than him. So I had to decide whether I'd back off and be very careful or care more about being in the limelight. In the end it wasn't hard, because I kept my eye on the [end] goal.

ESTABLISHING CREDIBILITY WITH PEERS

A new leader in the number-two position must establish lateral relationships with other division heads and functional leaders who report to the CEO, such as the CFO and general counsel.[3] Many of the same principles that promote credibility downward and upward—such as engaging in regular consultation and being seen as decisive but judicious, focused yet flexible, and able to make the tough calls—also apply to lateral relationships.

In building lateral relationships, the new leader should seek mutual respect and obligation but recognize the inevitability of competition. Often this is simply a matter of helping peers solve problems, recognizing their efforts, and showing interest in what is important to them. The resulting reservoir of obligation will generate impulses to reciprocate that the new leader can draw on. One leader gave this advice:

> Instead of thinking of it as all zero-sum, dog-eat-dog, realize that other people need to get things done. And if you become a source of help to them—if you [create] something where they're more likely to come away with a positive or helpful experience than a negative one—you're more likely to have more people turning to you. I help you get your job done and you help me get my job done, and we are both serving the organization and hurting no one. So the idea that you should be protective [of your turf] is profoundly mistaken, because, essentially, that means people may not encroach on your turf but they're not going to add to your turf. If they can provide you with information, they can support your position so your turf actually expands.

Becoming of the organization but not captive to it

Employees, bosses, and peers all want to know whether the new leader will champion things they care about. Does she identify with the core values they cherish? Will her initiatives be those they believe important? Will subordinates' hopes for advancement and development be realized? Should they anticipate stability or turmoil? Others' anxieties represent one more contradiction for the new leader to manage: becoming part of the organization while maintaining the flexibility to make the inevitable tough decisions. One leader emphasized the sense of all-being-in-it-together:

> The most important thing to do is to make sure that the people who are there understand that you're there as part of their team and they as part of your team . . . and that they recognize—largely by your actions, not by your words—that you understand you can't succeed without them . . . so that they know that their stake in the institution is recognized by you . . . that you're part of the team and

that you're not a free agent, and you are not trying to build your reputation as an individual at the expense of them.

Another emphasized demonstrating respect:

> You have to show the folks that you've inherited that you have some respect for their judgment and thoughts and work, and that you're not just going to throw all the cards up in the air and start anew. You should assume that a competent group will get it right 80 percent of the time, which means that you shouldn't be changing more than a fifth of the decisions. And if you are, it says that you've got real problems.

At the same time, the new leader has to maintain flexibility and avoid being captured by the agendas of employees. As one leader cautioned: "You can easily be shaped by them instead of you shaping them. And the people who allegedly are working for you will be trying to capture you for their purposes."

Another pointed out the subtle messages that one's choice of issues sends: "You need to be able to kind of pick and choose those issues that, in fact, demonstrate to them that you're committed institutionally, but at the same time that you're an independent person and you're not just going to pick up their agenda and go represent them . . . That's the leadership challenge."

How can a new leader demonstrate the value she places on past accomplishments without condoning performance below the standards she wants to set? Half of the answer is to point out straightforwardly what should not have happened or should have been done differently. Anything less would be treating employees as unable to recognize a better way to operate, and would squander an opportunity to make a strong statement about her expectations. The other half of the answer, however, is that honesty must be employed with care. Criticizing past efforts can easily come across as self-serving, and can cause the people associated with them to become angry adversaries or victims deserving of sympathy. The new leader also risks being perceived as unfair to predecessors who were reacting to the pressures of a different time. One leader put it this way:

By definition, you're dealing with something deeply entrenched and powerfully rationalized. There's a wonderful New England expression, "Don't tear down the fence 'til you know why it was built." There are reasons these structures—these cultural characteristics—exist, and they were initially by and large good ones. I believe one of the biggest mistakes you can make is to assume your predecessors were stupid. They did things for a reason. And, until you know what the reason is, you're probably better off being cautious about it.

"Separating the people from the problem" is a valuable survival skill that may help new leaders manage this tension.[4] What this maxim means is to focus on the substance of problems while avoiding personal criticism of predecessors. Besides casting the new leader himself in a negative light, personal criticism imposes strain on the people who remain loyal to their prior leaders and could sabotage the teamwork the new leader must foster. As one pointed out:

> When you first go in, don't go in like a bull in a china shop, unless the guy there before you has been fired, and maybe even then. There are going to be lots of people who will still respect him. To build teamwork, you want to move it firmly in the direction you want to go, but not by creating a lot of animosity you then have a problem getting rid of.

In sum, there are two ways to get into trouble while seeking to become of the organization but avoiding being captive to it. One is to denigrate the past; the other is to "go native." The best new leaders we interviewed had sensitive antennae and were able to avoid both traps. They could tell it as it is without doling out blame unnecessarily. At the same time, they were able to be sensitive to people's concerns without being mired in old ways of doing things.

Sending signals

Employees initially don't know much about the new leader. Some may have been given a biographical profile, and the most enterprising may even have ferreted out information about his reputation at his previous company. But even that provides no more than the briefest sketch of who the new leader is. As one leader put it: "Before you [arrive], it's always kind of a secret, because they don't want to announce you until they're sure you're the right one and they're sure that you're going to take the job and so on. So maybe you've met some people in the company, but a very small group."

People are understandably curious about the new leader's judgment, values, and energy. They also hope to discern (and, in some cases, shape) the new leader's intentions. Where does she think we should go? What will change? How will it affect me? Human beings share a powerful drive to make sense of what is going on by reducing uncertainty and identifying potential threats and opportunities.[5] Early in a transition, this drive may cause some employees to overinterpret scraps of information about the new leader. They may try to discern the new leader's behavior patterns and mindset on the slender basis of a few initial interactions and stories they hear from others.

The new leader, in turn, wants to shape people's early impressions, form relationships, establish expectations, and influence behavior. He immediately begins to send signals—consciously and unconsciously—through a series of small decisions, actions, and interactions with people who in turn share their impressions with others. Emblematic anecdotes about the leader begin to circulate as early impressions are elaborated and reinforced; eventually they begin to harden into conventional wisdom. For good or ill, the new leader may be pigeon-holed in a way that helps employees make sense of a changing situation. Once consigned to such a box, it's hard to escape.

Opinion formation is very challenging to manage.[6] Opinions are rarely shaped by a single defining event—unless it is so anomalous as to seem particularly telling about the new leader's character—although an event can confirm and crystallize a widely held opinion.

Instead, the process of building credibility tends to be incremental, since most of the signals the new leader sends will be small. It is the overall pattern that matters. Is what the new leader says consistent with what he does? Does he seem to be focused on the well-being of the organization or on self-aggrandizement? Does he keep confidences? How does he treat the people he deals with most closely? How does he treat people who are not powerful and thus may be less important to his success?

Let us look at three guidelines for managing the signal-sending process during the transition period.

Guideline One: Don't try to exert too much control over other's perceptions

A new leader can't hope to control every subtle aspect of his own behavior. Some of what we do is done unconsciously—it may be perceived by others but not by us. The new leader's true colors will come through in unguarded moments and in spontaneous reactions to unexpected events. While it is important to be self-aware, the new leader's credibility will be shaped by unconscious and sponta- neous acts over time as much as it is by careful, planned behavior. As one leader commented about the nuances of credibility building:

> I think you do that [build credibility] in almost subconscious ways. You just do it day by day, with people watching how you deal with meetings, how you deal with minor crises, whether you treat people fairly, whether you're articulate, whether you tell them why you did what you did, whether you've got some integrity when the pres- sure's on. So I don't think there's any formula for that. It really has to do with day-to-day performance, and since people's leadership styles are so different, I think they watch you kind of an inch at a time. It's not the big things.

Entering a complex social system with its own culture and power structure, the new leader can't fully anticipate or control others' reactions. At times, what she does will be interpreted through distorting (and perhaps self-serving) lenses over which she exercises little control, at least in the short run.

The point is to accept that neither one's impulses nor how they are perceived can be entirely controlled. This is often clear in hindsight, but hard for a new leader to accept when she is anxious to make her mark in a new environment. By anticipating the inevitable miscues that result from spontaneous reactions, new leaders will be better prepared to remedy them. An observer described one new leader's approach this way:

> [The new leader] handled that pretty well. He'd sometimes explode when things took too long or someone did something [the new leader] warned about [that should thus have been avoided]. But then he'd say, "Hey, I'm sorry I blew up like that, but it's not because I'm angry at you. It's just that I want this place to be all that it can be, and stuff like that just slows everything down." He was just passionate about doing things right, and people respected that once they understood that. By taking responsibility for it and admitting that he'd reacted without thinking, he took the sting out of it.

Guideline Two: Some actions resonate more than others

Sometimes the impact of early acts can spread far beyond the few people directly involved. The new leader's actions are likely to be communicated widely, told and retold, becoming defining stories that can powerfully shape the beliefs of people in the organization. People's curiosity about the new leader represents an opportunity to make these defining stories positive illustrations of the sort of place he wants the company to be. But if they are negative, they can cause potentially irreparable damage. Consider the following account:

> I used to go around and have what we call brown-bag lunches [with groups of employees], and I would give them the status of the company and then open the floor to any questions they wanted to ask me. And I told them, "Ask me any question you want. It's okay. There are no boundaries here." At one meeting we had 500 people, and a woman asked a question that was controversial in the area that she worked in. And after the meeting her manager went to her and said, "You never should have asked that ques-

tion." I had enough of a reputation at that point that people knew that I was fairly open . . . Word came back to me . . . I found out about it. So I called that manager into my office with his manager and the [next-level] manager who reported to me. And I looked at him and I said, "Look, I don't know who the hell you think you are. I said they could ask any question they want. You go back and say they shouldn't. I said I want an open environment." So I said to the manager, "You have a pure and simple choice. You either tell me you'll never do that again, that you believe in an open environment, and you personally go back to that person and apologize and tell her why what you did was wrong. Or you walk out the door today, 'cause I don't want you as part of the management team. And I want you to go back and tell every manager that you know how strongly I believe in this." I've got to tell you, the message went out! When I started, 90-some percent of all letters I received from employees were anonymous. Three years later I very seldom ever got an anonymous letter. They were all signed.

This leader acted intuitively, articulating forcefully what he believed was right, and the organization was energized by it. His action was seen as a statement of the new values of the company.

Guideline Three: Seize the moment

The leaders who were most successful at building credibility took advantage of the opportunities that happened to come their way. Attuned to the decisive importance of certain moments and situations, they seized these openings when they presented themselves.[7] One leader offered the following example:

Early on I went to tour the plants. The last one was a division that had been very profitable for a long time and had pretty much been left alone. [The CEO had] said to me that I ought to leave it alone and get on with other problems, that it was making a lot of money and he didn't want anything to get in the way. Everything I heard about it was positive, but everything had to do with the numbers, and I wasn't prepared for what I saw. The place was a [mess] . . . I hadn't seen a plant so dirty and so cluttered in years. Food on the floor, cobwebs in the corners, and trash cans overflowing. Lift trucks were operating too fast; the men's room hadn't been cleaned since the Civil War. There was inventory everywhere and parts and sub-assemblies were just thrown in piles.

I was speechless. It was a good thing that we had dominated in this market and that there was only one other big [manufacturer]. If there was more competition, and if [the product] was more price-sensitive, we would have been out of business.

I found out that I was the first [executive from headquarters] to visit the plant in twenty years. Everyone had just gone to [division headquarters]. Well, after I was able to speak again, I read the riot act to [the division president], his plant manager, and his head of HR. I could have just talked to the [division president] privately, but I had no faith that he'd translate what I felt. I told him the plant was a disgrace and they should be ashamed . . . that we couldn't expect the workforce to go out of their way for customers and cut costs or improve quality while the division was so disrespectful of them. I told them that I wanted a plan to fix up that plant on my desk within a week, and I was going to come back in thirty days, and if I couldn't eat off the floor I'd replace them all.

[The division president] started to complain that [the CEO] had never had a problem. I cut him off and went right up to him and said, "That's because he hasn't been out there to see that mess . . . and you work for me now and I'm telling you to get this done."

Well, I went back in exactly thirty days and it was like night and day. People had come in on weekends to paint the floor and clean the place up. The HR guy got the idea to buy uniforms for all the workers, and these guys were proud of them. I'm still not sure [the division president] will make it in the long run, but at least for now the quality and safety record is much better. The thing about all this, though, was that the visit sent a message that was very important . . . You know, the story got all around the corporation. [The CEO] knew about it before I got back to Corporate. And all of it in a visit that wasn't supposed to be a big deal in a division where everything was supposed to be fine.

Credibility is essential to mobilize the energy of employees. But it's hard to build, easy to lose, and difficult to regain. To build personal credibility, the new leader must come to be seen as having the judgment, values, and energy necessary to take people into unfamiliar territory. Chapter 5 will explore the process of determining what that territory should be.

5

GETTING
ORIENTED

If the beginning of a transition is like being at sea in a fog, it should be an early priority to figure out one's location and whether one's course is correct. Will the company's current course take it where it needs to go? Will it arrive there in the fastest and most efficient way? To answer such questions, one needs a map and compass. Hazards must be avoided and safe channels found. All the new leaders we spoke with devoted themselves early on to understanding the marketplace and matched it to the company's strategy and capabilities. A solid understanding of this relationship prepared them to fill in gaps and leverage resources.

This chapter looks first at assessing a company's strategy and organizational capabilities. It begins with mapping the stated strategy—what it says it is trying to do—and then the de facto strategy, as revealed in what people are actually doing. We will then turn to assessing the company's organizational capabilities through three distinct lenses—technical, cultural, and political—in order to identify gaps and underutilized resources. The chapter ends with a detailed set of guidelines to the aims, timing, and sequencing of one's information-gathering efforts. Chapter 6 will address in detail the *how* of the new leader's knowledge acquisition during the transition period, exploring tools and techniques for learning.

MAPPING THE EXISTING STRATEGY

How can a new leader determine quickly whether the strategy he has inherited is the best one? How can he pinpoint gaps between the prevailing state and the ideal state? If a different strategy is needed, when is the best time to change course?

Mapping the current strategy is a two-stage process. The first step is to grasp the stated strategy. The next task is to uncover the de facto strategy (represented by how people actually behave and how decisions are actually made) and identify differences between it and the stated strategy.[1]

The stated strategy

Without question, any new leader should undertake analysis of the industry, competitive positioning, and sources of competitive advantage.[2] Beyond understanding strategic position and driving forces, however, it is vital to assess the coherence and adequacy of the stated strategy.

Coherence. Is the stated strategy coherent? The coherence test probes the extent to which the strategy has a defensible logic. How can the new leader tell if the underlying logic is viable? One way is to disassemble the strategy into its component parts, arraying them side by side to see how they relate to each other, and then to ask diagnostic questions:

- Is there a logic that remains intact from one part of the strategy to another?

- When an analysis of market forces is compared to the five-year objectives, is there an obvious connection?

- Is the five-year new-product development budget in accord with the capital investments projected in the Operations portion of the strategy?

- Is projected investment in the sales force consistent with the market segments judged most likely to grow?

- Are plans in place to prepare the sales force for new products in the pipeline?

- If the strategy suggests that the marketplace is inexorably shifting in a new direction, is there a procedure in place to attract and train people to keep the company ahead of those shifts?

- Is the company's information-technology investment sufficient to keep pace with the systems change that the strategy will require?

Some of these questions can be answered during the fuzzy front end, though most will be answered after the new leader's entry when more strategic information will be available.

Consistency and coherence of these kinds are not difficult to find when the strategy has been well thought through; they will not appear if the strategy lacks logic. If logic is lacking or faulty to the point that the success of the first era is in doubt, the leader must raise her misgivings with the CEO.

Adequacy. Our new leaders all entered companies whose strategies were logically coherent, but some found strategies that were unable to adapt to market changes. This is a matter of adequacy: a strategy may be well thought through and logically integrated but in the final analysis insufficient for what the organization wants to accomplish. The new leader may find certain diagnostic questions useful in assessing adequacy:

- Will the toughest industry analysts conclude that the company has chosen a path that will provide enough return for the costs and effort expended?

- Are plans in place to secure, develop, or maintain enough resources?

- Are the long-term profit targets high enough? Is enough money budgeted for capital equipment? for research?

Since new leaders are typically brought into situations in which the Board (and perhaps the CEO) has decided that not enough is being done, the answers are not likely to be affirmative.

Much can be determined about the strategy's adequacy by probing the history of its creation:

- Who were the driving forces behind it?

- If a particular person or group had disproportionate influence on the strategy, what was their impact on its adequacy?

- Was the strategy development too hurried? If so, does its haste indicate that it was not well integrated with the day-to-day activities of the business? Alternatively, was the process too slow-paced, perhaps indicating a low priority?

The new leader can start this investigation before joining, but thorough assessments must await familiarity with the market, the company's customers, and the challenges those customers face.

The de facto strategy

After assessing the coherence and adequacy of the company's stated strategy, the new leader is ready to tease out the company's actual strategy and to compare the two. Useful questions include these:

- Are the metrics specified or suggested in the stated strategy used to make day-to-day decisions?

- Are the dimensions of performance tracked regularly by the management group those that are stressed or implied in the strategy?

- If the strategy requires teamwork and cross-functional integration, are people trying to act in such a way today?

- If the strategy requires employees to acquire new skills, is the training and development infrastructure in place to generate those skills? If not, is such an infrastructure being planned and pursued actively?

- If market-share growth requires being a low-cost producer, does the appropriate base exist to combine cost reduction, delivery capability, and speed?

- Does a cost-containment mentality prevail? What evidence is there? If so, what safeguards ensure that customers do not suffer as the company controls costs?

- Are hard data (as opposed to assumptions) being used to reduce the current cost base?

- If flexibility in manufacturing and delivery are called for, are production facilities, warehouses, and the systems that support them modified and upgraded on a regular basis?

The point here is to assess the extent to which the stated strategy and the de facto strategy are congruent and, if they are incongruent, whether the mismatch is due to problems on the formulation side or the implementation side.

Modifying the stated strategy

If the new leader discovers a seriously flawed strategy, is it possible during the transition period to bring about a radical change in how the strategy is implemented? Yes. Is it likely? Not unless impending doom is readily apparent and the new leader has superb persuasive skills. Most organizations with a history of success treat strategic planning as a serious undertaking and work carefully to secure Board approval. Significantly changing a strategy that the Board has approved will not be easy. Among the more than thirty senior executives we interviewed and many others we have observed and worked with through the years, only two mounted serious direct challenges to existing strategy during their initial six months on the job. One (not Andy) was fired by the CEO; the other, certain that prevailing strategy would lead to short-term failure, convinced his CEO to make a radical shift.

A new leader who believes the inherited strategy will bring trouble in the short term has a responsibility to raise questions. The nature and urgency of the questions, of course, depend on the magnitude of the new leader's alarm and the support she has garnered among people with influence.

If, by contrast, the existing strategy appears capable of moving the organization forward, but neither fast enough nor far enough, the wisest course is to adapt it as much as possible and plan for more substantial changes when appropriate. The ideal time to push for such changes will arrive when the leader has learned more about the company and its circumstances and has won broad support among important constituencies. The first natural opportunity after joining is typically the next strategic-planning update cycle, which often begins in the second or third quarter of each fiscal year. Even a new leader who joined immediately following such a cycle would have to wait only a year before participating formally in strategic planning—in most cases, barely enough time to have established the knowledge and power base necessary to alter the strategic path. It is likely that, for the first year or two, the leader will follow the strategic path set before she was hired. For this reason, she must understand its coherence and adequacy, as well as the capacity of the organization to change. This knowledge will be invaluable as she prepares an era plan to move the company forward.

ASSESSING ORGANIZATIONAL CAPABILITIES

After analysis of the company's stated and de facto strategies, the next step is to gauge the capabilities of the organization, identifying gaps to be filled in and resources to be leveraged. Why does the de facto strategy differ from the strategy that the organization's leaders have decided on? The answer usually resides in the capacity of the organization to change and to achieve more than it has before.

How can the new leader assess the organization's capabilities efficiently? Insight is maximized by viewing the organization through three separate lenses: a *technical lens* to assess the infrastructure of processes, technologies, and skills; a *cultural lens* to identify the underlying values and attitudes of employees; and a *political lens* to clarify how influence is distributed and used.[3] While the leaders we interviewed didn't explicitly articulate this distinction, their diagnostic efforts focused on these three realms.

The technical lens

The technical lens focuses attention on core processes, technologies, and supporting skills. The fundamental question to ask about core processes is how well the existing infrastructure positions the company to meet the demands posed by the strategy. Are existing processes capable of meeting and exceeding the requirements of customers and other key constituencies? Key constituencies and the core processes associated with each are summarized in Table 5-1.

The particulars of the investigation will depend on the type of business and the history of the company, but these questions may shed light on the strengths, vulnerabilities, and flexibility of existing processes and technologies, and of employees' knowledge and skills. New leaders can pursue these questions globally early on and progressively focus on particular units and facilities as the diagnostic process proceeds. To the greatest extent possible, impressions and insights should be captured briefly in writing to facilitate subsequent analysis.

- Are employee skills and procedures adequate to sustain high performance?

- What are the core technologies on which the company's equity, reputation, and industry standing depend? Are they the same as those the strategy calls for? In other words, does the strategy call for a change in the technologies that built the company's reputation?

- What is the history of investments to strengthen the company's technology base and how has their effectiveness been measured?

- Has the technical-training and education budget grown or shrunk over the past five years? What efforts have been made to ensure that employees stay up to date on technical developments?

- Have budgets for research staff and equipment, and other research-related technology assets, grown at the same pace as volume and profit growth?

TABLE 5-1   KEY CONSTITUENCIES AND CORE PROCESSES

Constituency	Core Processes
Customers	Production processes Service-delivery processes New-product development Supporting-technology development
Suppliers	Production planning systems Materials-handling systems Ordering and payment systems Quality and inspection systems
Employees	Work design Appraisal and reward systems Education and development systems Salary and benefits processing Information systems
Management	Planning systems Budgeting, measurement, and control systems Information systems

- Is the documentation on key technologies kept in a central location? Is it up to date? Is it widely accessible? Do employees take advantage of it?

- Does the company have an affiliation with one or more research institutions? Are they the optimal ones for this company? Are they utilized effectively? Are the company's best people involved?

The cultural lens

The cultural lens examines collective values and norms and their impact on the company's ability to sustain a high level of performance. It focuses attention on the norms the company promotes concerning employees' roles in the organization and the purpose of work in their lives and examines values on issues like authority and participation in decision making.[4]

To diagnose aspects of the corporate culture that may be undermining performance, the new leader might begin with questions like these:

- Are people capable of focusing sustained attention on key issues, establishing priorities, and marshaling the critical mass of resources necessary to pursue them, or are their efforts diffuse and unfocused?

- Do key processes and people deliver the necessary performance crisply and consistently, or are wide variations permitted in quality, cost, and speed?

- Is internal competition for turf more vigorous than external competition with other companies?

- Are innovative products and processes developed and brought to market as well as or better than they are by the company's best competitors?

- Does an appropriate sense of urgency prevail about pursuing priorities and responding to problems?

Table 5-2 summarizes some commonplace patterns and associated symptoms that stand in the way of high performance. Note that an organization can be highly energized but still unfocused and undisciplined. Alternatively, focus and discipline may be misplaced and may take a toll on the innovative spirit.

Assessments of the culture can also help the new leader understand how communication and information sharing actually work. These are the questions that our successful leaders recommended asking:

- How are communications systems and media used and by whom?

- Is there an active grapevine that carries messages throughout the organization, or do people tend to rely on more formal mechanisms to find out what is going on?

- Are top-level managers visible and accessible or remote?

- Has the vision of the CEO been disseminated and reinforced by senior managers, or do their messages indicate a different view of the company?

- Is the external image of the company consistent with how it communicates internally?

- How well does the text of the latest annual report correlate with the results of the latest employee-climate survey?

The political lens

Some companies depend on individuals to set the tone for change; in others, groups wield the most power. In some, being toughest or working the longest hours enhances influence, while in other settings the most influential people are those who are easiest to work with. Sometimes power depends primarily on the number of people one has mentored, while elsewhere it is a function of the size of one's department. There is no formula; the leader must master carefully and quickly the unique power structure in his new company.

TABLE 5-2 COMMON CULTURAL PROBLEMS

Shortcoming	Symptom
Focus	Organization is unable to define priorities or has too many priorities.
	Resources are spread too thin, leading to frequent crises and fire-fighting responses.
	People are rewarded for their ability to fight fires.
Discipline	Core processes and key people exhibit wide variations in performance.
	Employees don't understand that inconsistency carries negative consequences.
	Failure to meet commitments is excused.
Innovation	Focus is on internal benchmarks of performance rather than competitors' performance.
	Generation-to-generation progress in products and processes is slow and incremental.
	People are rewarded for maintaining stable performance, not for pushing the envelope.
Teamwork	Competitiveness is directed internally rather than externally.
	Functions vie to protect turf rather than cooperating to advance a shared agenda.
	People are rewarded for creating fiefdoms.
Urgency	Lack of focus on external and internal customers prevails.
	Responsiveness is not treated as an important value.
	Complacency is expressed in attitudes like "We are the best and always have been," or "It doesn't matter if we do it right now because it won't make a difference."

Three fundamental political questions are these:

1. Whose support is required to shape and implement a strategy to change the culture and improve performance?

2. How supportive are they likely to be?

3. Who will remain part of the team throughout the era and who will have to leave?

In order to answer these political questions, the new leader must identify the key centers of power and determine how influential they are. It is also crucial to become familiar with the issues, participants, and outcomes of past power struggles. The leaders we interviewed contributed a core list of helpful questions to ask:

• Are the most powerful subdivisions of the company line organizations (e.g., plants), line functions (e.g., Marketing), staff functions (e.g., Finance), or product organizations (e.g., a product category)?

• How did the most influential subdivisions acquire their power?

• How has support been rallied for past change efforts?

• What style of influence has worked most effectively? Have people responded to the use of data, logic, or precedent to support an argument? Have people been promised rewards in exchange for their support? Has an image of a compelling and attractive future rallied people? Have disincentives or implied threats been used?

Identifying gaps and underutilized resources

The ultimate goal of assessing the company's technical, cultural, and political landscape is to identify key gaps and underutilized resources. Gaps exist wherever the organization's capabilities are inadequate to support the strategy and sustain improvement. Closing these gaps successfully creates a basis for improvements in performance. Resources are underutilized if they are unrecognized or expended on secondary or peripheral undertakings. Identifying gaps and underutilized resources helps the leader to focus and leverage her change effort.

In the technical domain, gaps might take the form of unprofitable product lines, underperforming production or service-delivery processes, structural misalignments that generate interunit conflicts, or management control systems that undermine productivity. Underutilized resources are likely to be technologies that have not been exploited and groups of experts whose talents are being wasted.

Cultural gaps might include poor attitudes toward customers on the part of front-line workers or either overly centralized or undisciplined approaches to decision making. Cultural resources include core values, such as pride in craftsmanship, that the new leader can tap to stimulate innovation.

In the political domain, groups and individuals who exert disproportionate influence over what gets done can function either as gaps or as resources. They can stand in the way of needed change; on the other hand, convincing powerful people to support change efforts is likely to translate into broader support.

PLANNING TO LEARN

Ideally, learning is a gradual process of accretion. But time is scarce for the new leader, the stakes are high, and the curve is steep. Hardheaded planning is crucial. Different stages of the transition process have different objectives, and one's learning goals should be sequenced accordingly. The period just after entry, for instance, is the time to reexamine earlier assessments about company strategy, probe technical capabilities, and get to know the key players.

The remainder of this chapter consists of objectives and questions to guide learning during the various phases of the transition period. The bulleted questions will help new leaders develop overarching priorities for each phase; the accompanying table lists questions whose answers will help the new leader with deeper diagnosis. Chapter 6 will delve more deeply into the mechanics and strategies of the learning process.

By the End of the Recruiting Process

Objective:

- To know enough to decide whether this job is right for me and whether I'm suited to it.

Questions:

- Do I really want this job? How much?
- Do the Board and CEO want me? How much?
- Does this organization fit my self-image? Why?
- Can I succeed here? What makes me think so?
- If a friend were in my shoes, what advice would I give?

Learning about Strategy	Learning about Technical Capabilities, Culture, and Politics
Does the company measure itself by the standard that the marketplace uses?	How has the organization performed in meeting its commitments?
What are the company's espoused strategy, mission, and core objectives?	Why have previous leaders made it or failed?
Which product categories/divisions have consistently reached their targets? Do they appear to know why?	What are turnover rates for key personnel? Where are they highest?
	How are standards set?
	What happens when standards are not met?
	Who seems to have the most power and why?

By the End of the Fuzzy Front End

Objectives:

- To develop working hypotheses about the big strategic, technical, and political challenges facing the company.
- To finalize a plan for joining the organization.

Questions:

- How do the company's challenges match up with my strengths and shortcomings?
- What signals do I wish to send early on?
- Whom should I talk to, and how, to acquire the simplest, truest picture of the company's strategy and capabilities?

Learning about Strategy	Learning about Technical Capabilities, Culture, and Politics
What gaps in logic are evident in the strategy?	What do analysts and Board members think about how the company is managed?
What do the detailed financials say about the company's real priorities?	What do operating reports reveal about how the place really runs?
What do outside experts believe to be the strengths and weaknesses of the strategy?	What do former employees have to say about the organization?
According to key documents, what does the organization know and not know about its competitors? about its customers?	How effective are the key interfunctional decision-making processes?
Does the sum of the departmental goals and plans match the strategic plan? (For instance, do market-share and growth objectives match new-product plans?)	What evidence is there that top management understands what is happening on the front lines?

By the End of the First Week

Objectives:

- To get off to a good start and figure out where to look more deeply.
- To begin to test hypotheses of how the organization actually works.

Questions:

- How does the place feel to me?
- What are my initial impressions of the top management team?

Learning about Strategy	Learning about Technical Capabilities, Culture, and Politics
What does senior management believe are the company's key short-term problems and opportunities?	Are people open about the problems they face?
Is there consistency in its assessments?	How much cooperation or conflict does there seem to be among key groups?
What do people believe are the longer-term strategic priorities?	Does the pace of the place match the urgency of solving short-term problems and/or realizing longer-term growth potential?
How much growth potential do people think the company has?	
Are barriers to growth apparent to people?	

By the End of the First Month

Objectives:

- To form working hypotheses about the capabilities of the top management team.
- To assess how the organization interacts with customers.
- To get an initial feel for the organization's technical capabilities.
- To begin to identify key power coalitions and information networks.

Questions:

- Where are key opportunities for growth evident?
- What are the biggest threats we face?
- Are the right people in the right places?
- Do we have the capacity to meet customers' expectations?

Learning about Strategy	Learning about Technical Capabilities, Culture, and Politics
Does an orientation to customers prevail among top managers?	Do people follow through on what they promise? Do they worry when commitments are missed?
How do customers rank our service, cost, and quality versus that of our competitors?	Who seems to defer to whom? Who seems to exercise power and why?
Do VPs and managers think about the competition?	Can we deliver what our customers need? Do we have the right operations, sales, and service capabilities?
	Have I heard people criticize or praise the level of skills and knowledge here?
	Do the new products in the pipeline look promising?
	How do the key intra- and interfunctional decision-making processes work?

By the End of the First Six Months

Objectives:

- To understand the power balance and how decisions get made.
- To rough out a plan to move forward on strategy and capability building over the next 18–36 months.
- To decide who stays and who goes.
- To rough out an image of the sort of place this has to become.

Questions:

- Which power coalitions are pivotal for the changes I need to make?
- What must be my A-item priorities?
- Who has to be replaced and how am I going to do it?
- What political support can I count on for what I decide to do?

Learning about Strategy	Learning about Technical Capabilities, Culture, and Politics
What are our best competitors up to? Why?	Does top management seem to work as a team? Who are the team players?
What are the conceptual flaws in the company's strategy? How serious are they?	Does a customer orientation prevail throughout the company?
What do front-line employees think of our service, cost, and quality versus that of our competitors?	Is the talent in place at the top to get the job done? Who is fired up and who isn't?
What do our distributors think of our service, cost, and quality versus that of our competitors?	Will I get the support I need if I move to replace top people?

Learning about Strategy	Learning about Technical Capabilities, Culture, and Politics
What do our suppliers think of us as customers? Are they the best suppliers for us?	What must happen to improve the effectiveness and timeliness of important decisions?
	How motivated are the people on the front line? Do they get the support they need?

Orientation is largely a process of self-education and analysis while the clock is ticking. In Chapter 6 we will look at the mechanics of the learning process, drawing heavily on the experiences of successful leaders.

Part II

ENABLING

TECHNOLOGIES

Part I outlined what new leaders need to do. Part II tells how. Chapters 6, 7, and 8 spell out the practical mechanics of learning, visioning, and coalition building—three technologies that enable the new leader to create momentum during the transition period.

By mastering learning, visioning, and coalition building during the transition period, the new leader builds momentum for change. Effective learning accelerates the clarification of an informed vision.[1] This vision helps the leader to create strong coalitions, which in turn stimulate more learning as the leader taps into supportive people for information and insight. The result is better decisions much earlier in the leader's tenure than would otherwise be possible. Those decisions further increase the pace of the leader's learning. These self-reinforcing *virtuous circles* (see Figure II-1) proved instrumental during the transitions of the successful leaders we spoke with.

By the same token, a new leader who fails to manage learning, visioning, and coalition building well in the first six months can become caught in a *vicious circle* (see Figure II-2). Failure to understand the organization leads to ill-conceived actions that raise employees' doubts, fuel opposition, and alienate potential supporters. Employees may in turn withhold important information and set up conditions for still more trouble. As a result, hypotheses developed prior to entry may not be adequately tested, and people may refuse to participate in the visioning process or to commit themselves to implementation of change initiatives.

Our interviews suggest that the relative amounts of time devoted to learning, visioning, and coalition building tend to shift in predictable ways as the transition period unfolds. The characteristic pattern is illustrated in Figure II-3. During the recruiting and fuzzy-front-end phases, the emphasis is overwhelmingly on learning. Of course, the leader may also make some very preliminary efforts to envision what the organization might become. After entry,

FIGURE II-1 VIRTUOUS CIRCLES

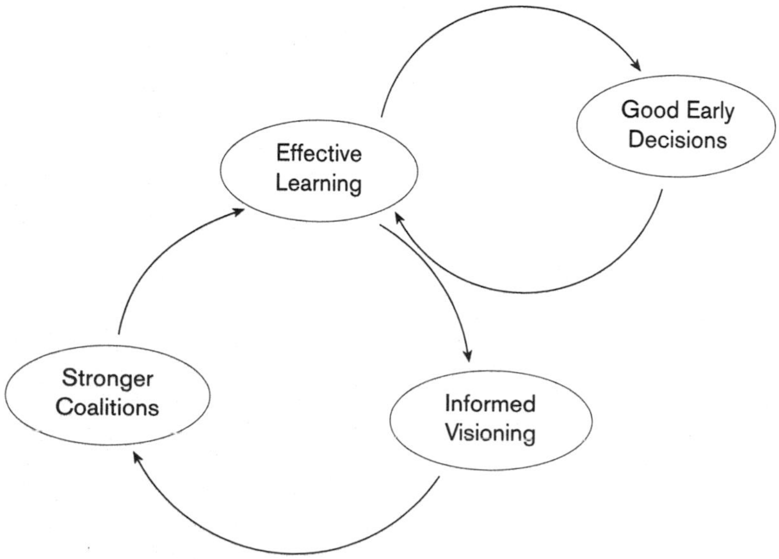

time devoted to visioning begins to increase, and the new leader begins to devote some effort to coalition building. By the end of the first few months, the primary emphasis has shifted from learning to visioning, and efforts at coalition building also begin to intensify. By the end of the transition period, the new leader is spending increasing amounts of time pursuing the support necessary to implement change initiatives.

Skill at all three enabling technologies helps the new leader to create virtuous and avoid vicious circles. Effective learning makes informed visioning possible and helps to identify the coalitions that must be built. Success at transforming a personal vision into a shared one helps to build support for the initiatives necessary to realize it. By the same token, inadequate learning can lead to poor early decisions and uninformed visioning, which in turn can undermine the new leader's ability to build powerful coalitions in support of change, creating a vicious circle.

Our interviews also suggest that the substance of learning, visioning, and coalition building shifts as time passes. During the fuzzy-front-end phase and immediately following formal entry, the

FIGURE II-2 VICIOUS CIRCLES

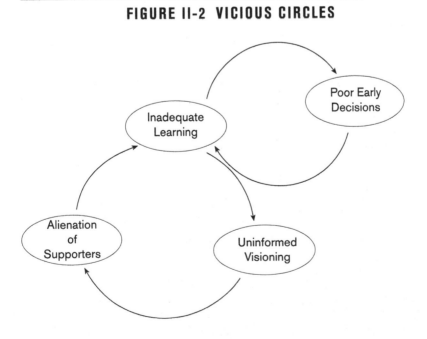

new leader's learning efforts are devoted to orientation. As he begins to map the organization's strategy and to understand its technical, cultural, and political landscape, his learning becomes more refined and interacts with visioning: a grasp of what is stimulates reflection about what should be. Meanwhile, his early coalition-building efforts are aimed at building credibility and pursuing some early wins. By the end of the transition period, coalition-building efforts should have shifted from identifying coalitions deserving of support to creating new coalitions to sustain improvements in performance.

FIGURE II-3 ALLOCATING EFFORT TO CORE TASKS

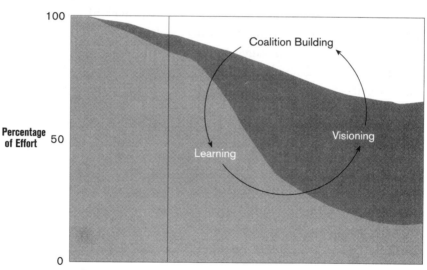

6

LEARNING

Because the new leader's situation is fraught with complexities, much is unknown, and because he is under pressure to make a positive mark quickly, efficient learning during the transition period is vital. The challenge is made trickier by competing demands on his time, systems that present information in unfamiliar ways, and people unaccustomed to his style. Initially, the new leader faces these conditions alone. As if sailing in a fog, the new leader must be deliberate and cautious yet flexible. This chapter offers some navigational aids drawn from the experience of seasoned leaders.

BARRIERS TO LEARNING

Faced with much to do during the transition period, some new leaders unwittingly sacrifice learning for action; they favor decisiveness over inquiry and reflection. Counseling against this approach, one leader observed: "You may feel you have to do things, but what you have to do is take the time to understand the culture and understand what's been happening while you try to understand the problems. Nobody comes to an organization understanding all the problems; you may think you do in the beginning, but you don't."

Putting too much stock in the applicability of one's own experience is a commonplace barrier to learning. Even if the leader has the right answers, employees whose support he needs may be alienated if he seems unwilling to recognize that what worked elsewhere may not be the best solution in this setting. Leaders who arrive behaving as if they have all the answers undermine their own ability to learn. As one leader commented: "I know I'm not smart enough to figure this out alone. I know I'm not smart enough to build in all the considerations that are important, to have all of the angles of perception that one needs to frame up something as important as what we're talking about."

A need to appear decisive can also block learning. Some new leaders believe they must prove themselves by projecting a confident, take-charge attitude. The danger once again is that the new leader will receive unbalanced input and thus will not hear the whole story. One leader explained: "You have to be able to be the student. People should feel like . . . you're helping them to fulfill their full potential. So it's okay to say you don't know everything. If you have to be the teacher all the time, you don't have the right people."

Some new leaders feel uncomfortable delving into organizational culture and politics, which calls for different approaches and a different pace than does reading technical and financial reports. But failure to master the company's culture and politics will surely generate vicious circles. Said one leader: "The most important stuff is what's not written down. It's how power and influence really flow in the organization: what kind of cultural expectations have been set up about what the real goal of the organization is, what the real values are, how it really operates."

At a more personal level, the new leader's own learning style can inhibit learning. Individuals learn in different ways. Some prefer to immerse themselves in detail, for instance, while others use conceptual models to guide their data gathering and analysis. Depending on the circumstances confronting the organization, different learning styles have strengths and weaknesses, as we will see in Chapter 9.

GUIDELINES FOR LEARNING

Five broad guidelines may help new leaders manage their learning during the transition period.

You can't learn everything right away–but you don't need to

Many important things have to be learned on the job. The new leader cannot hope to identify the sources of innovation in the organization or grasp the real political pecking order in the first six months on the job. It doesn't matter how hard he tries; finding the answers to such questions is not a matter of more intense effort. Typically the answers are complex and nuanced, and the only route to such knowledge is ongoing immersion in the organization:

> You stumble over a piece here, and it registers. Then you recognize that something you come across a week later over there has some relationship, but you don't know what it is yet until you hear someone say something for a totally different reason and it starts to come together. If there was a single answer that someone has and is keeping from you, it's easy. But most of the time, the problem is that no one has recognized the pieces and they haven't all been put together.

There is a circular logic to learning during the transition

To make a successful transition, the new leader must understand the organization's culture. But the first issues she encounters are typically performance problems, which she hears about during recruitment and the fuzzy-front-end stage. These performance problems are usually presented as gaps in technical capabilities that she is expected to close ("We can't ship on time because our logistics system doesn't work," or "We don't have a full enough pipeline of new products because Marketing isn't taking the lead," or "Our market share has been flat because Manufacturing can't make a breakthrough in the cost-quality equation"). An effective new leader avoids the temptation to concentrate on symptoms rather than root causes. She utilizes the technical gaps to better understand the organization's strategy and technical capabilities. By doing so, she begins to grasp its politics. Only then can she gain deeper insight into its culture. In this way, a new leader can use a cyclical problem-solving logic in the service of learning during the transition, moving from performance gaps to progressively deeper technical, political, and cultural realities.

You can't completely control your learning strategy

The need to respond to others' agendas will inevitably influence what a new leader can learn and when. New leaders also arrive with their own biases, which affect what they see and don't see. Personal learning styles—the way one prefers to learn—make it easier to learn certain things and harder to learn others. It is important both to understand your own style and to work to compensate for it. The views of trusted advisors, especially those with different perspectives and learning styles, can be precious resources to supplement your own preferred way of learning.

The hardest things to master are politics and culture

Helpful discussions of organizational politics and culture will not be found in financial or operating reports, though these documents may provide important clues. One can learn about politics and culture only from people who either work in or interact with the organization. But, to further complicate the picture, people will not necessarily be open about the politics or aware of the culture. Like an investigative reporter, the new leader must observe, look for patterns, develop theories, and evaluate evidence. In the world of organizational culture and politics, things are hardly ever what they seem.

It gets harder to learn as time passes

When a new leader first arrives, he is relatively pure: living in the organization hasn't yet affected the way he thinks. This may be both a vulnerability and a strength. He has little vested interest in what exists since he did not put it in place. He can view the organization through relatively objective eyes and can ask seemingly naive questions without loss of credibility.

With the passage of time, however, the new leader can become contaminated. As he becomes a part of the organization, relationships develop that begin to cloud his objectivity. He can't ask naive questions anymore. He will have made decisions and taken stands that he is personally invested in and feels the need to defend.

EMBRACING A LEARNING MINDSET

One key to overcoming learning barriers is to understand what you need to know and when you need to know it, which the framework presented in Chapter 5 will help clarify. Another key to effectiveness is to adopt a learning mindset, working to extract as much useful knowledge as possible from all available sources. A learning mindset can be seen as consisting of four interconnected elements: proactivity, learning with a point of view, active listening, and cultivating awareness. These are basic interpersonal competencies that many skilled leaders have developed by the time they approach the top. It is important to review them here because the pressures of the transition period can cause even the most interpersonally astute to lose sight of what they have learned.

Being proactive about finding problems

Effective learners don't collect and analyze information passively. Instead, they immerse themselves in information about their environments, searching for emerging threats and opportunities. They systematically identify and tap into good sources of information, and build internal and external networks of relationships to support intelligence gathering. As one leader put it:

> In my forty years of management experience, never once did I reach in my in basket and pick up something that said, "Hi, I'm a problem. Please solve me." The awareness of either opportunities or problems rarely comes packaged or even discrete. It comes from an accumulation of impressions, facts, observations, and opinions that gradually coalesce into "Uh-huh! Somewhere in there it looks like there's an opportunity, or somewhere in there it looks like there's a problem." And that's when you start directing resources to "Please help me understand this better," whether it's something that calls for action or whether it's something that calls for holding off, which is a harder decision. It's . . . relations with people that give you those kinds of soft information.

Another leader described a gradual approach to learning that worked for him:

> The first few months you go through and do reviews. You meet the people. You listen a lot. Ask a lot of questions. Make no judgments. Don't say, "This is good. This is bad." You listen. And you begin to ask them questions to get them thinking. At the end, you have pretty much formed judgments on people, on problems, because they will tell you the problems. Most companies know the problems. They really do. The issue is they don't know how to solve them because culturally there are so many people [who just aren't] interacting with each other. At the end of that time, you sit down with the management team and get them to agree on what the problems are.

Learning with a point of view

Fortune favors the prepared mind, particularly for a newcomer in a complex situation.[1] Learning that is disciplined and shaped by a point of view—which the new leader began to develop prior to entry—is far preferable to random information gathering. Here's what one leader said about this process.

> In any kind of transition you need a point of view coming in, [based] on research and analysis. But then you have to aggressively mold that point of view, round it out, expand it, embellish it. This means relentlessly pursuing and engaging folks, internal and external, to the enterprise that you are leading.

Another pointed out the importance of asking questions linked to working hypotheses:

> I had some hypotheses coming in that allowed me to engage with people in a dynamic interaction. I wanted to understand them—their perspective, their insight, their experience with the business—but I had hypotheses. So the questions that I asked weren't random. They were questions that helped me confirm or reject the hypotheses that I developed in my mind.

There are risks, however, to learning with a point of view. One is that tentative hypotheses can become constraining assumptions. Another is that hypotheses can influence the process of information gathering in ways that confirm and reinforce them—a process of selective perception leading to self-fulfilling prophecies.[2] These risks cause a fundamental tension in the learning process: a point of view focuses learning but can also distort the process of information gathering in ways that lead to erroneous conclusions. The leader can manage this tension by keeping in mind the distinction between assumptions and hypotheses. As one leader put it: "I think of a point of view as a work in progress, as opposed to a fixed position you are trying to just validate. I look for things that would lead me to reject it."

Keep in mind, however, that new leaders' efforts to test hypotheses are easily misread by employees, creating unnecessary apprehension and confusion. Such misunderstanding is best headed off by explicitly stating that you are merely testing hypotheses and stimulating discussion rather than formulating plans of action and making decisions.

On the other hand, some new leaders find it valuable to sow a bit of confusion and apprehension. One said "I'm not sure that people being clear about what I want is good all the time. I get some pretty good insight when I see people confused a little bit about what I really want. Some people will come back to check it out, and others will blindly go on even though there is a question. I want to know which way certain people will go and what they do when everything doesn't quite line up."

Listening actively

Learning from others requires insightful questions and active probing of initial responses. Active listening also involves demonstrating comprehension of what the other person is saying and deciphering the beliefs and emotions that underlie it.[3] Paraphrasing is an effective way to demonstrate understanding and to dissolve defensiveness and other barriers to communication. Simply saying, "So, if I understand you correctly, you're saying . . ," can elicit much more insight into a situation and its human ramifications.

The emotions that underlie an issue can sometimes be uncovered simply by saying something like, "It sounds as if you were pretty frustrated when that happened." A response like, "You bet I was! That was the fourth time I'd tried to get him to pay attention to what the customer was saying," deepens the leader's insight into what is at issue and at stake, and allows him to test a hypothesis: "It sounds like the history here has been not to pay as much attention as we should to what the customer wants."

On critical issues, testing hypotheses without appearing skeptical is a valuable skill that enhances learning. One of our leaders pointed out that good listening has multiple layers:

You need to understand how to communicate and how to listen. And you shouldn't assume that there's only one right way. Some of it is learning their perspective; some of it is learning their personality. It's not even an issue of framing a good question. You could frame a good question and, if the receiver is coming from a totally different angle, then he may not understand it the way you mean it even though you framed the question for 90 percent of the population. From dealing in the international world for so many years, what I discovered is: you want to make sure, first, that the person understands the question and, second, [that] the answer you've gotten back is what you really needed to know . . . So I made it a habit to ask the same question three different ways. It doesn't have to smell or act like the same question, but ultimately it's the same question. And when you get an inconsistency, that's where you probe.

Personal connections can pave the way for candor about organizational problems, politics, and culture. As one leader put it:

I think people respond tremendously to personal interest. So every meeting I have for the first time with people, I insist they give me a description of who they are and where they came from, what their family environment is like, what their key interests are. And then I do the same on me. And then I emphasize things like, you know, who the kids are and what the kids are up to. I talk about more obscure personal hobbies so they end up with a sense of depth around me, but also they sense that I want some depth around them. And that in turn creates a basic confessional paradigm. As soon as you tell something to someone, anybody, something intimate about yourself, there's a bond there. And I don't ask them to tell me the most intimate stuff, but, for some, to be asked to talk about their children is a shocking experience. And that opens things up. It is easy afterwards to sit down and say, you know, "I've been really thinking about how such and such works. Tell me about that."

Another leader told us:

You can say to almost anyone: "How long have you been here? Where have you worked in the past?" It doesn't take more than two or three mundane questions like that until you start to find out a whole lot about the person and the place. There is no magic question that causes them to just sort of unlock and spill their guts to you. It's two or three mundane questions where they think there is real interest on your part. You can also tell if you start to get the same sort of rote response to every question . . . Then you have to ask yourself, "Why are they all telling me this?" Sometimes . . . there's a belief that they have to tell you this. But you can get past that pretty quickly.

Cultivating awareness

Every interaction is an opportunity to gain useful knowledge. Cultivating the ability to recognize verbal and nonverbal cues can enhance your awareness of what is going on. Three types of awareness have parts to play:[4]

Integrated awareness is the ability to analyze and extract meaning from a combination of verbal and nonverbal information. As someone responds to your questions, what topics seem to evoke strong emotional responses? These hot buttons can provide important clues about motivation, and about reservoirs of emotional energy that can block or promote needed change. Does the person volunteer information, or does it have to be dragged out of him piece by piece? Does he acknowledge responsibility for problems or point fingers? What does he not say? Are his expressions and body language consistent with his words? One leader described his observations:

> I think people give you all kinds of signals if you are paying attention and look at the body language. I know if I'm asking deep questions people haven't thought about before; I know it immediately by their body language. If I am pressing a point of view of mine to the point that it overpowers them, I see it. I see their chairs back away. And if you do things that are inviting to people, it's interesting how you see them leaning over and getting closer to you. I don't think it's as difficult as most people believe it is.

Another leader said:

> I think a huge part of it is getting out and listening and trying to understand where people are coming from. Sometimes people will give me an inkling of certain things by their behavior, the way they said it, the way they move, the way they talk. I get the impression that

there's more to the story. I think a lot of it is just listening and trying to absorb everything, not just what they're saying but how
they're saying it, how important it is to them and that sort of thing.

Peripheral awareness is the ability to learn from what happens
on the sidelines. When one person in a group speaks, others react,
and their reactions contain important clues about attitudes, leadership, and alliances. As the new leader listens to one person in a
group, her peripheral awareness registers what is going on elsewhere in the group. Who seems to defer to whom on a given topic?
Who rolls their eyes or otherwise expresses disagreement or frustration? Who offers support? Who is conspicuously silent? Who
glances at whom?

Self-awareness is the ability to recognize and control one's own
reactions to other people's responses, and thus to avoid sabotaging
frank exchanges. However annoyed or disappointed the new
leader may be with responses to her questions, showing these emotions is certain to undermine communication. Deferring judgment
gives the new leader time to think about others' responses; she also
stays in control of the interaction and avoids prematurely revealing what she thinks.

IDENTIFYING SOURCES OF KNOWLEDGE

Our research suggests that it is a common trap for new leaders to
spend too much time reading and not enough time listening to people who possess valuable knowledge about the organization. Of
course, new leaders must analyze financial and operating reports,
strategic and functional plans, employee surveys, press accounts,
industry reports, and other data. But the information gleaned is
unlikely to become insight that the new leader can act on until he
draws on other people's critical knowledge about the organization's strategy, technical capabilities, culture, and politics.[5] One
leader alluded to the advantages of person-to-person contact:

I assess the health of an organization based on the attitude of people: the way they react to the manager they currently have and the

way they react to someone new coming in. I find that they tend to bring issues up pretty quickly once they get some personal contact.

Another agreed:

I think the first thing you look for is the attitude of the people. Is this an organization where there is some growth going on, and is there an exchange of ideas? Are there are a lot of interested people, or is this some sort of an operation where just one person is doing the thinking, or nobody is? You develop a pretty good feel for what's really going on just by talking to some of the people you run into.

One useful way to organize the learning process is to approach assessment of the company both from the outside in and from the inside out, as illustrated in Figure 6-1 and described in the pages that follow. Doing so involves looking at the organization through as many sets of eyes as possible. This approach thus equips the new leader to act as a bridge between external realities and internal perceptions and between the top of the hierarchy and the people on the front lines.

Practically speaking, a new leader cannot afford to spend time with everyone who might have relevant knowledge. The leaders we interviewed identified certain external and internal informants as particularly valuable sources of insight.

Learning externally

Industry analysts are important external sources of information. They offer relatively dispassionate assessments of the company's strategy and capabilities, as well as those of its competitors, and of the demands of the market. While an analyst's comments may be tinged with a critic's arrogance or a nonplayer's naiveté, significant differences between analysts' assessments and internal perceptions are warning signals. One leader described how he used analysts' reports and adopted their perspective:

I spent a lot of time looking at [the company] from the outside before I took this position. I looked at it from the point of view of analysts, read their reports, and thought about how they would value the company and where they see its strengths and weaknesses. I looked at it as if I were interested in a takeover: What might be the things that I'd be excited about and the things that I'd be concerned about? Did I think it was at its true valuation? Is it undervalued? How would I build shareholder value? I tried to build a frame of reference most insiders don't develop, because we aren't taught inside of most companies to look at it that way, except at the very senior levels: the CEO level, certainly, the chairman level, and maybe the operating president level. But if you go lower than those senior levels in corporations, most companies really don't teach executives how to look at a business that way.

The company's partners in the value chain—customers, distributors, and suppliers—can also provide perspectives and information unavailable internally. Meetings with customers offer a glimpse of the company in its role as a supplier; customers are in a position to assess the company's products and customer service,

FIGURE 6-1 SOURCES OF KNOWLEDGE

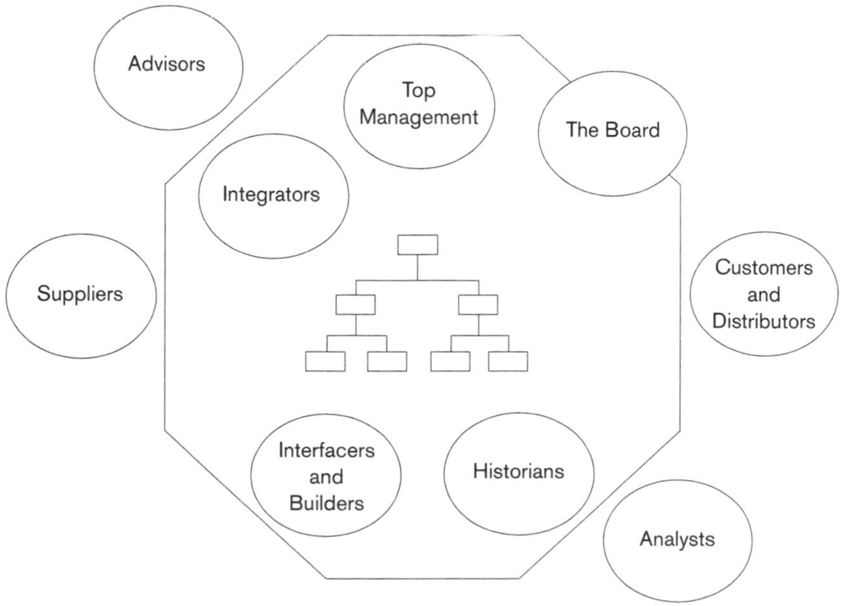

and to compare both to those of competitors. These visits can also predict the likely evolution of customer needs. Meetings with distributors can shed light on products, logistics, customer service, and competitors' offerings while giving the new leader an opportunity to assess the distributors' own capabilities. Finally, meetings with suppliers offer perspective on the organization in its role as a customer and on the shortcomings of internal operations management and systems.

Learning internally

Within the organization, key staff in Finance, Legal, and Human Resources are all important sources of insight into the way the organization really works. According to one leader: "The staff people can generally do pretty accurate character [profiles]. Of course, some are just angry, but many staff organizations will give you a pretty good assessment."

Less obvious as potential sources of valuable perspective on strategy and capabilities are the people we can characterize generically as the organization's interfacers, builders, integrators, and historians.

Interfacers are the people whose jobs put them in direct contact with customers, distributors, and suppliers.[6] Meetings with salespeople, customer-service representatives, and purchasing staff can afford the new leader a view of key organizational interfaces from the inside out. People in these front-line positions also offer more detailed, if narrower, assessments of products, services, and systems than those higher up in the organization. These meetings also offer opportunities to assess how the organization supports or undermines the efforts of the front line.

Builders design, build, and deliver the company's products, services, and systems. Meetings with working-level engineers in R&D, with members of the production workforce, and with information-systems developers provide a front-line view of the company's technical capabilities and of the skills necessary to translate those capabilities into customer value rapidly and effectively.

Meeting with *integrators*—those responsible for cross-functional integration—will shed light on the junctures where functions and processes mesh.[7] Integrators include business and product managers; project managers responsible for the development of new products, processes, and systems; and plant managers. From them, the leader can often learn about the organization's strengths and about who has power and how conflict among functions is managed.

Finally, new leaders should seek out the organization's *natural historians*—people who, for reasons of personality and memory, have become repositories of knowledge about what has come before. Often they are natural storytellers who can provide insight into the company's mythology and hence its politics and culture. One leader urged: "Get down to the floor where there's a little old man in the corner with the real books and find a way to get him to open up to you and tell you what's really going on."

In pursuing their inquiries, new leaders need to balance thoroughness with efficiency. It is not possible to talk to every member of each of these groups, and there may not be time to search out the best of them; during the transition period, the new leader will have to seek information opportunistically where it is most readily available. Listening actively and attentively, employing both peripheral awareness and self-awareness, will maximize the learning potential, as will the use of structured approaches whenever possible.

USING STRUCTURED APPROACHES TO ACCELERATE LEARNING

Significant learning takes place opportunistically during unstructured encounters, such as meetings. But learning can be enhanced by combining such unstructured learning with more structured approaches like interviews, case studies, market and plant tours, and pilot projects.

Interviews and group discussions

Since individuals often see the same events from different points of view, asking different people the same questions can be enlightening. Significant differences within the top management team, or between the top management team and its direct reports, can be particularly revealing. As one leader said:

> You start by asking the entire senior team about the strategy in separate meetings. It's a good sign if they agree about what they're trying to achieve, but then have somewhat different viewpoints on how to do it, because that means the team is marching to the same drummer. If they all say exactly the same thing, that's bad because you're either getting a bunch of brainwashed people or they're trying to tell you a consistent story.

Another described a format that worked well for him:

> You begin by asking questions: "Tell me about the business. Tell me about the competition. Tell me about the [market] shares. Tell me about the margins." You go through all these kinds of questions, and they either know the answers or they don't know them. And when there's a problem, you say, "Well, our share is down. What are we going to do?" Or "Why is that?" And you've got some people who will be very frank and open and will really explain what the situation is, real clear. Others will dance around and you will know it.

Structured interviews with "slices" of the organization are particularly useful as a way of quickly identifying problems and opportunities. These can be either horizontal slices of people at the same level in different departments or vertical slices through multiple levels. One leader described how she does this: "I try to talk to a good mixture of senior and key people in every division, every department—however the organization is organized—down to some of the younger people."

Needless to say, it is important to conduct these interviews deftly, not like interrogation sessions: "I try to keep it fun and upbeat: more an exploration than an inquisition. In the process, I disclose along the way some insights I have come to. It's not a one-way process. It is very much two-way communication."

If the new leader perceives differences within the top management team, or between levels, deeper probing will reveal whether these differences represent variations in functional perspectives, lack of shared understanding, or coalitional alignments. If differences between top management and direct reports are numerous, is it because senior managers have a broader view or because they lack understanding of the company's day-to-day operations?

Some of these differences can be explored usefully in group discussions. Convening people with different points of view to discuss an important issue will promote shared understanding of disparate perspectives, stimulate group learning, and set a standard of openness in dealing with sensitive issues.

The focus group is a particularly useful discussion format for learning from front-line personnel.[8] The objective is a broad-based, free-flowing conversation about subjects like organizational support for their work, incentive systems, or the changing needs of customers. Focus groups can also help to pinpoint natural leaders.

Case studies

Case studies can be used to assess patterns of decision making and to identify sources of power and influence. The new leader might select an important recent decision and probe how it was made, who participated, and who exerted influence at each stage, more or less as an investigative journalist would. This entails talking with the people involved, probing their perspectives, noting key differences in perceptions, and observing what is said and unsaid. Decisions about strategy, new-product development, and responses to critical problems are fertile ground for this kind of case analysis. Calling the case study "the best way to figure out how power and influence work in the organization," one leader elaborated:

> A good case is a situation where there is a particular stress. Every organization goes through crises, and how the organization reacts to them generally makes it pretty clear what the real values and real principles are. Bit by bit, you can piece together a mosaic of how people are viewed—which, for your top management team, is important. Basically, these case studies end up describing how the organization works and in turn how the key managers work.

Case studies are usually prepared by an aide or advisor to the new leader and initially used only by him. As he becomes more familiar with the organization's culture and politics, they can be useful in stimulating collective assessment or formulating strategy.

Market tours and plant tours

With careful preparation, new leaders can learn a great deal from the market tours and plant tours that will inevitably be part of their orientation. Market tours are opportunities to meet key customers and to interact with salespeople informally between meetings. Customers' complaints and insights become a springboard for discussions of causes and cures as well as product ideas. Plant tours offer exposure to the company's technical capabilities and its culture through a first-hand look at operations and meetings with sales and production staff.[9] By taking along some or all of the top management team, the leader can also see how they interact with people on the front lines and assess their technical knowledge. Here's how one leader described his approach:

> You take trips to the field with senior managers and you start to build a common vocabulary, a common understanding of things. You travel out to the field and see problems together. You say, "Okay, how can we do better?" So people get the idea: number one, he's listening; number two, he's not stupid. And you follow up on things that make sense. So you see that something happens. You build a trust base, not because you're sucking up to people but because you're genuinely interested in the business.

Another found it fruitful to sound out young employees:

> I go very far down in the organization, particularly to the young people. When I start to travel, I take the young people with me because they've got the energy; they're innovative. They haven't been molded, they haven't been tainted. I'll get the high-potential young people, and I'll say, "Hey, listen, I'm going to go visit [customers]

for three days. I want you to come with me." And I'll pick their minds—they won't know that. I don't think they'll know what I'm doing, but I'll get some real insight into the way this company is run and where the leadership is coming from and where it's not coming from.

Pilot projects

Pilot projects can provide the new leader important insight into the organization's technical capabilities, culture, and politics. As living case studies—microcosms of how the organization actually works from day to day—they reveal a lot if looked at with these multiple goals in mind. Borrowing a page from the psychoanalyst Erich Fromm, who pointed out that particularly insightful people listen with a "third ear," the leader ought to observe the group dynamics of the pilot team at feedback and report meetings. It is important not just to notice who talks most, but also to judge whether people say everything that is on their minds. Saying something like, "That's fine, and I understand that, but—tell me the truth here—is there more to it?" may elicit more candor from the presenter. Like many other techniques we have recommended, this approach benefits the new leader in the short term—she learns more about the issue at hand—and also has beneficial longer-term implications, establishing that it is appropriate for teams to discuss things that used to go unsaid.

STIMULATING ORGANIZATION-WIDE LEARNING

While testing the limits of their own ability to learn, new leaders can establish a standard for how others approach the learning process.[10] They can, for example, stimulate learning among subordinates by requiring decision making that is driven by hard data, providing structures for group problem solving, bringing new analytical frameworks to bear on existing problems, and encouraging sharing of information.

Requiring data-driven decision making

Advocating a data-driven approach to decision making means discouraging decisions made on the basis of opinion or conventional wisdom. Pressing people to gather data and revisit assumptions sets a new tone in many companies where people are accustomed to operating on the basis of old assumptions. Asking the management team, "What are our best competitors doing that we aren't?" should lead them to collect new data and set the stage for a collective learning process. Two leaders described their approaches as follows:

> You have to be real clear from day one to say, "Show me the facts; let me see the analysis." They'll say, "Well, it's a no-brainer, boss." I say, "Uh-uh, I want to see the facts." And when people go and get the facts, they say, "Hmm, I didn't know that."

> You make them go back and redo a lot of stuff—not in a difficult way, but just to say, "Hey, guys, you know, I need this redone so I can understand it. I need a lot of help on the subject. And you're the only guys who can give me that help, and you need to do that for me."

Adopting a rigorous approach to problem solving

Structured approaches to team problem solving can establish a model for collective learning. For example, the leader might require her team to adhere rigorously to the following sequence:

1. Define and reach consensus on what the problem is

2. Probe beyond symptoms to identify root causes

3. Develop inclusive sets of options and establish evaluative criteria

4. Evaluate options and make decisions[11]

Such an approach can also help the new leader build support for tough decisions. Consensus on the nature of a problem and its root causes makes the need to take action harder to dispute. Likewise, agreement on criteria for evaluating options makes it hard to argue for narrow political agendas. By the end of such a process, people may be willing to accept outcomes they would never have accepted at the outset. As one leader put it: "The benefit is that in the end the solution is ours, not mine, not theirs. It's ours. That's extraordinarily important. If they've all participated and argued and debated, and we got to the point where we finally agree, it's ours."

Introducing new analytical frameworks

New leaders also can stimulate learning by introducing new conceptual frameworks to guide analysis and problem solving. Conceptual frameworks are lenses through which to view the world; getting employees to adopt a new conceptual framework leads them to focus their attention differently, see the world differently, and make different choices. Strategies and visions are examples of what Bruce Henderson calls "powerful simplifications."[12] They provide frameworks for understanding the situation that the organization is facing, and guide choices that will lead in desired directions. Likewise, models for analyzing strategic position, such as Porter's five-forces model,[13] and management systems such as Total Quality (TQ)[14] are powerful simplifications that, once adopted, shape subsequent perceptions and choices.

While the new leader can profoundly influence decision making by introducing new conceptual frameworks to the organization, powerful simplifications can easily become useless oversimplifications. They may be applied indiscriminately or unthinkingly, leading to bad choices. As the saying goes, "To a man with a hammer, everything looks like a nail." Every conceptual framework has limitations that must be understood before using it.

Learning serves to build the foundation necessary for the new leader to address the next major challenge: envisioning an ideal future for the organization he intends to lead. It also provides him with clues as to appropriate pace and style.

7

VISIONING

Visioning—the process of creating a personal vision of an ideal future state and preparing to make it a shared vision—begins during the transition period but extends beyond it. Together, learning and visioning provide the basis for successful coalition building, enabling the new leader to build the support necessary to achieve early wins and prepare the way for sustainable improvement.

A *vision* is a compelling mental picture of how an organization will look and function when a particular strategy is fully realized.[1] A successful vision begins as an image in the leader's mind consistent with her style and situation. In the course of progressive and overlapping stages of clarification, testing, and exposure to facts and people, it can eventually evolve into a shared vision capable of providing both inspiration and a more communal sense of pur-pose.[2]

DEFINING VISION

An effective vision portrays a future that is both attractive and meaningful in the context of the present. It should answer the question "Given what this place has to do (the mission), its prior-ities (A-items), and how it expects to move forward (the strategy), what will it look like and how will people act when it has arrived?" In one leader's words, a vision is "a picture of the future distilled down to its crystalline, simplest form." Another pointed out that a vision must be descriptive and challenging: "A vision describes the way the organization is going to work in a reasonable time frame in the future. But it also stretches the organization, because if they're not stretching, it's not a vision."

A third commented on the magnetic potential of a compelling vision:

> I think leadership has two fundamental components: delivering business results and helping people get connected to the enterprise. And when I say "connected," I don't mean in the formal ways. I mean in a personal way . . . helping every individual understand how their contributions contribute to the success of the enterprise. The vision helps people make that connection.

To have an impact on people, a vision must be clear and spe-cific. It must be capable of eliciting passion in the new leader and others, and it must be linked to, but not a carbon copy of, other directional tools such as the mission statement. As one leader cau-tioned, "It can't be so broad, like 'excellence,' that it means noth-ing." Clarity and specificity grow out of an image that is vivid. What will one see and hear that is not seen and heard today? What will the ideal VP of manufacturing, for example, do differently? What actions will he take when there is a major product-availabili-ity problem? What does that imply about the VP's background, temperament, and style? What will be the results of an employee-climate survey performed several years hence, and how will it describe the organization's culture?

An effective vision also generates passion in the new leader—a passion that in turn motivates others. As organizational theorist Peter Senge explains, "Vision is different from purpose. Purpose is similar to direction, a general heading. Vision is a specific destination, a picture of a desired future. Purpose is 'advancing man's capability to explore the heavens.' Vision is 'a man on the moon by the end of the 1960s.'"[3] Because substantial positive change rarely happens without a strong motivating meaning, purpose and vision go hand in hand. A strong purpose without vision merely leads to directionless passion; many not-for-profit organizations, start-up businesses, and government initiatives have fallen prey to this weakness. In these cases, passionate and committed people work tirelessly to build something worthwhile, but what they bring about falls short of its potential and does not last. The combination of an inspiring purpose and a clear vision, by contrast, augments passion with direction. As one leader told us: "People want something to hang on to. They need an ennobling cause to work for. And we spent some time trying to define our business as an ennobling cause so people could say, 'I want to get up and do that.'"

To distinguish vision from related concepts like mission, core objectives, and strategy requires a steady grasp of what a vision is not:

- A vision is not a mission, which is what the organization's leaders want it to do and to be known for.

- A vision is not a set of core objectives or A-items, which specify targets in pursuit of the mission and are reflected in key personal and organizational objectives.

- A vision is not a strategy, which lays out the broad path by which the mission and core objectives will be realized.

A vision must, however, be consistent with the mission, core objectives, and strategy of the company it depicts. One leader put it this way:

People have to be able to say, "Oh, I see how all this [vision, mission, objectives, and strategy] fits together. I see where this guy is going," so eventually there has to be a shared vision of a desired outcome. Then there have to be some long-range, mid-term, and short-term goals for getting there. There has to be a road map that takes you through those goals. Everybody loves to say it's a journey rather than a destination [that's important]. That's true, but you have to have a pretty good idea in which direction the journey should be. That's why having a vision is key.

Even if senior managers agree on mission, objectives, and strategy, a vision can be essential to making the strategy come alive.

CREATING A PERSONAL VISION

An effective vision embodies the characteristics called for by all three segments of the pyramid shown in Figure 7-1: consistency with the new leader's A-item priorities, linkage to core values that provide meaning and purpose, and clear expression in the form of evocative descriptors.

Consistency with A-item priorities

The A-item priorities that the new leader has defined for the company flow directly from the strategy and expectations of the Board and the CEO. They are, in essence, the imperatives that will help to realize the strategy. A-items provide a foundation for effective visioning in two ways. First, the discipline of defining A-items and molding a vision consistent with them makes the resulting vision more practical and tangible than if it were based only on core values, regardless of how compelling they may be. Second, they offer milestones with which to track progress in achieving necessary new behaviors.

Linkage to core values

Consistency with A-items is necessary but not sufficient. An effective vision must be founded on values—such as integrity and loyalty—that imbue it with meaning and a sense of purpose. Table 7-1 borrows from the work of David Berlew on values and David Mc-Clelland on motivation to illustrate this point. Berlew identifies loyalty, commitment and contribution, individual worth and dignity, and integrity as core values that leaders draw on in clarifying a vision.[4] Our interactions with leaders at work on defining a vision for their companies suggest a relationship between these values and what McClelland calls "motivational dispositions."[5] McClelland contends that human beings are all spurred on by some combination of three basic social needs: achievement (the need to compete, do better, and win), affiliation (the need to be identified with a social group or team), and power (the need to control or to enjoy status). The degree to which a personal vision stresses achievement, affiliation, or power is a function both of the challenges facing the company and of the leader's personal values.

FIGURE 7-1 THE VISION HIERARCHY

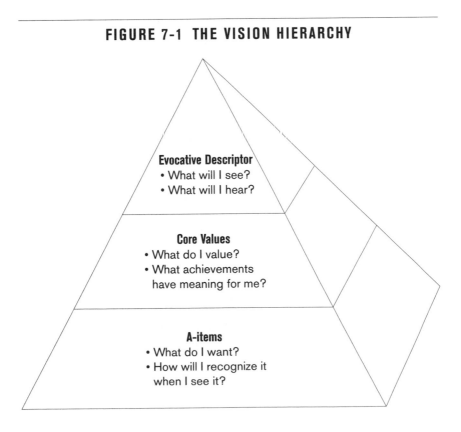

Evocative Descriptor
• What will I see?
• What will I hear?

Core Values
• What do I value?
• What achievements have meaning for me?

A-items
• What do I want?
• How will I recognize it when I see it?

Embodiment in Evocative Descriptors

The apex of the pyramid is occupied by what we call "evocative descriptors" of the vision. These are statements, embodying the A-items and core values, that describe in concrete terms what the organization should be: how it will be organized, how it will look different than it does today, what will be seen and heard, and what working at and doing business with the organization will be like. Some managers have trouble being as evocative as necessary. Say-

---

TABLE 7-1 VALUES AND MOTIVATIONAL DISPOSITIONS POTENTIALLY EMBODIED IN VISION

Values	Motivational Dispositions
Loyalty	*Achievement*
Commitment to an ideal	Drive for excellence, quality, and always doing better or best . . . continuous improvement
Sacrifice in order to realize that ideal	
Commitment and Contribution	Providing people challenging opportunities
Service to customers and suppliers	
Creating a better society or world	*Affiliation*
Individual Worth and Dignity	Teamwork, constant concern for the good of the team
Respect for the individual expressed as elimination of exploitative/patronizing practices, decency, and opportunity for all	Creating a climate that emphasizes personally rewarding work, especially in groups
Providing the means for individuals to reach their potential	*Power*
Integrity	Quest to be large, influential, dominant, and in control
Ethical and honest behavior	Rewards, recognition, and status, individually and for the organization
Fairness in all interactions	
Respect for the spirit as well as the letter of the law	

ing "I see a lot more teamwork," or "I see a place that responds to a new order in half the time we do now," is not good enough. Those are goal statements, not vision statements. More powerful vision statements might be: "I see people running to get the job done quickly and showing that they have a sense of urgency," and "I will know there is teamwork when I see an engineer, a supervisor, a quality-control manager, and a salesman huddled over a table looking at drawings and parts to solve a problem for a customer," and "We will be the fastest-response competitor when the product goes on a truck at our shipping dock and arrives at our customer's receiving dock without stopping at holding docks and secondary warehouses." Descriptors of this kind evoke a picture in the mind of the listener, while goal statements merely articulate a desire or a target. Table 7-2 provides categories that guide the development of evocative vision statements.

Defining and refining a vision

The new leader's early efforts to formulate a personal vision are likely to be more solitary than collaborative, because she has not yet mastered organizational politics or decided who will be on her team. This phase may be easier for leaders who tend toward a one-alone style than for those who customarily operate in collegial, team-based ways. But regardless of stylistic preferences, the new leader's early deliberations are likely to be undertaken alone. What is the nature of the visioning process during the transitional period? Our interviews suggest that effective visioning consists, more or less inevitably, of a three-stage sequence of observation, imaginative visualization, and clarification.

Observation. The new leaders who were best at formulating a vision of what they wanted to see were, by and large, the most careful observers of how their new organizations worked. Their scrutiny of the current situation and of the subtle ways in which behaviors were influencing performance provided the foundation for their efforts to imagine what could change.

Imaginative visualization. New leaders differed in the ways they formed an image of what the company might become. Some had to be disciplined and systematic, while for others it came spontaneously. As one explained: "I've just always been like that. I don't know why or where it came from. When I go to visit someone, to a dinner party or something, the first thing that comes to me is how I'd change walls, raise ceilings, put a built-in unit over there, eliminate those windows in the dining room and have French doors leading to a patio . . . that sort of thing."

Another said: "It's not easy for me to imagine something that isn't here yet. But I know that having a vision can motivate a lot of people to change. So what I do is make sure I've got people around me who are smart and real creative and I develop a system to use that so I can imagine an ideal [state]."

Whether or not visioning comes naturally, all leaders can enhance their capacity for imaginative visualization by writing down

TABLE 7-2   ORGANIZING DESCRIPTORS

Physical	Behavioral
How will the organization be structured?	What are the styles of managers and supervision?
How will information be shared?	How will the company be managed?
What kind of information? To whom? When?	How will coordination take place?
	How will big problems be solved?
How will products be developed?	
	How will small problems be prevented from becoming big problems?
How will products be distributed?	
What will the product supply chain look like?	How will employees be involved?
	What will be the nature of relationships with customers and suppliers?
How many suppliers? Where?	
	What will be the prevailing style of teamwork? How will I know?
	What will the organizational climate be like? How will I know?

thoughts and observations during the observation phase to serve as a basis for reflection, and by keeping a journal to capture insights during the imaginative-visualization phase; merely seeing items on a page can spark ideas.

Clarification. Whether it was with a vice president who was becoming a trusted aide or the CEO or an external advisor, the new leaders we interviewed all eventually subjected their ideas to reality checks by bouncing them off at least one other person. They tended to do so as a way of adding substance or examples after they were fairly sure what they themselves wanted. In this way, clarification also served as a way to test support.

Tables 7-1 and 7-2 provide a structure for organizing and refining ideas that emerge from visualization.

Frank's Case

Frank's experience illustrates how one new leader developed, refined, and clarified a vision of what he wanted his new company to become. His story also depicts a person who was not comfortable raising questions of vision or strategy until he had thought them through himself and was convinced he could stay in control of the debate. Finally, it describes how one leader made the transition from a personal vision to a shared one.

Frank had joined a Fortune 100 company to take over a large sector composed of seven businesses that served segments of the same market and sometimes the same customers. The market had consolidated considerably, and the company was increasingly selling to a few large distributors who were the keys to increased profitability of the sector. The sector had grown rapidly, largely through acquisition; Frank's predecessor had spent more time on acquisitions than on ensuring a synergistic fit among the companies. The good news was that he had fulfilled his mission to grow the sector's volume and market share. The bad news was that Frank had inherited an unwieldy collection of businesses that overlapped uncomfortably and lacked the discipline needed to grow profitably. Markets were also moving away from the high-priced, high-cost offerings that had been the foundation for the company's success.

Frank observed that some of the company's largest distributors were frustrated at the lack of coordination among the businesses, while others took advantage by pitting them against each other. Among the businesses, there was no cooperation in serving the same segments or the same customers. As these divisions had grown, they had been encouraged to survive and thrive independently. As a result, each had its own systems, benefit plans, marketing approaches, and administrative staff. But the realities of the new marketplace demanded more efficiency. That meant shared services and more cooperation.

Frank needed the managers who ran the divisions for their industry knowledge, and he was committed to keeping the divisions separate to maximize entrepreneurial potential. But he also recognized that the way the businesses operated had to change. He set out to decide how. He benchmarked by talking to people in other companies who had dealt with similar situations. He read. He brought in outside experts. He became a student of other corporations that had succeeded or failed at similar challenges; he invited executives from those companies to talk to his managers. Throughout, he kept his own counsel, never explaining to the division managers the purpose of such steps.

Since before joining, he had kept a journal of his thoughts on what the company could become. He regularly referred back to notes he had made days or weeks before. Often, doing so sparked a new idea; he built up his image to a vision one piece at time. After four months, he felt he had gone as far as he could on his own, and decided to test his emerging vision on others so their reactions could help him refine it further. He went first to his mentor, his former boss, who had retired before Frank left his previous company. Frank spent two days with him talking about what he had seen and experienced. He found his mentor's questions insightful and his reactions confirming. Before leaving, Frank asked his old boss to review a summary of his journal. The written critique that Frank soon received contributed a great deal of substance and refinement to the emerging image. Frank's former boss also offered to be an ongoing advisor.

Frank next talked to the corporate CFO of his new company, with whom he had struck up a friendship. The CFO had been with the company ten years, having formerly worked for one of its largest competitors, and he was a trusted aide to the chairman. Frank believed he could depend on the CFO to keep their conversations confidential, and he trusted that the CFO's experience could help him grasp nuances of the business he had not yet grasped. In addition, the area in which Frank felt most uncomfortable was corporate finance and balance-sheet management. His several conversations with the CFO exceeded Frank's expectations by providing a tutorial on the financial dynamics of the market and the competition. The CFO's financial depth also added richness and grounding to Frank's emerging vision. Through his consultations, Frank had progressed significantly in envisioning what his new company might ideally become. These two very different people—one an objective and sage outsider whose only purpose was to be helpful to a person he had hired and nurtured, and the other a financially oriented senior manager who knew the company's major financial levers and could contribute reality and grounding to Frank's ideas—offered just what Frank needed.

In consultation with his two confidants, Frank became much clearer about what he wanted to see and considered possible for his new company. At the same time, he became increasingly aware that deciding what he wanted and seeing it happen were quite different. His division managers had gotten used to operating autonomously, and simply dictating changes would not help realize Frank's image of what the sector could become. He emerged from his private deliberations convinced that it was feasible for the various divisions to maintain sovereignty while sharing administrative resources, communicating what they'd learned about common customers, and cooperating in marketing and new-product development.

Frank decided it was too soon to convene his division managers to talk about a vision of the future. First he had to find a way to encourage them to eliminate some barriers that had blocked their units from cooperating and learning from each other. If he succeeded, he reasoned, he'd be well on the way toward transforming his personal vision into a shared one. Rather than simply declaring that he wanted divisions to cooperate, he decided to create a situation in which he could observe whether they were able to do so. He therefore proposed a common set of profit and growth principles and an incentive system that rewarded cooperation and was linked to each division's P&L. Here's how he described the challenge.

> The key here was to get these division presidents excited about something that they hadn't done yet, but also to make sure that they saw it in their best interest to change. I could do some of that with a new compensation plan, but not all of it. They had to be involved in this, and also get to know each other better. The first step was to get them excited about creating a vision, which was not that difficult because all of these guys are pretty good businesspeople and each had done at least some visioning within his own unit. I aimed at defining a few core objectives that would be a basis for our new vision. If I could get them to articulate a few big objectives that we could all [use] as battle standards, I knew it would be easier to come up with a collective image of how we should be acting when we were ready to do that. We needed to agree on some goals that were logical reasons to cooperate. I wanted to get us as a group to the point of agreeing on objectives— and I didn't know what they would be beforehand—so that when you sit back and look at them, the only conclusion would be that to achieve them we'd have to share more between divisions than we [had been doing].
>
> We had several off-site meetings that were sometimes not much fun. But what emerged was a consensus on four [A-items]: customer focus on large key customers, fast response to everything, people taking responsibility for driving change, and employee involvement. It sounds like a neat package now, but it took a lot of work to get to these four . . . but we did, and everyone was committed to them because, I think, everyone was involved and had his say. And also we got pretty specific. At one

of our off-sites, it became clear that there were some parts of these [A-items] that some companies did better than others. And it wasn't a great task to get people to agree that one company could learn from another if they just visited each other and talked and shared some information. I set up teams after this off-site on each of these [A-items] that caused them to get to know each other a little bit better. They came back after a month or so with statements that described each [A-item].

To match changes in the market, Frank knew that costs had to be driven down and product-planning policies had to change. Manufacturing plants also had to make changes to reduce costs and improve speed and flexibility. But Frank also knew that the company's history of fine craftsmanship aimed at high-income consumers was a source of pride among employees. The move to lower-cost products would require some major changes that would upset long-standing cultural values. In order to broaden the product line, the division presidents had to lead the charge; if they weren't convinced it was important, Frank knew, there was little hope of persuading employees to make the required changes. He hadn't raised this topic at the first off-site meeting for fear of short-circuiting the progress he felt was taking place, but he knew the business would not grow without moving in this direction. Then something unexpected happened that he thought might move the agenda. Here's how he described it:

When I was interviewing here, the Board made it clear that the key to the stock price [growing] and overall value [increasing] was volume growth, and they wanted it quickly. New products were an obvious possibility, but over the years innovation had slowed here and the pipeline was not very full . . . It was going to take some time to grow through new products. One obvious answer was to make our products available to a wider range of customers by adjusting prices and creating line extensions and having lower-cost product lines but maintaining our quality. I was afraid that the top guys here would see it as heresy to lower prices and get into distribution channels in the mid-price range;

a few things had happened that made me think they'd see it as beneath them . . . and they'd really resist the notion.

Then we sort of just fell into something. I was at an analyst meeting and was asked how the company was going to grow with our products priced the way they were. What I said was not rehearsed, but it was from the heart. I got a little passionate in my answer. I have always been someone who roots for the underdog, and I never thought of myself as elite; I was an activist in college and have stayed that way throughout my life. I said to the analysts that I had not come to this company because it was exclusive, but because its products were the definition of quality and high performance . . . that there was no reason why these great products couldn't be within reach of every consumer, and that anyone who worked hard to make a living should be rewarded by being able to experience our quality and reliability. Well, one of the people there was a reporter, and [he] did this little piece on what I'd said. And the local papers picked up the story and quoted me . . . and in one of my plant tours, I had a meeting with the employees and it came up. The rank-and-file workers were really excited; it was all they wanted to talk about. I encouraged them and just listened. As it turned out, what they had always felt pride in was quality and reliability, but that had been sort of tempered by [another emotion]—almost embarrassment at these products that they were so proud of not being available to most people they knew, or to their relatives. I am sure that the changes we made in manufacturing practices and in reconfiguring the supply chain—some of them pretty big and fundamental ones—would never have happened if it weren't for this . . . It became a core value, and because of it the people on the front lines—the people who had to actually make the changes—were much more committed to making them.

Well, the president of that division was there, and we talked about it over dinner that night. I asked him what he thought the other [presidents] would think about this issue. He said that if their employees felt the same way about it as what we'd heard that day, that would be a pretty powerful argument to change.

As he related his story, Frank was planning another off-site meeting of his division presidents. He had asked the division president mentioned above to describe what had happened at the employee meeting, and hoped to test the division presidents' response to broadening the product line. He later reported that the division presidents were divided on this question and that he was not certain they could come to a consensus. Nevertheless he was ready to decide to broaden the product line, and he was confident of sufficient support, if not unanimity, to move in that direction.

Developing one's imaginative capacity

While some people are better than others at visualizing a desirable future, all leaders can develop a capacity for imaginative visualization. One approach, quite different from Frank's, is a visioning workshop in which a new leader and up to twenty managers meet off-site to explore the company's future collectively. The leader often begins by identifying conditions the organization is likely to face in the future, emphasizing competitive, regulatory, financial, and other dynamics that the strategy should have anticipated. After presenting some scenarios that depict the optimal organization's reactions to those conditions, the leader might then ask participants to imagine themselves walking through the organization today, noticing details that signify the culture: work pace, individual versus group work, frequency of eye contact, housekeeping, whether the layout encourages interaction or separateness, and whether feedback data are displayed. Participants are then asked to picture themselves walking through the front door and boarding a helicopter that rises through clouds and fog and eventually returns to the same spot. As they imagine themselves disembarking, they are told that the building is the same but something seems different: it soon becomes apparent that several years have passed. Participants are asked to imagine and discuss how, ideally, the company might appear. How is it laid out? What is the pace of work? Are customer-feedback data posted, and what do they show? What does one hear while listening to a customer call? What is seen and heard at a management staff meeting?

Participants then break up into small groups to describe what they envisioned. One member of each group acts as discussion leader, eliciting individual images and summarizing and presenting them to the full group in a plenary session. Such a session can serve a dual purpose: it helps the leader clarify her own personal vision and it reveals how radical a change the managers gathered at the session might accept.

The leader most likely to benefit from such a session is one who is open to the input of subordinates and finds teamwork and group decision making natural and fruitful for the business. Such a workshop is not as useful for leaders who prefer to keep their thinking private. Like Frank, such leaders keep their own counsel so as to maximize their decision-making flexibility. There is no single best way to proceed; there are only ways that fit some leadership styles better than others. Frank's method has the advantage of allowing him to stay more in control of the visioning process. Its downside is that subordinates' lack of early involvement in shaping the vision may affect their commitment to it.

Sometimes new leaders aren't sufficiently comfortable with their new companies to share their thinking openly:

When I came here it was clear that [the company] had to have a different image of itself, but that was something that few people understood. The person who had hired me [the chairman] and sponsored me with the Board was very supportive, and said a lot of the right things, but I couldn't really tell if he was ready to change; after all, he had been here for so long and had put his stamp on this place to such a degree that . . . I just felt that I needed to be careful. It was before I had formed my own organization, and I was still finding my way a bit. But the business was flat, and there were signs that some big investors were getting restless . . . and that was making the Board nervous. It first seemed that the three-year gradual, orderly transition that the Board and chairman had talked about was not really realistic. It had to happen faster. All the signs were there, and I didn't want to come in one day and be asked to do something that I wasn't prepared for . . . or, worse, be painted with the same brush as everyone else, and seen as part of the problem rather than as the solution.

I had acted in college, and afterwards had some thoughts of becoming an actress and did some off-Broadway shows and repertory and attended acting workshops. I had learned how to imagine being in different situations, and as I took on different roles and pretended to be the character, I had always wondered how I would actually handle some of the situations my characters faced. I had kept a journal back then, in these spiral-bound notebooks that students use; I had dozens of them. Going back and reading them was always helpful. So I started to think about the sort of place I really wanted this to be, and wrote down ideas in my journal whenever they occurred to me . . . coming back from [seeing a customer] after getting some straight feedback about something that we had done wrong, or after a roundtable meeting with our creative people, or after a particularly frustrating meeting where people just didn't seem to get it.

I was flying to the Far East after about four months on the job, and found myself spending the whole time on the plane reading my journal entries and thinking about what I really wanted to see happen here. Then, on the way back, I started to write down scenarios of what I imagined I wanted to see, hear, and feel when things were really clicking. I imagined the kinds of people that would be around me when we were growing at double-digit rates. One of the things that screamed out of my journal as I reread it was that the people around me just weren't communicators . . . They were nice people and well-meaning, with great industry knowledge, but it just never occurred to them to do things like articulating complaints from customers to lower-level workers and making sure that their subordinates really understood expectations and roles. Being aware of that seemed obvious after I had written it down, but really it wasn't so obvious until I began to read these signs of it over and over again in my journal. Well, that made me ask myself the question: "What kinds of people would help me here? . . . What do they think about? How do they react to some of the situations that I've seen my people underreact to?" Everyone probably has her own way of dealing with these things, but at least for me, you know, I have to be talking to someone to get clear about what I want . . . And when I didn't have anyone to talk to, talking to myself was the next best thing.

Private versus public?

As we've seen, it is sometimes best for the new leader not to share a developing personal vision until it is more completely formulated. In other situations, involving subordinates early on can help the leader clarify his thoughts and begin to build commitment.

Being private has the advantages noted above, but it could backfire and generate resistance if the new leader appears to be manipulating other people's reactions in the direction of a predetermined scheme. One leader described his efforts to avoid giving this impression:

> I generally don't tell anybody the full story of what I'm thinking and what I'm doing. But down the road, sooner or later, people say, "You know what? I feel great that we've got a vision. And I think a lot of issues have been dealt with, and that's been great. But at the heart of it, I'm still not sure what you [the leader] really think." One of the things I'm working on is showing enough of what I'm really thinking about when I do things, so folks don't think there's a [hidden] master plan. I think a vision and values are important . . . but a master plan per se implies a degree of all-mightiness which is not true—and also dangerous for people to think it exists.

Is there a single best way to manage this public–private tension? Not according to leaders who have faced this challenge. Their consensus was that it depends on personality and situation. But are there any guideposts a new leader can consult to decide how best to proceed as a personal vision is taking shape? Most new leaders put the question of whether key people will be replaced at the top of the list. As one leader explained: "You create a bonding experience, and then you fire a couple of people. And the people feel like 'Hey, maybe we didn't exactly bond as well as we thought, if so-and-so got canned.' " Most agreed that, if it is clear people will be replaced, it is best to do so before involving employees in collaboratively shaping a vision.

Another guidepost is the climate of the company. According to one leader: "You've got to move on this in [a way that's consistent with] the sort of place you're in. If you start acting in a way that is really different from what's been done in the past, people may be shocked instead of inspired or thankful that you're including them. No, you've got to be somewhat consistent and not too different, especially in [the transition period]." Others disagreed, pointing out that such a situation offers the new leader an opportunity to establish new standards of behavior, demonstrate what she stands for, and distinguish herself from what had been done in the past: "If you really believe in participation, and involving people in things like this, it's worth taking a risk." One leader interpreted this issue as a question of consistency with one's own values:

> Look, this isn't a real tough question to answer when you look at it as something you believe in. If you believe that people ought to be involved, and you know that eventually you are going to come out with something that expresses that real strongly as a core belief of yours, how's it going to look if you don't involve some people as you think it through? If you don't act out what you believe, it's going to come across as all words and your credibility is going to be shot.

What about sharing an emerging vision with the CEO? The answer is a resounding "It depends." Many new leaders prefer to wait until the vision is fully formed and there is a critical mass of support among influential managers before going to the CEO. Typically, the people who advocate this route do so because they fear the CEO will water down or block their vision. Often in these cases, the relationship between the new leader and the CEO is arm's length and consultation is reserved for major decisions. One leader described it this way:

> [The CEO] thinks in a way that just wouldn't help that much. He thinks in the present and the past [while] I think in the present and the future. When you come right down to it, he won't do things that haven't been done before—that's one reason we've suffered in terms of innovation and growth.

Other new leaders make it a practice to consult with their CEO on a regular basis and feel comfortable involving him in the formulation of their vision. Some believe that the CEO's influence will help them to enlist support. Others reason that doing so will avoid the risk that the CEO will resist because he is not involved in some way. A leader from this camp said:

> I want his opinion about this. He's been through a lot over the past forty years and I can use that experience. Anyway, there are some people who I need to be advocates for what I want who are skeptical. An endorsement [from the CEO] would help.

In the final analysis, it comes down to:

- How much the opinions of the new leader and the CEO differ regarding the ideal state of the organization. If the differences are fundamental and if the distance is great between firmly held positions, formulating a vision and getting support for it before going to the CEO may be the best approach. The downside is that the new leader then has to sell the vision to the CEO. This may result in disagreement and put subordinates in the position of having to take sides.

- The relationship that has formed between the CEO and the new leader. If styles are compatible and if both have invested in building as good a relationship as possible, the new leader can be in the position of clarifying a vision with the CEO as primary advisor.

Whichever approach the new leader chooses, he should ensure that the end result is a vision of a future ideal state that is the correct one for the business, that he is personally committed to, and that motivates a critical mass of employees.

Overall, three rules of thumb for deciding how soon to share one's developing ideas emerged from our discussions. First, link vision with values by proceeding in ways that you envision as commonplace when the organization is working at its best. Second, remain consistent with your own deeply held core values. If you believe deeply in involvement, for example, developing a vision in a manner that excludes involvement will surely backfire. Third, choose carefully when to take a stand on your values if they differ substantially from past practice.

In the final analysis, the primary goal is success at creating a new vision. If moving too soon imperils success, the new leader and the organization will both lose a significant opportunity. Most leaders encounter few real opportunities to establish a new path for the company, and the visioning process is an opportunity that must succeed. If personnel changes or the formation of new coalitions will increase its chances of success, it may be worthwhile to postpone involving others in the visioning process and address these agendas first.

TOWARD A SHARED VISION

The most a new leader can hope to achieve during the transition period is to form a personal vision and do some thinking about how to make it one that is shared by a critical mass of employees. None of the leaders we met had been able to instill a shared vision in less than roughly eighteen months. Because our focus is the transition period, we will not deal in detail with the process of transforming a personal vision into a shared vision. But because the new leader will eventually take this step, we will offer some guidelines for preparing to do so.

Shared vision and organizational change

How does a shared vision contribute to changing the culture of a company? A common vision influences employees in at least three ways: by aligning behavior, by "pulling" employees toward a desirable future in ways that energize them, and by containing anxiety about what the future will bring.

A shared vision helps to align people's actions by defining what the future should look like and spelling out the behaviors consistent with that future.[6] Along with other tools for molding behavior, such as the strategy and A-item priorities, the vision can become an objective benchmark for purposes of feedback and criticism as the new leader rewards behavior that advances it and discourages behavior that undermines it. By making the future attractive, the vision gives employees reasons for wanting the organization to work in ways consistent with it. It provides a rationale for abandoning the status quo and thus "pulls" employees toward it, in contrast to other motivational tools that "push" people to act in particular ways. A vision that is commonly held can also alleviate employees' anxieties about change if they can see how change is linked to the strategy and how it leads down a path that is clear rather than cloudy and uncertain.

Push and pull tools

How exactly does a vision pull employees forward? Figure 7-2 contrasts tools that pull with tools that push. Changes can undeniably come about through the use of push mechanisms that establish new rules, plans, and metrics, and provide incentives to behave in a certain way. Written strategies, compensation plans, measurement systems, mission statements, strategic plans, annual budgets, and so forth are powerful levers for influencing behavior; they push people in desired directions by specifying expectations and defining rewards and punishments. These push tools depend for their effectiveness on authority, loyalty, fear, and the expecta-

FIGURE 7-2 PUSH AND PULL TOOLS

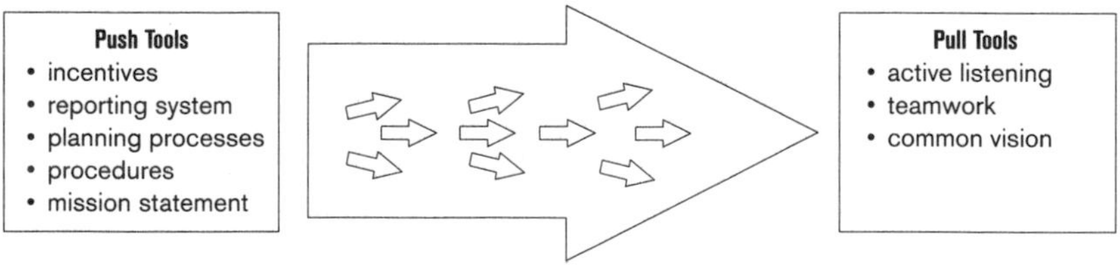

Push Tools
- incentives
- reporting system
- planning processes
- procedures
- mission statement

Pull Tools
- active listening
- teamwork
- common vision

Push and pull tools are used to align organizational forces that might otherwise go in many, inconsistent directions. Push tools align effort through authority, fear, and reward. Pull tools align effort through inspiration.

tion of reward. They can be especially effective in the short term, and are necessary in every situation to some degree.

But pushing people to conform to expectations is not enough. Employees must be pulled as well. Pull tools inspire. By defining an attractive future state, they cause people to want to change. Inspiration usually calls for employees to believe that new ways of operating will be substantially better than existing approaches at meeting their needs—for instance, that they will cause less frustration and wasted effort, or provide a more pleasant, team-oriented environment, or increase the likelihood of advancement.

Pull tools come in different sizes and shapes. The most basic are relationship-building skills honed to enhance communication. Examples are active listening and the ability to provide feedback in a way that strengthens relationships. Skill at team building is a higher-level pull tool. Still higher is the ability to transform a personal vision into a shared one in a way that inspires a critical mass of people. Pull tools depend on the leader's credibility and communication skills to a greater degree than do push tools.

Push and pull tools are complementary. Neither is sufficient on its own to alter deeply embedded habits and customary practices, or to create a critical mass of employees committed to change. For various reasons, though, most leaders come to rely on an unnecessarily narrow set of tools; they become adept at motivating people by either pulling or pushing. Our observations suggest that the best advice for a leader attempting to change a company's culture is (1) to identify which set of tools he is most adept at using, and (2) either to develop skills with the other set or to surround himself with people who can supplement his skills.

Preparing to make it commonly held

Based on our interviews, we have formulated four guidelines for laying the groundwork to transform a personal vision into one that is commonly held by employees.

Using consultation to gain commitment. The wise new leader will be clear about which core elements of the vision are nonnegotiable, but will otherwise be flexible enough to allow others to have input and to influence the vision-development process so that they share ownership. Here's how one leader described such an approach:

> You come in with a . . . good notion of a personal vision for what the place is going to be like when you're through, and 90 percent of it turns out to be what works. But along the way you want people to make it their own. So you meet, you have to have face-to-face time, and you have to have communications to get them involved. You make them a part of the process. You can meet with people and you can tell them . . . or you can engage people in a way that gets them involved. It's a delicate balance.

Another borrowed a page from Columbo, Peter Falk's wily TV detective:

> There are different ways to [make the vision shared]. I've used a group approach. You get people off in a room. You go through the process and you get consensus: "Here's what we ought to be trying to accomplish. Here's how we ought to do this." The alternative is Columbo. Deal with people separately. Talk to the suspects. Sit down and say, "You know, I don't quite understand it. Tell me what you think we're trying to do here, and what are your goals and what you want to accomplish." And you get a profile of where folks think they want to be. Then, sit down with them as a group and say, "Here's what I'm thinking about here, guys. First, here's where we stand. Here's what our competitive advantages are. Here's what our competitors' are. I've taken this from you, because you, Joe, said this . . . and you, Fred, said that . . . and Harry, you threw that in. Here's what you've been thinking, what you've been telling me. Here's what I believe, and so here's what I propose we do." Let them argue, but create a situation of ownership where you get them to the point where they agree on that decision. They have a lot of arguments about it, and they feel like it was generated by them rather than by you.

Is this motivation or manipulation? It depends on intent. The test is whether the leader's purpose was to control the process for personal gains that were more important to him than the common good.

Developing stories and metaphors to communicate the vision. Stories and metaphors are very potent ways to communicate the essence of a vision. As Howard Gardner notes in *Leading Minds,* "Leaders achieve their effectiveness chiefly through the stories they relate. . . . In addition to communicating stories, leaders embody those stories. That is, without necessarily relating their stories in so many words, [leaders] convey their stories by the kinds of lives they themselves lead."[7]

Parables are surprisingly powerful. When a good story is told at a meeting, people will remember the story long after the meeting is forgotten. Good stories just stick in our minds: their inner logic of heroes and villains, surprising turnabouts, courageous acts, and seemingly hopeless quests brought to fruition taps into our deepest needs and hopes. Works like Gardner's urge the new leader to communicate key elements of the vision through stories and metaphors. One leader agreed: "I use lots of stories. 'Good judgment comes from experience; experience comes from mistakes,' 'Life experience is a series of building on your mistakes. If you don't repeat the same mistakes, you're ahead of the game.' Getting [new attitudes] across to other people is tricky . . . Metaphors help a lot."

The ability to create a persuasive mythology about efforts to change the culture can be a powerful asset for new leaders.[8] Every effort to transform an organization is an epic waiting to be written. New leaders, no less than established leaders, create stories through their actions that characterize them as heroes or as villains. Leaders ignore the symbolism of their actions at their peril, especially early on when impressions are being formed. And by collecting and telling stories about other people in similar situations, new leaders can create a new organizational mythology. The best of these stories crystallize core lessons and illustrate the behavior the new leader wants to encourage. They should also resonate with the established mythology of the company, drawing on its best elements and channeling it in new ways.

Reinforcing the vision. Research on persuasive communication heavily emphasizes the power of repetition.[9] A new leader's vision is more likely to take root in people's minds if it consists of a few core themes that can be repeated until they sink in. As one leader observed: "You're so close to the situation that to you it's crystal-clear. But you have to pay attention to the fact it's not so clear to the rest of the organization." The new leader will know she has been successful at communicating the vision when employees start invoking the core themes without being aware that they are doing so. Said one leader:

> I work by the rule of seven. You have to say something seven times before people understand it or accept it or see it . . . and you have to say it in different modalities. Say it in a speech, write it in a letter, put it in the company magazine, capture it on videotape. Unless you've said something seven times, you have no hope anyone other than you and your secretary, who's typed several drafts, will get it.

Think about how you learn the lyrics of songs you hear on the radio; by the sixth or seventh hearing, the song has become part of your mental furniture even if you've never made an effort to learn it.

When people have begun to understand the message, the new leader must continue working to buttress and deepen their commitment to the vision. As Owen Harris points out in "Primer for Polemicists," reinforcement helps ensure that support doesn't slip away and expands the new leader's persuasive reach: "Preaching to the converted, far from being a superfluous activity, is vital. Preachers do it every Sunday. Strengthening the commitment, intellectual performance and morale of those already on your side is an essential task, both in order to bind them more securely to the cause and to make them more effective exponents of it."[10]

In doing so, the new leader is also showing subordinates how to promulgate the vision throughout the organization:

> [Making a vision common] is a very, very complex process that consists of articulation, images, constant reiteration, and communication at very many levels, over and over again. You spread it among the top leadership, and then they have to go down with it in their

organizations. It has to go many, many levels down, and it also has to be communicated [outside the company].

Developing channels for communicating the vision. It is impossible to communicate a vision directly to each person in the company. Thus, in addition to working with small groups such as a top team, the new leader must be effective at persuading from a distance. The transition period is the ideal time to develop communication channels for eventual use to promulgate the vision broadly.

In the absence of adequate formal communication channels, the grapevine will be the source of information people rely on. Just as nature abhors a vacuum, informal networks spring up to fill communication voids in organizations. Inevitably, a rumor network introduces substantial distortion into the communication process; thus it may be necessary to create new formal communication channels to gain control of the medium as well as the message. This may be as simple a matter as publishing a new in-house newsletter or devoting a regular column in an existing house organ to the new leader's vision. Other approaches are teleconferencing and distributing videotapes throughout the company each quarter. Some leaders identify people who have influence with their own constituencies and convene them semiannually to focus on the vision and progress toward it. Here's what one leader said about making the communication process work:

> If you're running an organization of, say, a thousand or so people, and you're there for a few years, you can get eyeball-to-eyeball feedback. But as numbers go into the tens of thousands, the communication process is real tricky. Remember the game of telephone we used to play as kids at birthday parties? It takes just two or three people and the signal is completely distorted—I mean completely distorted. So, when I say "communicate," I'm not talking about just transmitting . . . I'm talking about understanding whether the signal has been perceived and received properly. That means developing good communications channels.

Living the vision: walking the walk. Personal credibility is one of the most potent of persuasive resources. Leaders are better able to influence people's perceptions of their interests and alternatives when they are respected, considered trustworthy, and perceived as having expertise that gives them the standing to make judgments.[11] A leader's judgment is also trusted more if his own behavior is consistent with the behavior he seeks from others. Colloquially, "you can't just talk the talk. You have to walk the walk." A leader's inconsistency, or the appearance of pursuing self-serving goals, affords employees the psychological "wiggle room" to avoid difficult choices.

The new leader probably cannot convert a personal vision to a shared vision during the transition period, but can prepare a strategy for doing so. Vision is only one of several tools the new leader can use to align behavior, but it is a very important one. Rather than pushing people, a compelling vision can prompt people to commit themselves to moving in a desired direction. Visioning therefore makes an important contribution to coalition building, the process of creating a critical mass of support.

8

COALITION
BUILDING

No matter how effective they are at learning and visioning, new leaders will fail if they are unable to muster a critical mass of support for their initiatives. The support of the CEO and the Board, even in combination with the formal authority to allocate resources and make decisions, is not enough to make change happen. That's where coalition building—the third enabling technology—comes in. Learning and visioning are largely private activities, but coalition building is an external and political challenge.

If the organization is to be transformed, powerful individuals and groups must see it as in their interest to help the new leader realize his goals for the company. A compelling vision and personal credibility are indispensable in making the case for change; so are a grasp of company politics and a supportive coalition. Efforts at political management should begin while the new leader is still learning about the culture of the organization and the motivations of its key people.

RULES FOR SUCCESSFUL COALITION BUILDING

Several propositions for successful coalition building emerged from our interviews with leaders.

Proposition One: Ignore organizational politics at your peril

Political networks—informal bonds of solidarity and support among individuals and groups—can marshal the power either to resist change or to get things done. Divisive factional conflicts, contests over power, and self-serving efforts to protect prerogatives can unquestionably undermine organizational performance. But by the same token, the ability of respected people to mobilize support is an indispensable aid in making needed change happen. In the words of one executive:"You need to understand the total power structure of the organization, and what constituencies people have outside the immediate hierarchy, [what loyalties] they hold to the Board and key stakeholders."

Proposition Two: Technical change is never enough

Technical change characterizes every serious effort to introduce fundamental change in an organization. The focus of technical modifications might be the formal organizational structure, information systems and technologies, or business processes. But it's never enough to make changes in the technical realm. If the organization is to sustain improvements in performance, the new leader can't ignore the cultural and political dimensions.[1] Employees may resist change out of fear that they lack the necessary technical skills, but far stiffer resistance will materialize if the proposed change challenges norms and deeply held values or threatens status and political power. New leaders must anticipate and manage the cultural and political implications of any changes they choose to undertake.

Proposition Three: Effective political management is different from being political

Legitimate efforts to influence perceptions differ from manipulation. One leader equated politics with legitimate influence:

> Politics has a negative connotation, because when someone's being political, it suggests that it's wrong. But sometimes what it means is that there is a culture within the organization, and there are people who have more influence. It's just the way it is. If that means [other] people go more to them, and put more weight on what they're saying [and the leader has to take that into account], that's not being political in a negative way.

Clearly, intent is decisive in political management. People will not be willing to make sacrifices if they suspect that a leader is pursuing personal benefit at their expense or that of the organization. Similarly, divisive power games tend to encourage overtly political behavior among subordinates and peers. The leader's behavior, and the values embodied in how she uses influence, reveal underlying motives that will be apparent to employees.

Proposition Four: The goal is to build winning coalitions and prevent the formation of blocking coalitions

Managing cultural change involves the hard work of building what David Lax and Tim Sebenius call "winning coalitions"—coalitions with the power to take action and the robustness to survive inevitable opposition and crises.[2] Often leaders must also forestall the formation of blocking coalitions by those seeking to protect the status quo or lead the organization down a different path. Inevitably, there will be preexisting coalitions that came into being to support the old leader or to resist change during the old regime. All these challenges require figuring out who will offer support and who will raise opposition. This task in turn is inseparable from one's efforts to learn, gain early wins, and develop a compelling personal vision. Coalition building should be well under way by the end of the transition period, so that the leader can count on winning coalitions to help achieve the goals of the first era.

Proposition Five: Build up your political capital

New leaders enter companies with an array of personal resources—formal authority, agreements on expectations, reputation, personal energy, and skills. But being new, the leader lacks a reservoir of support and obligation on which to draw. He must accumulate political capital before he can hope to secure support for key initiatives. As we have seen, one does so in part by achieving some early wins and channeling the resulting support into broader initiatives. Another necessary step is to help others in strategic positions advance their own agendas in exchange for their support. And leaders can also build support by taking advantage of unplanned opportunities. One leader commented:

> If I had to do it all over again, I'd do a better job of taking advantage of meetings or [chance encounters] with people. When I prepared for a planned event or something like that, it went fine, but I learned you've always got to be ready to make a strong point about your agenda when you have the chance. A comment from the boss during an elevator ride, thanking someone for what they did, or stopping during an important meeting to point out an award someone got can go a long way when you need it.

Another leader recounted:

> My last boss before I came here was a master at that. He kept talking to people who were on the fence about something he wanted them to support, pointing out how, if they did it, it would help them get something that they really cared about. A lot of times he'd do it with humor, you know, so that the other guy never felt his arm was being twisted. He was relentless, never missed a chance. And eventually he got the support he needed.

The rest of this chapter will build on these propositions by presenting approaches to analyzing organizational politics and strategies for creating winning coalitions.

MAPPING AND MANAGING THE POLITICAL LANDSCAPE

It all begins with the task of mapping the organization's political landscape, described this way by one leader: "You've got to be aware of who's for what and who's got an ax to grind on what kinds of issues . . . You need a lot of intelligence. If you don't get that information, you can't protect yourself." Building support in key political arenas requires identifying groups instrumental in the processes that drive day-to-day activities, identifying influence networks, and determining key individuals' sources of power.

Analyzing the key political arenas

To build supportive coalitions, the new leader needs to analyze three political arenas: top management, middle management, and the workforce.

Success in the first arena rests on cultivating and retaining the confidence of the CEO and building productive working relationships with peers and top-level subordinates as discussed in Chapter 4. The CEO will be sensitive about questions concerning the transfer of power, such as exactly when he intends to leave and how power will be transferred. He may also see certain segments of the business as central to his legacy. Some CEOs want to protect their long-time allies, and some are not ready to let go of power. In each of these cases, the CEO's behavior may be interpreted by top managers as opposition to the new leader's efforts. As for peers and subordinates, needed changes may require shifts in power relationships that create winners and losers; some people may have to leave. Others may have sought the job that the new leader was hired to fill. It is likely that some have had long-standing relationships with the CEO and each other that enabled them to work independent agendas and shape the perceptions of others.

Because of these circumstances the senior management arena may pose the most treacherous challenge, especially if the new leader is seen as representing unwanted change. Achieving some quick wins could help dampen the impact of resistance, while a failure to post improvements in business results might strengthen it. The support of one or two of the most influential senior managers can make a big difference, and this support may be enhanced if the new leader helps them to promote causes or projects that are important to them.

In the middle-management arena, the new leader must build supportive coalitions among those who influence key decision-making processes and can rally enthusiastic support for necessary changes. She must identify and tap into existing managerial coalitions and build new ones. The support of managers in the middle of the organization chart is often as crucial as that of senior-level managers, especially in downsized companies with few mid-managers and large spans of control. As the field commanders, they have great sway over the attitudes of those on the forward edge of battle. By paying attention to the structure of power in the mid-management ranks, the new leader can accrue substantial political capital. One leader affirmed the importance of this principle, but pointed out a potential danger:

> You need to [figure out] the informal chain of command. Where are the very influential lower-level people you really need to be plugged into? But you also need to be careful not to start dealing with somebody three levels down on a pretty intensive basis too early . . . It sends the wrong signals about how you are going to do things.

In the workforce arena, new leaders must build a base of trust and respect so that workers in key organizational units will not reflexively resist needed change. More broadly, the new leader must build personal credibility, as discussed in Chapter 4, while demonstrating commitment to doing whatever it takes to get superior performance at the working level. One new leader cited a very positive reaction when he visited the shop floor in the company's smallest plant and the more remote parts of the field sales force—the first person in his position to do so. Another who regularly ate lunch with small groups of people at the lowest organizational levels reported a similar reaction: employees were simply pleased that a senior-level manager would take the time to listen and to talk to them. Several people cited employee surveys as a vehicle for understanding the workforce arena and noted that efforts to feed back results and begin to take corrective actions had a powerful impact.

Identifying key groups

Much of the day-to-day work of an organization is accomplished by processes that do not appear on any organization chart. Often these processes are managed by standing committees or ad-hoc groups of people from different departments; though typically quite visible, these groups operate independently of the organization chart. From information-technology steering committees to distributor advisory groups, they often represent important concentrations of power that operate horizontally across the organization.

Coalitions within and among other established social groups in the organization also arise. Important types of groups include:

1. **Organizational units** consisting of employees bound together by similar training and expertise or by shared tasks and supervision;

2. **Identity groups** bound together by occupation, age, gender, race, or social class, which value solidarity to protect their interests; and

3. **Power coalitions** of people who have banded together opportunistically to advance or protect shared interests, but who may not otherwise identify or socialize with each other.[3]

The new leader should seek to understand the forces that bind these groups and to identify their interests, the issues likely to evoke powerful responses from them, and their scope for opposing or supporting her agenda.

In the process, it will be helpful to keep in mind that there are two primary bases for alliances: *shared interests* (things we both care about) and *opportunistic trades* (you support me on matters I care about and I'll support you).[4] A shared-interest alliance might spring up if influential managers and employees have already been advocating changes the new leader seeks. By contrast, an opportunistic trade might be possible with the general manager of a sister division, who could decide to redeploy some manufacturing assets to make subassemblies for the new leader's business, saving her the cost of changing factories, in return for joint marketing or bundling of products and services.

Awareness of the history of coalitions and analysis of their characteristic patterns of cooperation and conflict can offer insight into how to deal with them. Coalitions tend to be fluid, depending on the particular issue at hand. Because winning coalitions can emerge from any of a number of sources, the leader's intelligence-gathering mechanisms must always be sharp and at the ready.

Analyzing influence networks and communication channels

Once important groups have been identified, their internal structure can be grasped by mapping their influence networks—who defers to whom on crucial issues.[5] Communication networks—the channels through which information is shared within groups—can also be mapped.[6]

Such analysis often helps to pinpoint the identity of opinion leaders, who may exert disproportionate influence outside the group and even across the entire organization.[7] Convincing these pivotal people of the need for change translates into much broader acceptance, while resistance on their part can cripple support.

Compiling an accurate map of influence networks and communications channels is easier said than done. Ideally, such knowledge accumulates over the course of long experience with the organization. As we saw in Chapter 6, however, there is a range of techniques for accelerating political learning.

Assessing individuals' sources of power

Assessing pivotal people's sources of power involves assessing the resources at their command and the nature of the people who follow them.[8] One way to structure such an assessment is to answer the following questions:

- **Expertise:** Does unique know-how equip her to solve critical problems for others and to ensure the smooth performance of crucially important processes?[9]

- **Information:** Does she have a monopoly over the flow of, or unique access to, crucial information?

- **Status:** Is he someone to whom others turn for guidance? Does he provide cues to others about how to think and act? Do others take cues from him?

- **Resources:** Does he have the power to distribute or withhold desirable rewards, or does he control resources that others need? Does he control large or important sectors of the organization?

- **Loyalty:** Has she built up a reservoir of loyalty or indebtedness by, for example, protecting others and helping them realize their goals?

- **Lieutenants:** Is he an essential component of the power base of a more powerful person? If his loyalty were to shift, would the power of his patron be seriously affected?

Deciphering the company

Listing potential sources of power is one thing; acquiring useful insights may be quite another, both because the leader is new to the company and because of her position at the top.[10] Where can she turn to learn about power and influence whose effects are more evident than their sources? The first step is to listen and watch. Said one leader:

You go to meetings, and the same people are there a couple of different times. You see others in a group commonly looking at an informal leader or an idea person or someone who's [particularly articulate] on a given subject. It clues you in on who the people are who can and will tell you what you need to know [about the way the organization really works].

A couple of approaches to deciphering organizational politics that were discussed in Chapter 6 deserve mention again here. Case-study analyses of how a particular decision was made or why a particular effort to implement change succeeded or failed can highlight coalitional alignments. So can the company's natural historians (people with a long history in the organization, good memories, and insight into its culture and politics). Such individuals can provide feedback on planned initiatives, identify potential pitfalls, and help to package change in ways likely to increase its acceptability.

The new leader can also learn a lot about politics—and foster new coalitions—by broadening participation in decision making:

Every place I've gone, I've expanded the number of managers who participate in making decisions. It's my style to get more people involved in [grappling] with the company's problems. It helps me learn [about the organization]. It also makes it much easier to effect changes when you have to, because you've got the support of a much broader group.

While working to understand the political dynamics of the past, it is important to keep abreast of current developments. Doing so could mean building a network of people who see it as their responsibility to keep you informed, and who themselves have rich networks of contacts. One leader reported: "I had to find out [whom] I could trust and couldn't trust, who was aligned with the new way of doing things versus who wasn't. So I tried to get some informal networks going quickly." People who are known to have the leader's ear are sought out, if they prove themselves to be trustworthy, and become natural conduits for information from people at lower organizational levels. As another leader put it: "You have to have some people around you who are of the institution, who understand it and can give you advice."

Identifying and tapping into the places where dissatisfaction tends to flow can provide an early-warning system. Human Resources, for example, is often privy to early signs of dissatisfaction in the workforce and can be an invaluable source of information about what is really going on:

> I relied heavily on Human Resources. The head of Human Resources here [in our division] and I had clicked earlier, and we had very open discussions on almost any issue. That was good, because he knew the culture and could reality-test my own thinking. He could coach me through things, and he was also a good sounding board just one-on-one.

In organizations whose HR departments are less competent or helpful, it is likely that some other unit plays this role either formally or informally. Discontented employees usually seek help somewhere. The new leader can get ahead of the game by identifying these repositories of knowledge and tapping into what they know.

Organization-wide climate and satisfaction surveys, if well designed and administered, can also provide insight into employees' collective state of mind and the culture in general. Another option is to undertake less formal "tracking polls" of particular departments or processes in order to chart trends in key plants or departments.

MAPPING OPPOSITION AND SUPPORT

As the transition proceeds, efforts to map organizational politics begin to interact with planning to implement change. As key initiatives begin to take shape, the key is to identify likely allies and opponents and those who are on the fence. Then the new leader can craft a strategy for consolidating support and overcoming resistance.

Reasons for resistance

New leaders inevitably face resistance when they make changes.[11] While some pivotal people and groups will genuinely and actively support a new agenda, others will be indifferent, undecided, or even implacably opposed. Three main reasons for such resistance emerged repeatedly in our research: negative past experiences with change, anticipated loss, and a poorly designed change process.

Negative past experiences. Someone once wrote that a cat who has been bitten by a snake will even fear a rope. Similarly, people resist change in organizations when their past experiences with it have been traumatic. One leader told us about a reengineering program introduced with great fanfare several years before he joined the company; it had been billed as promising greater efficiency and more interesting work. Eighteen months and several million dollars later, the company had a new information system that didn't work effectively. Meanwhile, the indirect workforce had been cut by 20 percent, leaving frustrated, angry employees overloaded during a period of sales growth. He rightly feared that any discussion of a "change initiative" or "organizational improvement effort" would meet with cynicism and resistance. The prevailing attitude in his new company was not so much open resistance to change as resigned, this-too-shall-pass apathy. Such attitudes greatly complicate the task of creating momentum.

Anticipated loss. Resistance is triggered when people fear loss in areas that matter to them. Four types of loss that elicit particularly defensive responses are:

- **Loss of a comfortable status quo:** Employees who are comfortable with the current situation may see no reason to change it. They may fear changes in work flow that will likely alter patterns of interaction and disrupt well-established working relationships. If there is no apparent crisis, many people will not want to invest energy in change.

- **Loss of a sense of competence:** Resistance may arise from fear of feeling incompetent or being unable to perform as required in post-change environments. This kind of resistance is commonplace when change involves the introduction of complex new technologies, rendering obsolete skills that were previously highly valued.

- **Threats to self-defining values:** People avoid innovation if they expect it to require them to behave in ways that are antithetical to their values and self-images. One example is a push for speed and flexibility, requiring more individual initiative and cross-functional coordination, in a company where silo-like vertical decision making has been prized.

- **Insecurity due to uncertainty about the future:** Uncertainty about the consequences of a proposed change can bring to the fore people's most fundamental fears. Employees may fear that change will lead to downsizing and job loss. Even when this anxiety is baseless, it can result in reluctance to pursue change.

Underlying each of these sources of resistance is a perceived threat to the "social contract" between employees and the company: the explicit and implicit understanding that it is the duty of employees to work hard and be loyal and of the employer to provide security and treat people fairly.[12] Even the appearance of a breach of this contract can trigger intense feelings of betrayal and generate opposition that can be very difficult to reverse.

Because the new leader has a mandate for change, it is likely that some aspects of the social contract will be affected by what he is advocating. It is therefore particularly important for him to take the time to understand the social contract between the company and its employees and to think through how it will be renegotiated. The same points apply when renegotiating relationships with suppliers, customers, and the communities in which the company operates: informal understandings can be as important as formal written contracts.

Poor design of the change process. The process used to implement change can itself contribute to resistance. Inadequate consultation and communication triggers feelings of alienation and lack of control. The perception that gains and losses are being distributed inequitably or indiscriminately quickly crystallizes opposition. And the feeling that too much is happening too fast overwhelms those who might otherwise be positively disposed. The new leader must devote at least as much attention to the process by which change is introduced as to its substance.

A good change-management process pays attention to: *preparation, presentation, preservation,* and *pace.* Successful new leaders prepare the organization for change, making the case for it in ways and in terms suited to the company's unique climate. They present changes comprehensibly and allow for questions and clarification openly and often. Degrees of involvement vary with the leaders' styles, but all successful new leaders always provide enough involvement to make acceptance more likely. The right process will also preserve existing arrangements that deserve protection, such as a long-standing contract with a supplier that has provided extraordinary service during difficult times. Finally, pacing is the delicate balancing act of tackling difficult problems quickly without overwhelming employees. As we saw in Chapter 5, each organization exhibits distinct warning signs, and the new leader will need experienced advisors to help interpret them.

Resistance strategies

People who have reasons to resist change don't necessarily do so openly or directly. The new leader's efforts can be seriously jeopardized if others can prevent her from learning, securing early wins, laying a foundation, and building credibility. Key people may withhold support or resources by not providing the best talent and full information. More subtly, they may express alarm in private about the risks inherent in the new leader's proposals. Such campaigns to weaken the new leader's change agenda may be waged individually or by an established coalition. An observer described one leader's experience:

> [The heir apparent] was being groomed as a successor to [the CEO], and the guys underneath him cut the legs out from under him. They

let him make some foolish decisions and then didn't support him when he needed it. It was basically "See, this guy did it again today." After a while it became so bad that [the heir apparent] moved out and went to another role, where he added a lot of value to the company . . . but the net effect of it is that it put back his moving into the CEO role by two or three years. He is now CEO and doing a great job . . . but it was a long road and it wasted a lot of time.

A dispassionate assessment of the strength of opposing coalitions helps to predict their impact. How long have efforts to galvanize opposition been under way and how vigorous are they? Is the opposition united through long-standing relationships and shared interests or by short-term opportunism? Are there linchpins who might be won over, and whose conversion would substantially weaken resistance? Is resistance likely to be active or passive? What forms might it take?

More broadly, how do key people perceive their alternatives in the face of impending change, and how might their perceptions be altered? A clear understanding of how key people define their alternatives helps the new leader hone and polish change strategies in order to win their support.

The following case study of a new leader facing significant political resistance in a tradition-bound organization illustrates one set of answers to these questions.

Steve's Experience

Steve was hired from the outside as COO of a highly respected printing company. Early in his transition, Steve selected the core production process in the company's largest printing plant as his center of gravity. He and the CEO agreed that this production process had to be converted from a low-technology, high-skill operation with a rigid functional organization to an automated process that would be lower-cost and team-based. If successful, these changes would significantly boost the plant's quality and efficiency while freeing up capacity. They would also create a template for transforming the company's other plants.

Steve had learned that the production and maintenance foremen exerted vast influence over plant operations. The workforce consisted of highly skilled craftsmen, among whom press operators enjoyed the highest status. The foremen had been promoted from the ranks because of their skill at solving difficult production problems. Each department headed by a foreman occupied a separate part of the plant.

Five years before, a quality-circle initiative had failed due to resistance from a coalition of production and maintenance foremen and some middle managers. The story of its demise told Steve quite a bit about the company culture and about how resistance took shape. The blocking coalition had resented the imposition of quality circles, and resistance had galvanized when several of the circles degenerated into forums for airing complaints about supervisors. Some good ideas emerged from the quality circles, but few were adopted because the quality circles lacked implementation authority. When members of one circle made unauthorized modifications to a press and caused extended downtime, supervisors lobbied their managers, questioning the impact of quality circles on safety and productivity. In response, the circles were discontinued. This story told Steve that supervisors and middle managers could band together when necessary, and that they were unlikely to be open about their real concerns. Instead they would find a pretext to discredit a program they opposed. He also noted that the blocking coalition had not been overruled by senior management.

Steve recognized that the planned automation would threaten production workers' sense of competence and identity as craftsmen. They would anticipate that the new equipment might turn them into mere technicians, or require skills and behavior they could not master. The new production process would also require team-based decision making, which the higher-status production workers, such as the press operators, were apt to resist.

The production foremen also had reasons to resist. They would be required to become team supervisors, accountable for the work of multiple specialties. They could no longer rely so exclusively on their own technical expertise, and would have to share authority with the maintenance foremen responsible for keeping the new capital-intensive equipment running.

Steve summarized the resistance he foresaw in tabular form so as to better understand its sources and impact. The result was a resistance matrix (Table 8-1) listing key groups, their probable reasons for resisting anticipated change, their degree of cohesion, the extent of their organization, and their ability to block the change process.

Let us look at some broadly applicable approaches to building supportive coalitions. Then we will return to Steve's story to see how he handled the situation.

BUILDING WINNING COALITIONS

Resistance to change is, of course, only part of the story. The other piece is identifying potential sources of support. The new leader's efforts to understand key groups—their interests, alternatives, and internal networks of influence—will shed light on who is likely to be supportive of change. Those likely to be undecided or indifferent to change, in turn, may represent crucial "swing votes."

Alongside efforts to understand pockets of resistance to change, the new leader must build powerful coalitions to support change. This process involves selecting the pivotal people with whom to form alliances and determining how best to recruit them. As one leader pointed out: "I'm looking for people that I know will be supporters or advocates for this, and seeing those where I know there's going to be resistance. [It is best to do] all these things very early in the game before you jump right in." Another added: "You have a strategy to grow the top line and one to get the right IT, HR, financial management, and so forth stuff in place. Why wouldn't you have an influence strategy too? After all, if you don't do that part of this right, the best marketing strategy will fail." The new leader's coalition-building strategy typically has two components:

TABLE 8-1 RESISTANCE MATRIX

	Group	Reasons for Resistance	Extent of Organization	Ability to Block
	Production workforce	Threat to competence	Some cohesion, well-developed networks	Minimal—few alternatives for good jobs
	Maintenance workforce	Threat to competence	Greater cohesion	Some—very high mechanical skills
	Production foremen	Threat to competence Threat to power (shift to team organization) Previous negative experience with quality circles	Significant cohesion Press foremen have strongest internal networks and highest status	Significant ability to influence productivity and attitudes of workforce
Potential blocking coalition with previous history of cooperation	Maintenance foremen	Threat to competence Threat to power (shift to team organization) Previous negative experience with quality circles	Strong internal cohesion, but small numbers in comparison to production foremen	Some ability to influence machine up time
	Middle managers	Threat to power (shift to team organization, potential for job losses)	Strong internal cohesion in production control	Some ability to influence installation, testing, and scheduling of new equipment

(1) identifying and consolidating potential sources of support, and
(2) persuading undecided people who are persuadable.

Consolidating sources of support

Two categories of employees represent likely sources of support for
change: the undecided contingent (to be discussed in the next section) and those who, frustrated by how the company operates,
have pushed for changes like those the new leader advocates. These
individuals may have been branded rebels or troublemakers, or
they may have been quietly working for change on a small scale.
Both groups represent change agents to whom the new leader can
turn for support, as illustrated by a division president's account of
his early efforts to get to know his new company:

> After a few months [in my job], I started to see examples of what
> some people had made happen in spite of the [prevailing] way of
> doing business here. One guy created a new layout in his depart-
> ment in one of our plants. I saw it on a plant tour and realized he
> had created a manufacturing cell with almost no work-in-process
> inventory, better housekeeping, and better throughput . . . This cell
> operation was so efficient that final inspection just couldn't keep up.
> Anyone with eyes could see the problem . . . in the cell operation
> you could eat off the floor—it was clean and orderly—but in the
> final-inspection area it was a mess. Well, I asked to meet the super-
> visor of this cell department. It was this guy who'd been in the plant
> for twenty-five years, and had been in plant engineering, mainte-
> nance, the warehouse, and production control. He said he'd always
> been [concerned] about the waste in the plant and he taught himself
> about flexible manufacturing by reading whatever he could and de-
> cided to try out some of the things he read about. He never called it
> a cell, never used [the term] just-in-time, and never asked for much
> money because he was afraid the plant manager would notice and
> stop what he was trying to do and didn't want to bring attention to
> himself. He and a few of his people and friends from plant engi-
> neering and maintenance came in during a shutdown and moved the
> equipment around and cleaned up the department. He just did it

quietly, and stayed under the radar. And by the time I saw it, it was the most productive department in the plant.

Pockets of innovation are to be expected in traditionally successful companies, but it is not always easy to find them. If, once discovered, they exemplify how the new leader wants the organization as a whole to operate, she must encourage them and support the innovators. In the case above, the division president convinced the plant manager to retire and temporarily took over the plant himself (acquiring first-hand knowledge of manufacturing in the process); he promoted the department supervisor to manage not only the last part of the production process but also final inspection, and eventually made him plant manager.

Another new leader created a support group from scratch by convening new employees from different parts of a consumer packaged goods company. He hired a new HR director with a strong management-development background and asked her to identify the highest-potential brand-new employees, explaining that he wanted to encourage them to be change agents before they became acculturated to the company's normal mode of operation.

He convened the group three times per year; one off-site multi-day meeting was devoted to discussing possible change initiatives and exploring how other companies operated. As he explained his reasoning:

> When we get out of high school we have minds that are open . . . then we go to college and specialize, and then graduate school and specialize even more. Then [when we join a company] we get slotted into a function and spend years learning discrete parts of it. Our perspective gets more and more narrow. The result sometimes is that you have general managers who are not innovative enough, because they aren't broad enough by the time they get to that point.

The primary rationale for organizing the group was to mold more innovative managers for the future, but the leader found an unexpected benefit:

> These guys are pistols . . . they have active, quick minds and they're impatient, and I love it. What's happened over the past year is that

they've gone back to their jobs and been advocates—that's what they are, really: advocates for fundamental change. I'm convinced that one of these kids is going to run this company someday. But they've become my Delta Team, you know. I can get them engaged on a real important project, and I don't have to look back. Because I know they are going to push for change and they will work night and day until it's right.

Identifying and consolidating existing support may not be enough to build a winning coalition. It is almost always desirable, if not necessary, to make strenuous efforts to convince people who initially are neither supporters nor opponents.

Persuading the persuadable

Early in the transition, many employees will be neither dedicated supporters nor implacable opponents; they will be indifferent or undecided, and hence persuadable. Tools of interpersonal influence and persuasion can transform people's perceptions of their interests and alternatives in ways that make them more likely to support change. The goal is to intensify the forces pushing people in the direction of support and weaken those provoking them to resist. In previous chapters we have talked about changing incentives, drawing on personal credibility, developing and communicating a vision, and educating and involving people. A new leader who has been successful in building political capital with key people can also draw on reciprocity, a very powerful norm to gain a buy-in.[13] But the new leader also has other tools, including *quid pro quo* negotiations and influence through relationship networks.

Quid pro quo negotiation. If key people cannot be swayed otherwise, it may be necessary to enter into a this-for-that negotiation, agreeing to support a project or initiative they care about in exchange for their support for the larger change effort. Success rests on understanding the full set of interests at stake, which may include reputation and prestige as well as more tangible needs, and on knowing how to craft attractive deals. It also means understanding what one is sacrificing in the long term to gain support in the short term. Support can almost always be bought. The question is: at what cost? Leaders who don't know when to stop buying support can end up making compromises that dilute their efforts and undermine their long-term success.

Leveraging relationship networks. People rarely make important decisions in isolation.[14] When deciding whether to support a change initiative, many will be influenced by their networks of relationships and the opinions of key advisors inside and outside the organization. If a new leader understands and can influence these relationship networks, his ability to persuade key people and build momentum increases dramatically. Awareness that a highly respected person has already endorsed an initiative alters others' assessments of its attractiveness, its likelihood of success, and the potential costs of not getting on board. The willingness of these opinion leaders to mobilize their own networks has a powerful leveraging effect.

Back to Steve's Story

Steve's first move was a program of memos, outside speakers, and comments in his monthly operating updates to educate the workforce on developments in the printing industry, efforts by competitors to cut costs and become more efficient, and the disadvantages their plant would have if it remained as it was. Articulating his vision of what the plant could become, he stressed new team and technical skills and committed to expand the training budget as necessary to prepare people for the environment in which the plant had to compete. To present the case for change and to preempt resistance, Steve used both memos and question-and-answer sessions. He also enlisted the support of a group of workers who had expressed interest in upgrading the facility.

During his initial orientation meetings, Steve had discovered several groups of people who were anxious to improve the plant. One group of production workers—most of them new to the company—seemed eager to learn how to operate new automated equipment that had already been purchased, but they hadn't been given a chance because assignments to this equipment had been based on seniority. (Even those assigned to it had not been trained and productivity was low and downtime frequent.) Another group of foremen in Maintenance seemed eager to move into production supervision and were willing to learn new ways of operating. Again, the seniority system blocked them in favor of longer-term production foremen who resisted changing the status quo.

Steve's cautious reorganization of the plant took several months to complete. It unfroze the prevailing rigid hierarchy by creating new supervisory positions, three of which were filled by the maintenance foremen seeking jobs in production. He then scheduled an off-site meeting of supervisors and managers to discuss his vision of what the plant had to become. He had shared many of these thoughts at earlier workforce meetings, but, after learning more in the interim, he could now convey them more vividly and forcefully to this smaller group.

The new foremen were more open-minded than their longer-term counterparts during this session. Steve reached out to those who appeared to be "on the fence." He then sketched out a new compensation plan for supervisory people who increased their knowledge and skills. The more they learned and the more broadly they could apply that learning, the bigger their bonuses. By Steve's own assessment, the results of the meeting were "Okay, in the sense that the group was divided in thirds: one-third was really pumped, one-third didn't like it at all, and one-third was in the middle."

What tipped the balance was how he structured a project to install new equipment that had been ordered before Steve arrived. A team of up-and-coming middle managers under the leadership of a highly respected senior manager was assigned to develop and oversee the installation of this new integrated production line. Rather than setting it up in a remote location as originally planned, Steve directed that it would be placed in a highly visible section of the plant where many workers would pass it during shift changes. The supervisory team, complemented by a multidisciplinary group of production workers, received training in teamwork as well as the technical skills required to plan the new layout, installation of the new equipment, selection of operators, training of operators and maintenance people, and the details of startup. The project came in under budget and on time, and was described very positively by the people on the project team. It was the first of a series of initiatives through which Steve ultimately transformed the organization.

Managing the pace

In implementing change, there is a fundamental tradeoff between giving employees time to adjust and losing momentum or allowing opposition to coalesce. It is crucial to set the right pace; if there is too little momentum, the leader can accelerate the pace by inaugurating new initiatives or changing key players.[15] Conversely, he can also ensure that things don't get too hot. For example, Steve had daily contact with the installation team, and visited the site of the new line at least once a week as it was being installed and tested.

Both enthusiasm and opposition have predictable phases. Pent-up demand for change typically generates unrealistic hopes, which can lead in turn to disappointment and sometimes frustration or cynicism. Once substantial changes begin to be apparent, however, support may catch fire again. In other cases, reflexive resistance and anxiety about the new leader's plans may decline as people become familiar with her style and as her motives become clear. More focused resistance may arise again later when the leader begins to articulate a vision and initiate deeper changes. A standoff may force the leader to use blunt power of position to squash resistance, and perhaps ultimately to fire those who are most stubbornly opposed.

The leader who is still new to the company should seek to avoid such a no-win confrontation. The objective is to build a bridge from the past to the future, not to run people off a cliff. A leader who focuses laser-like on changing what needs to be changed, where and when it needs to be changed, and who builds winning coalitions should be able to construct such a bridge. By strengthening features of the company that provide familiarity and comfort, by drawing on traditional values such as pride in craftsmanship, and by treating even the most ardent opponents with courtesy and respect, the leader can render even radical change safe and worthy of broad-based support.

At the same time, it is rare for any organization to undergo culture-altering change without senior-level people getting fired or asking to retire. Every one of the new leaders with whom we spoke eventually faced this reality and concluded that some people had to go if the organization was to move forward. Such decisions, however, are seldom made during the transition period.

The long-term cost of winning

When coalition-building efforts are blocked by obstructionist opposition, more aggressive tactics might appear desirable. Two tempting neutralizing tactics are reorganizing for the purpose of disrupting a blocking coalition and forcing the early retirement of an influential opposition leader. Such tactics are sometimes appropriate and in certain circumstances routine in running a business, but we have come to believe that the transition period is not the time to use them. We came to this conclusion for two reasons.

First, the new leader has joined the company for reasons of future opportunity. The ultimate goal is to win the top job. A new leader coming in as number two with the expectation of becoming CEO is making the move of her career. She expects to stay for some time, perhaps for the remainder of her working life. Thus political actions must be taken with an eye to the long term. Causing hard feelings during the transition period will work against her ultimate goal, even if the action is justified.

The second reason to avoid aggressive tactics at the outset is that the long-term objective is to sustain improved performance over time. Doing so means creating a culture in which employees exhibit the same commitment to cost-consciousness, innovation, and growth as the CEO. The creation of such a culture is in large part a function of employees' respect for the leader of the company. If their respect is eroded, so too is her ability to gain their support. By using aggressive tactics against those who disagree with her, the new leader—whose motives are not yet fully understood—runs the risk of being seen as a bully. If there is one single leadership lesson that stood out in our interviews, it is that respect for new leaders' motives and values is more decisive in the long run than whether they win any particular contest for influence.

The people who ascend to the top levels of corporate leadership by going through a Board-sponsored search are usually able to win respect for their motives and values. Whether they do so in their new companies, however, is a function of how adroitly they handle the stresses and continuing demands of a new situation. Success at doing so requires self-management.

Part III

MANAGING
ONESELF

Taking charge successfully calls for more than effectiveness in learning, visioning, and coalition building. It takes a clear head and emotional balance. The inevitable stresses of the transition make it imperative that the new leader remain disciplined and calm so that she can remain on the rested edge and avoid the ragged edge.

In a sense, this entire book is about how new leaders should manage themselves during the transition period. What additional insight can we provide about the intrapersonal dimensions of this challenge? We will not review the mundane aspects of personal management, such as time and schedule coordination, which leaders have already mastered. Nor will we explore the deep psychological forces that shape individual perceptions and sometimes hobble good intentions; interested readers are referred elsewhere.[1]

Part III will instead examine three aspects of self-management—self-awareness, leadership style, and advice and counsel—that offer concrete tools with which to diagnose and gain perspective on one's situation and actions.

Chapter 9, on self-awareness and style, offers guidelines for self-diagnosis and midcourse corrections. It also provides a framework for understanding individual differences in leadership style. Chapter 10 explores the art of setting up a balanced network of advisors and counselors and provides guidelines for how to use advice and counsel effectively.

9

SELF-AWARENESS
AND
STYLE

Preparation is essential for a successful transition, but it doesn't eliminate ambiguities and uncertainties. For those unaccustomed to dealing with the pressures faced by new leaders, and those more comfortable in unambiguous situations, it can be difficult to keep a clear head and maintain emotional balance. But it's crucially important to work at staying on the "rested edge." As one leader put it: "It's easy to be overwhelmed by all of what you have to do. You have to be able to detach yourself and do some self-assessment. Remember you're in a marathon, so you have to take your time, learn the job, and not worry too much about what other people are saying."

New leaders must also be emotionally prepared for the role of heir apparent when the pace of ascension is under someone else's control. The resulting internal tensions will test the new leader's maturity. As one leader described it:

> You have to have an enormous amount of patience. I think there's a tendency when you enter an organization from the outside, and you're not the CEO, to come up with a wide variety of things that you believe need fixing. And the day you enter the scene, in most cases, you're not in a position to fix them . . . It's sort of like being [the vice president of the United States]. I mean, it's more dramatic, I think, in politics than it is in business, because if you're coming in as chief operating officer, there are a lot of changes you can make. But you often really cannot reshape the organization until you are CEO. And even then you may not be able to do it. But for people who come in to a number-two spot, I would advise them not to expect their impact to be substantial so quickly. They have to really have patience to be able to shape things.

The new leader has to be prepared for the long haul, and prepared to invest emotionally. The decision to accept the number-two position is a life choice; it differs fundamentally from a turnaround, in which those who come in from the outside to save a troubled company intend to leave after the job is complete, usually within two or three years. Building the relationships necessary to transform a company that one intends someday to lead is a more complex personal challenge. As one leader expressed it:

> It's a very difficult position. You constantly are battling within yourself. And you're never quite sure whether you're passive enough, or aggressive enough, or whether you're serving the CEO enough, or you're handling the [units under you] in the best way . . . You're constantly trying to meander down a very unbalanced path. And I think, at least with me, I debated for the first year almost every day whether I was too tough or too weak. So I think there's a lot of self-doubt as to how you're handling it.

This chapter explores how to manage the stresses of a personal transition while beginning to transform an organization. It emphasizes self-assessment and the use of structured reflection to refine one's coping strategies and make some midcourse corrections. Finally, the chapter looks at the impact of differences in leadership style on interpersonal conflict and proposes some compensating strategies.

SO WHAT TO DO?

Faced with high expectations, much to learn, and few teachers to turn to, what can the new leader do? When we posed this question to the leaders we interviewed, their responses clustered around two dominant themes. First, they used self-diagnosis and reflection to gain perspective and understand what was going on. Second, they established control over their surroundings and schedules in order to cope better with inevitable stresses.[1]

Diane's Experience

The need for self-diagnosis and adaptation is well illustrated by Diane's first days on the job:

> I had more of a problem at first than I ever thought I would. On one hand, I loved the work, the people here were great, it was exciting . . . I was really loving every minute of it during the day. But at the end of the day, I wasn't satisfied. I'd never been in a situation where there was so much to do and where I felt I wasn't getting it done. It was really frustrating for a couple of weeks early on. I was going from one thing to another during the day, and would go back to the apartment at the end of the night and feel like I hadn't done anything worthwhile. I remember I just went home to see my parents for a weekend and took a long walk with my dad. We were talking about my new job, and I told him how I felt I wasn't getting anything done even though there wasn't a free minute during the day. He said to me, "Sounds like you don't feel you're in control of things." Well, I hadn't thought of it that way, but of course he was right. I was going from one thing to another on someone else's schedule. I'd

get a briefing from someone before I went into a Finance meeting that was someone else's meeting, where I didn't know enough to say much. And then I'd get in a car and be driven to a field office, where I didn't know enough to contribute anything. I wasn't used to not being in control, and I was starting to feel useless, like I didn't deserve what I was getting paid.

For Diane, the need to be in control functioned as a strong motivator and an indicator of self-worth. Simply recognizing that her sense of lack of control was the issue helped her gain perspective: "That in itself was helpful, because I knew it was temporary. It was something I just had to get behind me." Awareness also enabled her to take action to hasten the process.

I started to be a little bit more assertive when it came to my schedule, and made sure I got more prepared before meetings so I had in mind one or two questions on what seemed to me the most important issues to find out about. It sounds like a simple thing now, but back then it really helped me. The big thing was to find a way to have more say on the agenda, so I wasn't as dependent on someone else.

UNDERTAKING SELF-DIAGNOSIS

Without exception, the successful new leaders we interviewed all spoke of self-assessment as having been important to them.[2] As one said: "It's very important to have self-awareness, because if you don't, then you're likely to misread both yourself and everybody else."

Our leaders' approaches to self-assessment were of two general types: private reflection and talking to someone else. One recalled:

I got into the habit of dictating what was on my mind every night. At first I was staying in the company apartment, and I was alone when I got back there at night, and I'd just talk into this hand-held thing. It helped a lot to play the tapes back every once in a while.

Another used a simpler tool:

> I carry around these three-by-five index cards, and whenever something happened, or something would occur to me, I'd just jot it down on these cards.

A third leader leaned on his wife:

> She's always been a confidante to me, and she knows me probably better than anyone else. It also got her ready for this place once we sold our house and moved here. She knew more what to expect and what sort of place it was.

A fourth confided in a mentor:

> I turned to a guy who had been a mentor to me for some time. He didn't know much about this industry or this company . . . [but] we'd stayed in touch, and it was really helpful to call someone who was just interested in me. He didn't have any agenda. He just wanted me to succeed here.

Whether alone or with someone else, by writing, dictating, or talking to an advisor, all found a way to diagnose what they were experiencing and gain insight into themselves at the same time. Some paused for a formal ninety-day assessment. One leader described hers this way: "I just decided, after about three months on the job, I should take a step back to see what I liked and didn't like about what I was doing and how I was getting started. I wrote in my journal. It was a good way for me to reflect and just pause a bit."

Another reported: "I periodically step back and say, Okay, what is important here? What has emerged? There's a pattern I'm seeing over and over. And also, what's the time urgency of the issues?" He added that the perspective he gained gave him a sense of greater control.

Ideally, self-reflection is continuous, but certain natural junctures during the transition period lend themselves to deeper assessments and midcourse corrections. As we saw in Chapter 1, the transition period consists of three phases: learning tends to dominate the first third, visioning the second, and visioning and coalition building the third. These shifts in emphasis provide natural opportunities for self-diagnosis and corrective action. For this reason, it can be particularly productive to set aside time at roughly two-month intervals for some structured reflection and assessment.

Our research identified some useful questions to guide the process of self-reflection. One set has to do with thoughts and emotions, another with early opportunities missed or profited from, and the third with people and events that have had an impact on the new leader and could be significant as she moves forward.

Posing these questions at two-month intervals—and augmenting and refining them—can be a tool for generating insight into one's early impressions and emotional reactions.

About Myself

What do I think so far about my fit in this situation? On a scale of 1–10, how good is the fit?

- What seems possible? Impossible?

- Is this place geared to my strengths?

- What can I do in the next several weeks to improve the fit?

What do I believe so far?

- What two strengths do I bring that this company needs most?

- What evidence leads me to believe that?

- If I could take one action to make this a better organization, what would it be?

How do I feel so far?

- On a scale of high (intense and certain) to low (occasional), do I feel:

  ☐ Excited? If not, why not? What have I done to block feeling excited?

☐　Happy? If not, why not? What have I done to block feeling happy?

☐　Confident? If not, why not? What have I done to block feeling confident?

- Is my success under my control? If not, what must I personally do to gain more control?

What has bothered me so far?

- With whom have I gotten along badly? Why? What have I done to cause conflict?

- Of the meetings I have attended, which has been most troubling?

- Of what I have seen and heard, what has disturbed me most?

- What changes will I make, at the right time, to the things that have bothered me most?

About Missed and Exploited Opportunities

- Of the interactions I've had, which would I handle differently if I had the chance? What did I do to cause them to go badly? Which exceeded my expectations? Why?

- Which of my decisions have turned out particularly well? Why?

- Are the most significant missed opportunities attributable to me or something I had control of or to something outside my control? What was it?

About Impact

- Who has had positive and negative impact on me so far? Why?

- What are the pluses and minuses of each of my direct reports?

- If I had no constraints and could wave a wand, what would I do that would increase my impact here?

All these questions seek to pinpoint whether a given perceived difficulty is the result of the situation (world blocks) or of explanations that lie within the leader (personal blocks).[3] Most of us have a powerful bias toward attributing our problems to the situations we are facing rather than to our own actions or oversights.[4] Because we feel we have less control over situations (world blocks) than over ourselves (personal blocks), the net result is missed opportunities to take effective action. This does not mean that the leader is unable to eliminate or minimize blocks that the situation presents; it only means that he has more control over those within himself. Awareness of which type of block one is facing will help make it much more likely that appropriate action can be taken.

REFINING COPING STRATEGIES

Most leaders have already developed effective mechanisms for managing stress, but these strategies have typically been geared to less demanding jobs and more familiar and supportive surroundings. It is because of the extraordinary demands of the new leader's situation that self-diagnosis is important; for it to be most useful, that diagnosis must be translated into coping strategies.

The leaders we interviewed employed four main strategies to cope with the pressures they faced during transition: asserting control over their immediate environments, taking a long view, finding ways to relax, and balancing family life and work.

Asserting control locally

Like Diane, new leaders gained a sense of control by rapidly forming personal support systems and asserting more discipline over their calendars. Establishing predictability in their immediate environments better equipped them to tolerate their lack of control over the larger organizational environment. Actions in pursuit of this aim ranged from carefully selecting a secretary to requiring final approval on scheduled trips. Total predictability proved impossible, but our leaders found partial or even temporary steps to that end helpful.

Taking the long view

With so much at stake, the pressure is intense to make all decisions right away. But experienced leaders advocate taking the long view whenever possible. As one observed:

> I think the most important thing I would tell people is that this is a marathon, not a sprint. You should take your time, learn your job, and not worry too much about exactly what people are saying early on.

Said another:

> It's easy to be overwhelmed by the magnitude of what it is you're trying to do, and the fact that most people coming to you, particularly early on, aren't going to give it to you straight. But having been through a [few] of these, I guess I learned a long time ago to settle down and do your job and not worry about it too much. Because, in fact, most of what you really want to think about you won't [have] to deal with 'til you've been there sixty or ninety days at least. You can roll them over in your mind, but you're not really able to engage in them until you've been around a while.

Finding ways to relax

Most of the leaders we interviewed found ways to relax that operated as personal safety valves. For some, exercise was the answer: "I'm almost obsessed with athletics. I do something [athletic] every day regardless of what is going on." Others found refuge in humor and other tension-relieving social activities. One said: "Humor is an amazing thing. If you can't laugh when you're in the middle of a stressful situation, your brain gets congested. You have to be creative. Creative environments are environments where people are lighthearted and can laugh. That's how I maintain my sanity." Another said: "Getting outdoors is essential for me. It restores my sense of balance and equilibrium. And family is essential. I've been fortunate to have a very supportive wife. Maintaining a private life and investing in it are essential for strength over the long run." Another described it this way: "I think in almost any job you can drive yourself crazy if you don't have some mechanism for separating yourself from the job. If you don't do that, I think eventually you are going to reach a point where you are not particularly effective. I also think your family life is very much at risk if you are unable to separate yourself from your work."

Balancing family life and work

While some leaders turned to their spouses or partners as advisors, several spoke of the importance of separating their private and public lives. As one put it:

> You can drive yourself crazy if you don't have some mechanism for separating yourself from the job. One of the things I have tried to do over the years is not take a lot of baggage home . . . You can't run off and leave a very serious problem, but you need to be able to leave the issues and problems on the desk or in the office. If you don't do that, I think eventually you are going to reach a point where you are not particularly effective. I also think your family life is very much at risk if you are unable to separate yourself from your work.

Practically speaking, the demands of a transition substantially cut into the time new leaders can spend with family and friends. But a number of the people we interviewed stressed reestablishing balance as soon as possible and not getting trapped in permanent overdrive. Said one:

> In any job you [forgo] some personal pleasures. And until you feel like you're coping, it's hard to keep a balance. But once you feel you're going to swim rather than sink, even though you're not doing a very elegant stroke, you can begin to get the balance back. And then eventually you can get to a point where you can pace yourself, and keep enough of these private satisfactions in life, so your public side isn't all-consuming. There are some people who do seem to have their public side become themselves, which I think makes you fragile. Because then if you get a blow to your public persona, you have nothing to fall back on.

Sound advice and counsel also emerged as a crucial source of support and perspective. We will devote Chapter 10 to exploring the nuances of advice and counsel.

UNDERSTANDING LEADERSHIP STYLE

Leadership style came up often in our discussions with new leaders, CEOs, and members of Boards. Style was often a factor in selection, as the Board sought to match the new leader to the organization's perceived problems. Indeed, many new leaders were selected precisely because they embodied a particular style.

New leaders' styles often differed significantly from those of the CEOs they were slated to succeed and those who were to report to them. Because such differences have the potential to cause friction, it is particularly important to assess one's own style in light of the culture of the company and the styles of key people and to develop ways to compensate for stylistic differences. As one leader explained: "I tend to be authoritarian. I have to check myself, really to listen and to try to build consensus. I say to myself, 'Be careful. Listen. Listen more.' I learned to do that by making mistakes and letting opposition build."

Defining style

By *style,* we mean how a person prefers to learn, make decisions, and motivate others. Personal style reflects preferences, not capabilities. Generally speaking, a new leader who is aware of his style and its limitations will be better at using it effectively.

Stylistic preferences grow out of formative personal and professional experiences, including formal and informal education and choices of professions, jobs, and mentors. Style has also been reinforced by promotion and other rewards to the point that most leaders' styles are deeply entrenched. A basic style that has evolved over years of formation, testing, and reinforcement is unlikely to change dramatically, short of a serious personal crisis that forces fundamental reassessment.

This does not mean that one's ability to learn, influence, and so forth does not continue to evolve and sharpen. But while new leaders hone and refine their styles, becoming more adept, they are not likely to adopt methods very different from those that have worked for them in the past. Some who are good at building teams prefer group decision making, while others find they are better one-on-one. Some learn best by dealing with abstract concepts, while others require concrete experience to internalize new learning. Some influence others most effectively with facts, logic, and precedents, while others are more adept at using involvement and participation.

The impact of style

Our interviews produced three sets of guidelines for dealing with stylistic differences as one approaches the apex of a company:

Anticipate stylistic inconsistency. Stylistic congruence with the existing culture is not usually a primary criterion for selecting leaders at this level. The Board and CEO expect the new leader to introduce a certain degree of cultural change. Thus the company's culture will not necessarily be consistent with the new leader's strengths. Several new leaders we interviewed excelled at building relationships with customers and suppliers and, because of their outward-looking orientations, at anticipating market shifts; the businesses they entered had stagnated because their top managers had capabilities other than those. Others moved from very large corporations to midsized companies hoping to grow; the new leaders' styles and mindsets thus represented what their new companies aimed at, but differed strikingly from those of their new colleagues and subordinates. Differences in perspectives as well as skills are to be expected in these situations.

A new leader who is functioning as a pioneer, introducing new ideas and ways of operating, may find the terrain and the natives unforgiving and hostile at times. If Lewis and Clark had assumed a friendly, compatible environment in the Louisiana Territory in 1803, they never would have reached the Pacific and the history of the United States might well have been irrevocably altered. Figuratively speaking, the potential cost of unrealistic assumptions is just as great for the new leader.

Take responsibility for understanding stylistic differences. The new leader bears the responsibility for grasping the differences between her style and the culture of the company, and the impact of those differences. Otherwise she runs the risk of misjudging the pace at which the company can change and of communicating unclearly what she expects employees to do differently and where she wants to take the company.

Some frustrated leaders overlooked their own failure to understand how employees in the new company learn and make decisions. One complained: "Sometimes I get frustrated . . . I'm trying to take this place to a new level so everyone will be better off. But most of the people just don't seem to get it, or just don't want to." This particular manager learns best through abstract concepts; he settles on a course of action by forming and testing a concept in his mind. He also tends to pursue this process alone, rather than in discussions with others, and he lacks experience managing people who learn differently. Many midlevel managers he considers unable or unwilling to grasp his ideas are people who learn differently, from concrete experience or direct observation. Thus people from whom he had expected enthusiastic buy-in had difficulty understanding what this leader was suggesting. Benchmarking visits, pilot projects, or use of influential employees as interpreters might have bridged the gap.

Choose subordinates with complementary styles. Should a new leader try to surround himself with people whose styles are similar to his, or choose subordinates whose styles are different but compatible?

The leaders we interviewed suggested searching out direct reports who complement the new leader's style, skills, and experience. This approach provides for balanced perspectives within the top team, and surrounds the new leader with styles that are already valued and probably widespread within the company. Change efforts can be thwarted, however, if subordinates' divergent styles are interpreted by employees as evidence of lack of support for the leader's agenda. It is very important for the new leader's direct reports who represent different strengths and styles to demonstrate commitment to the new leader's agenda.

Assessing style

"Know thyself" may be the most important piece of advice that can be given to any leader.[5] To do so, she must be willing to probe her core assumptions and become aware of stylistic patterns and preferences. In particular, any leader should ask herself:

- Does my experience match the problems facing the organization? If, for example, the new leader is drawn to product problems but the company's fundamental problems are cultural and political, the mismatch may waste valuable problem-solving effort.

- Does my experience match the expectations of my superiors? The CEO and key members of the Board of Directors will have their own preferred ways of operating and beliefs about what works and what doesn't. Knowing whether they match those of the new leader will help ensure that the relationship begins on the right note.

- Does my experience match the expectations of subordinates? Subordinates' expectations and priorities concerning what should be fixed, how, and when will have been formed by their employment experience. A mismatch could cause confusion when the new leader begins to test a personal vision.

During the transition period, new leaders will be well served by assessing how their own preferred ways of learning, building coalitions, and developing visions jibe with their new companies' normal mode of operation. The questions that follow provide a framework for self-diagnosis and self-evaluation.

About what do you prefer to learn? New leaders are hired for their knowledge and experience, acquired in various positions and perhaps in different companies or industries. That very experience, however, reinforces and shapes preferences about the kinds of problems that particular leaders like to solve and how they tend to do so. Research has shown, unsurprisingly, that managers' functional roots continue to influence their perceptions long after they have entered the ranks of management.[6] Even those with extensive cross-disciplinary experience continue to draw on their functional knowledge to make sense of an organization during a transition.

But blind spots can arise from *functional myopia*—relying too much on functional expertise at the expense of other concerns. The learning challenges posed by entering a new company at a next-to-the-top position require moving beyond reliance on one's existing expertise. Some leaders may resist doing so because of the associated uncertainty and feelings of vulnerability.[7] Meanwhile, knowing less than one's key subordinates while trying to establish authority over them tempts a new leader to play to his strengths, to focus on familiar areas, and to avoid delving into issues with which he is uncomfortable.

When the hiring process successfully matches a new leader's expertise to the key problems facing the company, the leader's learning preferences will be a strength. But when deeper examination reveals that the company's real problems are not those that the executive recruiter and CEO described, mismatches of preferences and situation can be devastating.

This is true of functional training and experience. It also applies to the new leader's preferred lens—technical, political, or cultural—for viewing organizational life. A given leader may prefer, for instance, to focus on the technical aspects of markets, products, and finances at the expense of understanding power and coalitions. Such a preference may match the company's presenting problems, but the root causes of those problems—and therefore their solutions—may lie in different domains.

The assessment matrix in Table 9-1 is a simple tool for pinpointing personal learning preferences. The columns represent the technical, cultural, and political lenses through which leaders can view organizations; the rows represent functional specialties. The cells of the matrix represent functional domains within which organizational problems can arise—for example, technical problems in Operations or cultural problems in Finance. On a scale of 1 (not at all) to 10 (very much), rank your intrinsic interest in learning about and solving problems in the realm represented by each cell.

Summing the columns will indicate your relative orientation to technical, cultural, and political problems; significant differences among the three scores may reveal a blind side that bears watching. Likewise, summing the rows will offer a rough idea of your comfort level in key functional areas. Rows with low scores indicate a need to compensate either by paying more attention to the functions they represent or by engaging the help of people strong in those areas.

TABLE 9-1　ASSESSING LEARNING PREFERENCES

	LENS			
Function	*Technical*	*Political*	*Cultural*	**Row Totals**
Human Resources	appraisal and reward systems design	employee morale	organizational equity	
	____	____	____	____
Finance	management of financial risk	relationships with shareholders and analysts	cost-consciousness	
	____	____	____	____
Marketing	product positioning	relationships with customers	customer focus	
	____	____	____	____
Operations	product or service quality	relationships with distributors and suppliers	continuous improvement	
	____	____	____	____
Research and Development	project-management systems	relationships among R&D, Marketing, and Operations	design for manufacturability	
Column Totals	____	____	____	____

How do you prefer to learn? Leaders also differ in how they prefer to gather data about the organization and use the information to reach conclusions.

With respect to gathering information, the central question is one's preference for *hard data* or *soft data*. Neither is inherently superior, but this preference will dictate how one seeks to learn: hard-data people rely on numbers and analysis, while soft-data people gain insight by talking to employees and probing their experience and opinions.

Then there is the question of how many problems one prefers to work on at once. Some new leaders tend to be *single-track problem solvers,* while others are more comfortable proceeding on multiple tracks simultaneously. Single trackers tend to be highly focused and to devote themselves to a particular problem until it is solved. This approach works well if the company is facing only one or a few major problems, but less well if many issues must be tackled simultaneously. *Multiple trackers* tend to keep many balls in the air at the same time, usually moving fluidly from issue to issue. But they may be inclined to devote insufficient time to certain issues or to lose interest in a problem before it is solved.

In addition, some leaders are *inquisitive* in their orientation to learning, while others are more *argumentative.* Inquisitive leaders devote extensive time to listening, and work gradually to fit the pieces together. They tend not to take strong positions; instead, they construct flexible positions and revise them, sometimes too easily, in response to new information. Argumentative learners spend far less time questioning. Instead, they take a quick reading of the situation and adopt positions about key problems and solutions. They then explicitly challenge others to prove them wrong, and learn from the resulting argument. Both approaches have strengths and weaknesses: in brief, inquisitive learners may take too long to reach conclusions, while argumentative learners may reach the wrong conclusions.

Finally, leaders tend to be *experiential* or *conceptual* in their approaches to learning.[8] Faced with a novel situation, experiential learners immerse themselves and search out hands-on experience; they often experiment with minor changes to test the new culture as they pursue understanding incrementally. Conceptual learners, on the other hand, tend to step back in pursuit of a global view and a broad conceptual framework. Again, each approach has its advantages and disadvantages. Experiential leaders' bias toward action can cause them to miss the big picture, to solve the immediate problem but create new ones, or to overlook the key levers that must be pulled to effect deeper change. Conceptual leaders seek a global view of the situation, but may take too long acquiring the global view they seek; they may also see the forest but end up so remote from the trees that they make poor short-term decisions.

The optimal outcome is to understand the lenses through which one views the world, to recognize the strengths and weaknesses of particular learning styles, and to compensate for the weaknesses by means of staffing or deliberate corrective efforts. Differences in learning styles are summarized in Table 9-2.

How do you prefer to make decisions? Leaders also have preferences about the timing and nature of their involvement in the decision-making cycle. Some take the lead in framing the agenda and then back off; others involve themselves in developing detailed options for consideration.

Delegation of decision-making authority is another sphere in which personal preferences vary strikingly. Some leaders encourage decentralized decision making; others prefer to keep control more centralized. Some retain control over certain issues while expecting others to be taken care of. Different leaders also have different thresholds for giving subordinates responsibility for results and discretion over how to achieve them.

How a given leader exerts control over information gathering is closely linked to decision-making style. There are three basic approaches:

1. Those with a *competitive* style believe the best decisions emerge from encouraging competition among subordinates, keeping subordinates guessing about the leader's real intent, and creating multiple competing networks for intelligence gathering.

2. Those with a more *formal* style tend to rely on a formal staff-based procedure-driven system to gather information and synthesize it in a way that equips the leader to make a decision easily.

3. Those with a more *collegial* style believe the best decisions are made by teamwork and a sense of mutual obligation among subordinates. They encourage consensus and tend to favor give-and-take discussions over solitary deliberation as a way to reach clarity on a decision.[9]

The impact of each preference varies with the situation. Internal competition can stimulate innovation, but it can also be counterproductive in situations that require cross-functional collaboration. Formal systems can bring to bear needed predictability and in-depth analysis, but tend to be slow and to insulate the leader from diverse points of view. Collegial processes stimulate commitment to implementation, but can suppress internal dissent and result in low-est-common-denominator compromises.

TABLE 9-2 DIAGNOSING YOUR LEARNING STYLE

Dimension of Learning Style	Diagnostic Question
Hard data or soft data?	When you are seeking insight into a complex problem, do you prefer quantitative analysis or qualitative assessments from people close to the situation?
Single-track or multiple-track?	Do you prefer to concentrate on a single problem until you have it solved or to work on multiple problems in parallel?
Inquisitive or argumentative?	When seeking to learn from others, do you prefer to question them gently or to take a strong position and see what reactions it provokes?
Experiential or conceptual?	Do you prefer to immerse yourself deeply in a situation before reaching conclusions or to begin with a conceptual framework and working hypotheses?

The leader's decision-making style also embodies preferences among speed, quality, and acceptance.[10] All operational decisions involve tradeoffs; the elements in the tradeoff are the speed with which the decision is made, the thoroughness and care with which the choices are considered, and the acceptance of those who implement the decision. A stress on speed tends to bear a cost in complete analysis (quality) or buy-in from those affected (acceptance). Likewise, emphasis on covering all the bases analytically or ensuring broad buy-in comes at the cost of speed. For many reasons, leaders may inadvertently skew decision making toward speed, for example, even in situations where quality or acceptance is very important.

How do you deal with preexisting power structures? Strategies for dealing with existing power structures vary with circumstances, but most leaders tend to rely on one of three strategies: (1) to co-opt them; (2) to neutralize them and build their own supportive coalitions; and (3) to ignore them and get on with the business at hand. For leaders whose preferred strategy is co-optation, preexisting power structures represent resources to be tapped into and shaped. These leaders seek to cut deals and to support powerful people's goals in return for support for their agendas. The built-in risk is that their agendas will become watered down, but leaders with this political style may also gain a head start on building a powerful political base.

Then there are those who see existing power structures as fundamentally loyal to the status quo, and hence as obstacles to needed change. Typically, they seek to bring in new people and to neutralize existing power bases through reorganization. Leaders who adopt this approach avoid diluting their vision through deal making, but they risk alienating people who can mobilize support for change initiatives.

Those who try to concentrate on the business at hand, assuming that they can win over necessary support with the logic of their case, tend to view dealing with the existing power structure as a necessary evil. They neither seek to co-opt it nor actively build their own base of support. Here the risk is that opposition to change will coalesce. Like the leader described below, those who ignore organizational politics will almost certainly contribute to their own undoing.

Bruce, a new leader who concentrated too much on technical challenges, was blindsided because he missed important political cues. The CEO of a fast-growing high-technology manufacturing company had enticed him away from the smaller company where he had spent his whole career. He had become senior vice president of Operations. He had never looked for a job elsewhere, but was ultimately lured by the CEO's promise to consider him as a successor and by the challenge of putting in shape the company's fast-growing and unwieldy supply chain. He had never failed in a job, and believed that success would result from bringing discipline to a company that was on a steep trajectory, working hard, and offering a sense of purpose to people under him. Eighteen months later he was fired by the CEO, who gave him a very generous severance package and some advice. In Bruce's words:

> He said that I'd done a great job, that all the things I'd said were needed were right, that Operations had never been working better, and that this was a very hard thing for him to do. But he added that I had spent so much time managing down, I missed the fact that I was doing things that really got my peers mad and I didn't have any support from them. They went to him as a group and said they couldn't work with me. Looking back now, there were meetings [and one-on-one encounters] where I should have been smarter and more aware of what I was doing, and I should have looked at things from their point of view. But I'd never been in that kind of situation before.

This leader failed because his achievement-oriented nature turned out to have some serious drawbacks in an environment where power mattered more than achieving shipping targets.

How do you motivate people? Some leaders lean to the push side of the motivational spectrum, believing it best to use logical, factual arguments or incentives to move employees in a particular direction with rewards or threats. In their view, these approaches establish clear expectations and provide tangible rewards for desired behavior. Others gravitate to the pull side, in the belief that logic and incentives are less powerful than an inspiring vision and a supportive environment. They tend to motivate through inspiration and participation, stressing shared commitment and a sense of community.

Most leaders appear to employ a mixture of push and pull mechanisms but tend to favor one over the other.[11] We believe that this preference is linked to how leaders themselves prefer to be motivated. For purposes of establishing credibility and a base of support, it is essential to know which side of the motivational spectrum one prefers. One way to find out is to ask oneself which leadership activity elicits the most personal satisfaction and satisfies basic social needs. Exercising power over others? Achieving something unique, or winning in a competition with others? Feeling part of a group or team? Another approach is to think back on one's most satisfying jobs and projects, and analyze them to determine why they were gratifying: How did the boss act? Was there an atmosphere of teamwork and community, or of independence and accountability?

As is true of all aspects of leadership style, there is no single right way to motivate others. Push tools work well when they are appropriate to the culture, when goals and the behavior they call for are clear, and when the right rewards can be bestowed for achieving these goals. But leaders who rely too much on push methods run the risk that employees will do precisely what they are rewarded to do and no more, or that they will revert to old behaviors when the rewards end. Pull tools are best when employees are asked to do what are, for them, extraordinary deeds. The danger is that they could demotivate or confuse people if the prevailing reward system encourages behavior different from what is being asked of them.

How do you develop a vision of the company's future? Some new leaders with a mission to change incline naturally to speculate about what the company would be like if it were ideal. Others tend to take things as they are and do the best they can. Some can quickly consider what-if scenarios, while others require a structure or model.

How leaders prefer to craft a personal vision seems to be correlated with their preferences for pull or push motivational tools: those who prefer push mechanisms seem to envision orderly organizations in which problems are under control or avoided, while leaders who rely on pull mechanisms picture groups of people who are energized and excited. A leader's personal vision is also affected by personal social drives. Those with high needs for achievement usually envision competitive, fast-paced environments that meet challenging objectives; those with a strong need for affiliation form mental pictures of people working together closely to attain shared organizational goals; those who seek a sense of control and influence over others may picture the future company dominated by its leader, and the company at the center of its industry, dominating competitors.

In sum, there is no single best approach. The point is that the leaders who are aware of their own styles and preferences are most likely to master the three tasks that our research deems central to success—learning, visioning, and coalition building.

Compensating for one's style

This chapter argues that a new leader's effectiveness during the transition period is to a large degree a function of being self-aware. A concomitant aspect of self-awareness is recognizing how one's stylistic preferences fit the culture of the company and the styles of bosses and subordinates. As a group, effective new leaders appear to be highly aware of their own preferences, and to work hard at identifying potential mismatches with the demands of the organization.

Several leaders we interviewed cautioned, however, against trying to be all things to all people. Said one:

I would just tell them to be confident in their own style, because your own style shows when you get under pressure and adversity. You cannot be who you're not, and true colors come through. So if you're trying to act a certain way because you think you'll be perceived as a leader or perceived as presidential, it won't work. It's maturity; it's being comfortable with yourself.

Another put it this way:

It's important to be respectful of [other people's] styles and not come in with guns blazing, but at the same time I learned that I didn't have to worry too much. I held back a lot because I didn't want to come across as though [I had all the answers] . . . Then [one of our Board members] said to me one day that I was being too tentative, that it seemed I was hesitating—knew what had to happen but was holding back. He reminded me that one reason I was hired was my aggressiveness and [willingness] to charge up the hill.

Some degree of mismatch between the new leader's style and the styles of bosses and key subordinates should be expected. Tension and conflict can flare even if the new leader was hired to bring a new approach, and even if the boss promoted his candidacy for that reason. As in any relationship, what appears to be a slight stylistic friction can mushroom into a significant disagreement. To prevent minor friction from becoming debilitating, it is up to the new leader to be aware of stylistic preferences—his own and others'— and to understand their roots and potential impact during the transition.

One of the most effective ways to augment self-awareness, compensate for stylistic differences, and fill in gaps in experience is through the use of advice and counsel.

10

ADVICE
AND
COUNSEL

The experience of being thrust into new situations is rarely debilitating for those who are preparing to come lead a company. The typical new leader has confidence and well-honed survival skills as well as a sense of adventure. He sees the move to a new company as a challenge worth tackling, another step on life's journey. Still, he has traded in familiar relationships and systems to sail solo in a situation that offers no easy answers and no formula for success. He has many initial reactions, even more questions, myriad ideas about what might be done, a desire to move forward, but he needs to proceed carefully and deliberately.

Having left behind familiar support systems, however, the new leader does risk becoming isolated and losing perspective. Paradoxically, the same high personal expectations and confidence that enabled him to win the job can contribute to his downfall if they lead him to decide he can do it all alone. Speaking of this danger, Ronald Heifetz has written, "The myth of leadership is the myth of the lone warrior: the solitary individual whose heroism and brilliance enable him to lead the way . . . [But] even if the weight of carrying people's hopes and pains may fall mainly, for a time, on one person's shoulders, leadership cannot be exercised alone. The lone warrior model of leadership is heroic suicide. Each of us has blind spots that require the vision of others. Each of us has passions that need to be contained by others."[1]

Beyond the strategies for self-diagnosis and coping offered in Chapter 9, what can the new leader do to avoid becoming isolated or overwhelmed? The best answer is often to search out and take advantage of the right kind of advice and counsel. Our research suggests that successful new leaders use strong external and internal networks of advisors and counselors to help them in their transitions. As one leader put it, "when you're flying close to the ground, the top of the trees go by real fast and it's difficult to determine what's down there and what you have to do. But when you gain some altitude [by talking it over with others], things start to slow down a little bit and you get a broader picture even though you are traveling just as fast."

Many situations we have already described call for the perspectives, feedback, and recommendations of expert helpers. One example is dealing with successor's syndrome, where what begins as a cordial relationship between the new leader and his boss—the CEO whom he expects to succeed—sours over time, leading to lack of communication and, ultimately, loss of trust. It is all too easy for such problems to arise. The new leader is struggling to get oriented and is intent on learning, visioning, and coalition building. He will be keeping a hectic pace and concentrating on gaining some early wins. It is no surprise that he might miss subtle clues that the CEO is feeling left out. An effective counselor can make all the difference by slowing down the new leader, being an objective sounding board, and providing examples of others' successes and failures from which he can learn.

What is counsel and how does it differ from advice? Is one more appropriate than the other for new leaders during the transition? Is counsel more helpful at some times than others? How can new leaders best recruit and use networks of advisors and counselors? This chapter offers a framework for creating a balanced and effective support network. It discusses blocks to taking advantage of this help—some inherent in the new leader's situation, others outgrowths of his particular style—and concludes with suggestions for mastering the art of counsel taking.[2]

AN ANCIENT AND MYSTERIOUS ART

Though history offers numerous illustrations of the importance of advice and counsel, few studies have examined the process of taking and using advice effectively.[3] The works of thinkers as varied as Homer, Plato, Han Fei Zu, St. Benedict, and Francis Bacon, as well as the Bible and Koran, are replete with stories of counsel taken by kings, generals, and prophets. Much of Aristotle's status and influence rested on his counsel-giving relationship to Alexander the Great. Though Machiavelli, perhaps the best-known pre-modern commentator on taking counsel, has become synonymous in the contemporary mind with manipulation, his writings offer valuable insight on the art of counsel taking. *The Prince* (1513) includes passages like the following:

> [The prince must] safeguard against flatterers . . . by letting people understand that you are not offended by the truth. So a shrewd prince should adopt a middle way, choosing wise men for his government and allowing only those the freedom to speak the truth to him, and then only concerning matters on which he asks their opinion. But he should also question them thoroughly and listen to what they say; then he should make his own mind up and by himself. And his attitude toward his councils and toward each one of his advisors should be such that they recognize that the more they speak out the more acceptable they will be.[4]

Two thousand years earlier, the historian Herodotus wrote that multiple sources of advice elicited the best decisions from the leader; he records Artabanus as telling Xerxes, the King of Persia, "Only if there is an alternative can you have a choice; we must make a decision for better or for worse, and that will only be possible if an opposite opinion is expressed. It is like gold: you can't tell whether gold is pure unless you strike it against another piece of gold."[5]

Many preindustrial-era commentaries emphasize that counsel taking can strengthen a leader's hold on his position. A thousand years after Herodotus and a thousand years before Machiavelli, St. Benedict wrote that even an abbot who has absolute and unquestionable power over a community of monks must take counsel. He goes on to explain how, by taking counsel in a particular way from the monks he governs, the abbot actually enhances his power.[6] Francis Bacon agreed when he wrote (circa 1620) of "an inseparable conjunction of counsel [and] Kings."[7]

In modern times, counsel taking often attracts attention in the political arena. Most recent U.S. presidents have had close relationships with counselors. Franklin Roosevelt had Louis Howe and, later, Harry Hopkins; Dwight Eisenhower turned to Lucius Clay and Sherman Adams; John Kennedy relied on Clark Clifford and Robert Kennedy; George Bush looked to James Baker and Brent Scowcroft, depending on the issue. During the 1996 presidential campaign, Bob Dole was criticized for not availing himself sufficiently of advice and counsel.[8]

Because it has been so well documented, the giving of advice and counsel to U.S. presidents can yield useful insights for new leaders of corporations. Clark Clifford summarized the relationship between leader and counselor this way:

> I have been asked many times, what is the role of an outside advisor? How should Presidents use them? My answer is simple; even if he ignores the advice, every President should ensure that he gets a third opinion from selected and seasoned private citizens he trusts. (The second opinion should come from congressional leaders.) Though cabinet members and senior White House aides often resent outside advisors, a President takes too many risks when he relies solely on his own staff and the Federal bureaucracy for advice. Each has its own personal or institutional priorities to protect. An outside advisor can serve the role of a Doubting Thomas when the bureaucracies line up behind a single position, or help the President reach

a judgment where there is a dispute within the government. They can give the President a different perspective on his own situation; they can be frank with him when White House aides are not. [9]

Clifford points out that how a counselor's help is utilized depends on the leader's style and personality:

> For years I resisted any and all suggestions that I join the Johnson administration, just as I had with President Kennedy. However, the relationship I had with each man was quite different. When Kennedy called on me, it was usually to play a clearly-defined role on a specific problem—from the aftermath of the Bay of Pigs to the steel crisis. Johnson, on the other hand, wanted my advice or observations on almost anything that might confront him. Johnson also asked me to participate in important national security meetings which otherwise involved only government officials, something Kennedy never did. In these meetings, I would say little unless asked to comment by the President—and even then I shared my views with him later, only in private. [10]

In sum, Clifford emphasizes that advice and counsel from independent, unofficial sources can provide a needed counterweight to internal, official perspectives, and that such advice and counsel is best given privately. Whether in government or in a corporation, the effectiveness of advisors and counselors depends on the leader's trust that they are loyal and seek only to help him make the best possible decisions.

What useful conclusions can we draw from all this? First, that leaders have always relied on advice and counsel to attain and retain power. Second, that counsel taking is as mysterious as it is ubiquitous. Its mystery lies, in part, in its variety and specificity since it depends on the particulars of each leader's circumstances. It also tends to take place one-on-one and in private. The key questions for the new leader are what sorts of advice and counsel can be of most help and when, how to find the best combination, and how best to use it. Our conversations with leaders gave rise to three basic propositions.

Proposition One: Counsel is different from advice

Advice consists of the transmission from expert to leader of knowledge drawn from analysis of strategic, operational, or technical information. Facing many complex issues and expected to produce quick results, the new leader needs to locate the right information, to elicit the best analysis, and to use both efficiently and effectively. When it comes to the nature of new technologies, the dynamics of markets, and the strength of competitors, the new leader needs accurate analysis in order to decide on a course of action. She should seek advisors who possess specialized technical expertise as well as the ability to analyze data and to communicate the results in such a way that she is better prepared to decide what to do next.

Counsel is something quite different. The essence of good counsel lies in the leader gaining insight (including self-knowledge) through dialogue. The contribution of the gifted counselor arises not from technical expertise but from his understanding of inter- and intrapersonal dynamics. Much more than is the case with advice, the relationship between leader and counselor is a reciprocal one. To offer insight into the complex political and personal challenges the new leader faces, the counselor must gain a deep appreciation of the leader's personality and the particular ways she learns, influences, motivates, and is motivated.

Advice and counsel play complementary, indispensable roles for the new leader. Counsel does not supersede advice; it is a different kind of help. Analysis can help the new leader better understand the strategic, operational, and technical issues facing her new company, but success in changing it requires her to face complex political conundrums and personal choices. Being the one responsible for changing a company's culture requires a level of experience that most new leaders haven't attained. Wise counsel utilized in the right way can help to bridge that gap.

The right combination of advice and counsel can make all the difference. A compelling illustration comes from recently released transcripts of presidential decision making during the Cuban Missile Crisis, those thirteen dangerous days in October 1962 when the fate of the world hung in the balance. President Kennedy had the benefit of much advice about the capabilities of the Soviets, but

their intentions were largely unknown to him. He had solid assessments of Soviet military capabilities and intelligence analyses
of the missile buildup in Cuba, but they did not spell out a clear
course of action. Tapes of the proceedings reveal Kennedy as
highly skilled in the art of counsel taking. He managed a process
of debate and exploration of options in which individuals and
small groups—sometimes working alone and at other times
jointly—tested possible actions, anticipated reactions, and crafted
responses to the moves of the Soviet leaders. In these accounts,
some in Kennedy's inner circle are revealed to be counselors of the
first order, while others were best not listened to. Fortunately,
Kennedy knew the difference.[11]

Proposition Two: There are three principal kinds of help: technical advice, political counsel, and personal counsel

Technical advice consists of information about and analysis of
technologies, technical/scientific matters, and strategy. It could
consist, for example, of recommendations on the effects of the
manufacturing process on a product's reliability, the application of
a new technology, or entering a new market. One leader described
benefits that can flow from competent advice:

> When I came here, I was coming into a brand new industry with
> new dynamics. I was spending all my time trying to figure out this
> place and its culture and I got worried that I wasn't getting up to
> speed on what our customers in the marketplace were reacting to. I
> had scheduled customer visits in the first 90 days and I'd brought in
> [a technical advisor] to give me a profile of the market, our com
> petitors, stuff like that. They've done work for me before and they
> know how I think . . . I didn't have time to orient someone else. I
> also got an added benefit when they found a few [employees] who
> worked with them on the survey. These [employees] got exposure to
> me in a way they wouldn't have otherwise and they learned new
> ways to analyze the markets [from the technical advisor].

Technical advice could also include information on the culture
or the political climate of the organization; for instance, an em

ployee climate survey is one form of technical advice. As one leader put it:

> I had been in one company my whole career before coming here and I'd never really paid much attention to [organization culture]. When I started here in the president's job, I was really struck by the different ways things were done. [In particular] a division or department was separate like its own company and had always been encouraged to stay that way. They had different cultures. If I was going to upgrade performance overall, I had to get a handle on how things were done and what was on employees' minds. I didn't have time to go ask them all, so I had our strategic planning guy go out and find a [technical advisor] to do a survey of the culture. I'll tell you, the information was invaluable to me, and it was the thing that really got our change process going.

Having the right technical advisor can be indispensable during the transition period. As one leader put it:

> I came from an industry with different dynamics and where the economics were also very different. My background and abilities were ideal for the [leadership] challenges, but I had to get up the learning curve fast. The consultants I used were industry experts, and they did an outstanding job getting me oriented and prepared. Without that help it would have taken a lot longer [to make a successful transition].

The keys to success in taking technical advice are timeliness (having the information when it is needed), accuracy (the pertinence of the advisor's knowledge given the problem or opportunity), and connection (matching the advisor's ability to deliver the knowledge with the executive's ability to understand it).

Political counsel helps the leader in a different way; for example, in dealing with the culture, politics, and relationships in the new organization. More of a give-and-take process, it is not based on a particular body of knowledge. A technical advisor could pinpoint a strategy likely to double sales; a political counselor would help the leader implement it, given the prevailing realities, the leader's style, and the capacity of the company to change. The political counselor is typically a sounding board for the leader as he thinks through and tests ways to implement his agenda. In this role, the counselor also provides a methodology to help the leader decide on the best route. An important task taken on by the political counselor is to ensure that the decision-making methodology is compatible with the leader's style. She might prepare an implementation plan for the leader, incorporating insight into what has succeeded in the past and how other companies have implemented similar strategies. She might also line up support within the company, identify likely opposition, and recommend ways it can be dealt with. Lining up support might involve gathering and translating the hopes and worries of people who would hesitate to express them to the leader. Implementation recommendations could include laying out the ideal sequence of meetings the leader must conduct to begin the culture change and coaching him in how to best communicate his vision to ensure commitment from key employees.

The effective counselor will also challenge the leader through direct feedback and what-if questions. Often she is the only one whose explicit role it is to play devil's advocate for the leader. As one leader put it:

> The downside of being [inspiring] in front of people and being a strong leader is that people sometimes hesitate to disagree. I've [also] learned about myself through the years that when I make up my mind about the right thing to do, I get tunnel vision and go for the goal line. Well, sometimes that [determination] causes me to not pay attention to people who have a different opinion, especially if they don't just come out and say it [forcefully]. I have [a counselor] who knows me real well who hits me between the eyes sometimes . . . he's probably the only one who gives me feedback on what I'm doing and how I'm coming across. It makes me slow down.

Personal counsel is help offered out of concern for the new leader's personal well-being rather than the cultural or political challenges he faces. Because of their long-standing relationship and/or intimacy, the personal counselor sees the leader at private, relaxed, or vulnerable moments and in a light that others do not. The bond that results allows the personal counselor to understand motives that might not be obvious to others. It also gives the license to offer feedback in a direct and unflattering way that the leader would probably reject coming from others. Often this personal concern is accompanied by clarity that can be uniquely helpful. An example is the help Diane received from her father, described in Chapter 9. One leader recounted another example:

> There was a fellow in undergraduate school I got to know when I was there. He ran the counseling office and gave me a lot of opportunity to learn and mature outside of the classroom. He was always there for me, to offer help and to give me some encouragement. We stayed close after I graduated, and he followed my career. Anytime I was in town, I'd go to his house to just sit and talk even long after he retired. Even then, he wouldn't hesitate to challenge me, especially on [issues of] values. He really didn't understand a lot about my business or the work I did, but he knew me and all he cared about was that I was doing okay.

Another example is a recollection of the relationship between President Harry Truman and his wife Bess:

> Bess Truman was a pillar of strength to her husband, a person of sound judgment to whom he was devoted. Because she was so retiring in public, most people did not realize how important her role was in President Truman's life. They made a splendid team. President Truman was not always analytical or sufficiently detached in evaluating the people around him. Mrs. Truman often had better insight than her husband into the quality and trustworthiness of the people who had gathered around him, and helped to steer him away from the people [who might have gotten the Administration in trouble].[12]

Mrs. Truman's value as a counselor grew out of years as President Truman's best friend, understanding him in a way that others could not, and giving feedback that he would have rejected coming from anyone else.[13]

Proposition Three: Most executives are better at seeking and using technical advice than at gaining help in the political and personal realms

When asked about sources of help, all the leaders with whom we spoke listed technical advisors, including lawyers, accountants, and consultants in strategy or related areas such as market analysis and information technology. Some of these helpers might also offer political counsel, but they do not specialize in it, and few have been trained to do so. When asked where they seek political help, leaders' answers ranged from "inside the company, maybe Human Resources, depending on the skill of the HR guy" to "my old boss" to "I'd never really thought about it." In other words, political counsel is more haphazard and less accessible.

This greater openness to technical advice than to help in dealing with cultural and political problems is a phenomenon we have observed for some time. In the late 1970s, the early gurus of the Total Quality movement stressed statistical process control and analysis, and treated the culture of a company as a forbidding black swamp that stood between management and a more predictable, profitable operation. Apply our analytical tools, they said, and you can skirt the black swamp. But as these tools began to be used on a large scale in actual situations, it became painfully obvious that culture cannot be ignored and that it is less murky and impenetrable than it may at first appear. In another example, Robert McNamara once pointed out that, when he was making decisions about the Vietnam War, he lacked political counsel. He was influenced almost exclusively by military strategists, guerrilla-war experts, ordinance and materiel specialists, and so forth; no one was at his side to help him understand the mood of the American public or how to build support in Congress. [14]

The preference for technical advice may stem in part from how businesspeople are trained. Many of our leaders observed that insufficient attention is paid to preparing graduates of colleges and graduate schools for the realities of organizational culture change and politics; they also agreed that the business world does not offer much on-the-job education. Many believed that there were no resources inside their companies (including HR departments) that could provide them with training or advice on changing the organization culture. Even though the hiring criteria for senior executives typically include the ability to change organizational cultures, our research turned up little evidence that such skills are fostered in the way we educate, train, and develop our future leaders.

To be effective, however, the leader must anticipate and avoid stress when possible and deal with it adequately when it is inevitable. Alex George, a scholar of presidential decision making, attributed stress to leaders' confrontations with two kinds of complexity: *cognitive complexity* prevails when one must make decisions with inadequate information and uncertainty about the consequences; *value complexity* sets in when decisions require compromising one's core beliefs or those of others affected by one's decisions.[15] Anyone who has been in a leadership position knows the tradeoffs that these two forms of complexity present. The more complicated the tradeoffs, and the more they involve personal values, the greater the stress. When either kind of complexity becomes acute, and in particular when both types arise simultaneously, stress builds. Counsel taking is one way to deal with it. But by no means have all of the people we talked with taken advantage of, or endorsed the value of, good political and personal counsel.

One example is an executive who had just taken over day-to-day operations at a holding company with half a dozen independent operating divisions. He prides himself on being a problem solver and working hard to stay on top of what is going on in his businesses. Peers and subordinates describe his interpersonal style as "friendly," but he also admits that his friendly demeanor fades quickly when something not to his liking happens, at which point he can become very angry; one person described him as "easily combustible." This executive made it plain that he did not need political counsel unless it could be proven beforehand that such help would produce a quantitative return and had been successful in companies just like his. The CEO to whom he reported suggested that he find someone to serve as a sounding board, but he rejected the idea; the CEO also proposed a climate survey of the divisions, which he decided to postpone. This executive's style and the stress it produced resulted in two problems that negatively affected both him and his company.

The first stemmed from his "combustible" nature. This underlying emotional volatility discouraged those around him from offering feedback or bringing him negative news. As a result, he was surprised when cost and profit problems surfaced in two of the businesses that reported to him but were least familiar to him. Even more disturbing was his discovery that the signs of impending problems had existed for some time. As he looked for root causes, he realized that he did not have the mechanisms at hand to anticipate problems or identify their precursors because those he had prided himself on in more familiar situations had proven insufficient. Furthermore, the people in the divisions and at corporate who were aware of the danger signs did not warn him of impending problems. When asked, they admitted that they had hesitated from fear of his reaction. Instead, they kept checking to verify the problems they foresaw, which erupted even as their likelihood was still being assessed.

The second problem this leader faced stemmed from his insistence on personal involvement in operating decisions and problem solving. A style that had worked well for him in positions with less scope overwhelmed him when he ascended to the number-two spot of a multidivision corporation: given all he had to learn, he simply could not keep up with the amount of detail he needed in order to feel comfortable. His stress increased with the surfacing of problems that he believed he should have anticipated. Within six months of assuming his new role, he experienced chest pains and fainted. He was released from the hospital after a few days, relieved that what had happened was only, as he put it, "a wake-up call." Later, a case of flu turned into pneumonia that lasted several weeks; his doctor blamed a suppressed immune system.

Would some combination of advice and counsel have helped this leader avoid these problems? Could counsel have better prepared him for the pressures of his new job? Perhaps not. What is clear is that, had trusted counselors relayed the concerns of those whose information he needed but who were afraid to offer it, he could have avoided expensive operational problems. Advice and counsel might not have prevented his problems, but would not have made his situation any worse and probably would have enabled him to anticipate and deal with them more effectively.

CREATING A BALANCED ADVICE AND COUNSEL NETWORK

While technical advice is more prevalent than political or personal counsel, many of our leaders agreed that political and personal problems hinder leaders' efforts more frequently than do technical problems or gaps in knowledge. For this reason access to all three kinds of help contributes to the new leader's success. An equal number of technical, political, and personal advisors and counselors is not necessary; what matters is the right help at the time it's needed.

Some leaders who think they have access to advice and counsel later find that the quality of help is uneven, or that help is unavailable when it is most needed. If an advice-and-counsel network is not already in place when a crisis approaches, it will be difficult to construct one and orient its members in time to benefit from their help.

Furthermore, one person almost certainly cannot provide first-rate help in all three areas. People better at offering technical advice than political counsel tend to look at the world in a more concrete, black-and-white way, relying on rational, fact-based capabilities. They are at their best when addressing questions whose answers can be drawn from concrete bodies of knowledge. Examples are pollsters who inform politicians about the mood of the electorate, an auditor who analyzes the impact of the latest changes in accounting regulations, and a strategy consultant who charts a plan for introducing mature products into emerging markets.

Political counselors, on the other hand, are best when grappling with situations that lack definite yes-no answers. Examples include changing organizational cultures or dealing with others' personalities and styles. Here political counselors can offer the leader ways to think about the alternatives and guide him as he selects a promising path.

The quintessential example of a political counselor was Clark Clifford, who counseled four U.S. presidents. After the 1960 election, Clifford wrote president-elect Kennedy a memo on how to

make a smooth but thorough transition from the previous administration. In his memo, Clifford told Kennedy, in effect, "Here is
how past presidents who achieved dramatic change organized their
administrations. Given what you face, what you want to do, and
your experience and style, here are ways to transform the government and organize the White House that will work for you. Here
are the ramifications and possible dangers of doing so, and here's
how to decide the best way to set up your administration." Over
the next few years, Clifford became indispensable to Kennedy. He
did not shape policy alternatives, but Kennedy routinely turned to
him for counsel on the political ramifications of a particular path
or the implementation of new policy.[16]

An effective political counselor has to have worked with other
leaders facing the same challenges and/or grappled with them himself. It is difficult to give competent political help without having
personally experienced a similar situation, characterized by imper-
fect options and sharp value conflicts. Clifford had spent the previous twenty years in such roles as an aide to President Truman
and an architect of the national security system and the Department of Defense.

Balanced political and technical help calls for a strong mix of
internal and external advisors and counselors. As one leader explained:

> Advice inside is basically making sure that you get honest and open
> feedback from people who work for you. But there is another [im-
> portant type of advice]—advisors from outside [from whom] you
> can get frank advice about how it looks dispassionately to an out-
> side observer . . . you don't want to just take advice from people
> who are going to be friends, and particularly you don't want advice
> from people [who] flatter you too much, because it's dangerous if
> you start to believe it.

Effective external advisors and counselors often belong to the
new leader's portable lifelong network. They are loyal to the
leader, not to the new organization, and have no personal political
agenda. They may have seen the new leader develop and mature,
and they have come to know him well. They provide much-needed

continuity as the leader moves through life and from one organization to another. As one leader expressed it:

> I have a few people who I trust and I talk to them [when I need to]. They're people who don't have a vested interest [in the organization I'm a part of]. When I was exploring taking this job I talked to them, and even now I check in [when I need] another point of view. I always have lunch with [my old boss] at least once or twice a year.

Another pointed out the importance of outside advisors who understand the sort of culture the new leader faces:

> I cultivate some people from outside who understand [the organization]. These cultures are so peculiar, you know. So get some people who know it but are not now part of it, who don't have their own agenda.

Then there are the internal advisors and counselors who will form the new leader's network inside the organization. The people we talked to stressed the importance of rapidly identifying such people during the process of political learning. Said one:

> I have never been in a place where I couldn't find somebody that I could trust and build a relationship with, that I could come to and say, "Listen, I need you to tell me if I'm doing something stupid. Tell me if I'm doing something in the wrong way. I'm not sure which way to turn here." I've had people that would even report [organizationally] to someone else, that there was enough trust that they would tell me what really was happening inside that organization, knowing I had just the best interest of the company at heart, and never would be betrayed. What I have told people is "I don't expect you to trust me right away, but we will have these conversations. You will give me this input, and if you give me this input you will find over time that you will not be betrayed and it won't cause you difficulty and that it will help the joint cause."

Several leaders pointed out a key tradeoff in selection of internal advisors. They wanted advisors who didn't have their own agendas, and who would offer straight and accurate advice; at the same time, they wanted people who represented key constituencies. Often the answer was a mix of independent people—some in staff roles—and representatives of key coalitions. One leader told us:

> Inside the organization, I looked for individuals who didn't have an agenda. They didn't seem to have anything to gain if power shifted from one division to another. I also [sought out] individuals that I thought had respect within the organization. These would be people who could not only give me advice, but who could potentially be a goodwill ambassador [on my behalf] to others. Usually they were individuals that also were, in their way, opinion leaders. They would help me in translating [the vision], and in working [within the organization] to make the transition successful, because they had the respect of some of the people that I needed.

The risk, of course, is ending up with unbalanced political representation, some constituencies presenting their cases and others not having a voice. One person proposed two principles in this regard:

> I think if you're not very careful, you can become captured by those that are right around you [who are] always putting a particular spin on it. [That is] number one. Number two is, I think, having a divergence of views on particular issues—[building an] intelligence network that will be very helpful to you in terms of your strategy, and where you think you need to go, and where you need to tweak your game plan, so to speak.

CHOOSING ADVISORS AND COUNSELORS

Contemplating the time it takes to build a solid and balanced network for advice and counsel brings to mind an anecdote about John F. Kennedy. He had ordered a young tree planted, and kept asking the gardener why it hadn't been done. The gardener said, "What's the hurry? You won't see it full grown for years anyway." Kennedy replied, "Well then, you'd better plant it right now!" The message is: when you know something important will take time to mature, start it now.

How does a new leader form a network of advisors and counselors? Let's step back and consider selection criteria.

Selection criteria

The three most important selection criteria for advisors and counselors—and the order in which they should be assessed—are competence, trustworthiness, and enhancement of the leader's status. Anyone who doesn't meet all three standards should not be considered.

In assessing the competence of people who might provide advice or counsel, the key questions to ask include: Have they provided the sort of help I need to others? What do others say about their competence? How many times have they dealt with the kind of situation I face? What is their analysis of my situation? Are their arguments clear and well thought through? Are they able to zero in on the vital elements of a complex problem and to summarize their analysis effectively? One leader put it succinctly: "What I look for in advice is well-considered ideas. You know, the difference between [what] somebody just thought of off the top of the head and a well-considered idea."

The next step is to assess trustworthiness. While it is not easy to determine whether someone is trustworthy before being tested, in the absence of first-hand experience, the best assessment tools are usually background checks, references, and one's inner voice. Will this person keep what I say confidential? Will she fulfill promises and be available when needed? Have I heard or sensed anything indicating that I cannot trust her?

The third major criterion is the potential impact on the new leader's reputation and standing of having the person as an advisor. As Machiavelli wrote, "The first opinion that is formed of a ruler's intelligence is based on the quality of the men he has around him. When they are competent and loyal, he can always be considered wise."[17] The new leader should ask: what will Board members think of me if they meet this advisor? What will the CEO think? My senior managers?

Candidates who pass these first three tests have earned the right to be considered. Selection is then based on evaluations of three additional attributes: chemistry, ability to implement, and the ability to tailor recommendations to the new leader's situation.

Without chemistry, the openness that a leader–advisor relationship calls for will not develop. Do I feel comfortable talking with this person? Does she listen attentively to me? How do I feel when and after we speak? Do our interactions enhance my confidence and enthusiasm? If the right chemistry is lacking, the most competent, trustworthy, image-enhancing advisor will not provide the leader with the best help.

For a technical advisor, implementation ability means a grasp of what makes a good idea work in the leader's organization. As one leader pointed out: "It's one thing to come up with the ideal answer when you are a step removed and don't have to live with the results. But coming up with an answer that's practical and that can be implemented is what separates the [pros from the amateurs]." The technical advisor has to give advice that acknowledges the realities and constraints the new leader faces. Good advisors balance practicality against what is best and most innovative technically. They start with the ideal solution and mold it to overcome existing obstacles. They might say to the new leader, for example, "What I just presented is the best way to go, and it is a solution that eventually you must implement here . . . but we're in the real world and some of this can't be done yet. So here's an implementation path that will solve some immediate problems and move you down the road toward the ideal solution." The ability to balance what is best with what is practical is a defining trait of a good advisor. Those who too quickly advocate what is practical without considering what is best will not help the leader change his organization; those who only consider the ideal run the risk of ending up with no change at all.

The political counselor takes on responsibility for implementation in a different way. Alongside hands-on experience with comparable situations and demonstrated ability to make seasoned judgments about key players, the political environment, and likely support and opposition, political counselors must also take into account the leader's decision making, influence, and learning styles. To the experienced political counselor, *how* the leader deliberates and implements decisions is at least as important as their content. The counselor will factor in assessments of the underlying motives of key players (including the leader) and will help the leader anticipate others' reactions and craft responses. Counselors are more likely than advisors to combine strong recommendations about what to do with strategies for proceeding and for overcoming resistance. They are also more likely to be actively involved in implementing decisions and interacting or negotiating with employees on behalf of the leader. "Go and talk to Sam and come back to me, and let's figure out what I need to do to get him on board" is the way one leader characterized a typical interaction with a counselor who had won the trust of various senior managers.

Assessing a potential political counselor calls for answering questions such as: Do her observations and her "read" on my situation offer me insights I didn't have about how to get things done? Can she help me implement my policies? Will she vigorously represent my point of view with others I have to influence? Can she do it in such a way that they will trust her and tell her what they want to say directly to me?

Then there's the ability to customize advice. For the technical advisor, customization requires an in-depth understanding of the company's strategy, its external challenges, and its internal strengths and constraints. A political counselor too must grasp these factors, but must also understand the leader's style, the barriers to achieving the leader's vision, and the political and cultural dynamics that could compromise the leader's success. The leader might judge ability to customize by asking questions such as: Is the advisor adept at applying a general concept to specific conditions? Are there more generalities than specifics in his recommendations, or are they clear and detailed, listing measurable steps for moving forward? Is the counselor suggesting ways of doing things that fit how I think about them? Are ideas laid out in such a way that I can quickly grasp the point? Is he laying out something that I can identify with? If I follow his suggestions, is it likely I will be proud of the results?

The criteria for selecting advisors and counselors are summarized in Table 10-1

What to avoid

Perhaps the most common selection mistake is to assume that a trusted friend will necessarily make a competent advisor or counselor. The comfort one feels with a trusted friend has little to do with that person's capacity to analyze complexity and recommend a way to proceed or to counsel the leader safely through political minefields.

A second trap is to assume that a technical advisor can be an equally competent political counselor. As we have seen, people who excel at one may look at the world quite differently than those expert at the other. It is usually best to find a technical advisor and a political counselor who are compatible, share the same values and perspectives, and can work together closely.

A third mistake is to assume that someone who proved helpful in the past can be equally useful in a new situation involving different problems. The perfect advisor in the leader's old organization may be the wrong person to advise him in the new one. As one leader put it:

TABLE 10-1   CRITERIA FOR SELECTING ADVISORS AND COUNSELORS

To earn the right to be considered
- Competence
- Trustworthiness
- Enhancement of leader's status

To select the best from that pool
- Chemistry
- Ability to implement
- Ability to tailor

A trap you can fall into is overreliance on the same advisors for very different problems and situations. You have developed a good relationship with somebody who gave you good advice, but now the problem set has shifted radically. It may be that they are so intuitive, so smart, that they are able to give you good advice on the new problem. But you have to make sure and be careful [before assuming that they can].

ADVICE AND COUNSEL-TAKING GUIDELINES

The following guidelines for advice and counsel taking can be particularly useful during the transition period.

Make sure the network is geared to your style

Several CEOs told us that they had built up advice and counsel networks over the years, mostly informally, and that their successors could now reap the benefits fully; indeed, in several cases the CEO's advice network contributed directly to the hiring of the new leader. But now some of these leaders were recognizing that their networks were not transferable. One might assume that a new leader could inherit an existing network that understands the company and its culture, but it rarely seems to works that way. As one leader reflected:

> When I came here, [the CEO] encouraged me to get together with some of the guys he'd used over the years. I really appreciated that, [because] it was such an open gesture and he wanted to make sure I knew I could take advantage of [help that had been important to him]. But they really didn't grasp what I was trying to do here, because they were more [oriented] to what this place was rather than what I wanted to make it into. I met with one or two of them, but then over time we didn't see each other very often.

Effective advice and counsel are geared to the individual leader, to the situation she faces, and to what she wishes to create. It is the stylistic and experiential match between leader and advisor or counselor that makes for excellent help. The key is familiarity that grows out of the relationship, and effective relationships are built over time.

Manage the network actively

Once a network is in place, the real work begins. There is no substitute for taking time to orient your advisors and counselors, and to ensure that they understand how you view the situation your hopes and aspirations, and the role you play today and intend to play in the future. The first step may be as simple as asking yourself, "What do they need to know about me and this situation and what I want in order to be most helpful to me?" The complicated part is what comes next: ensuring that everyone is on the same wavelength, and that the advisors and counselors understand what they must know. Doing so depends on the leader's openness and the listening skills and experience of those brought in to help. The task is shared, but the primary burden falls on the leader, who has the most to gain and the most to lose.

How often leaders and advisors or counselors meet, and in what way, depends on the issues at hand. Competent advisors will always make themselves available in an emergency, but in the normal course of events the style of the leader will determine the pace of interaction. Some reach out whenever they feel the need to test an idea. Others select projects with clear objectives and agreed-on deliverables. Some leaders convene their advisors two or three times a year, so that they can hear and build on each other's perspectives; others always meet with them separately. The best approach is usually to solicit advisors' opinions early on about how best to stay in touch, and then to experiment with different approaches.

Overcome personal blocks to effective advice and counsel taking

When barriers to effective use of advice and counsel arise, they are usually personal blocks. Three common blocks we have observed are insufficient openness, impetuousness, and careless listening.

An advisor or counselor can be helpful only to the degree that the leader reveals what he thinks, believes, and feels. Sometimes, such openness requires interpersonal risk taking, such as expressing uncertainty and lack of confidence. A new leader who is comfortable with himself and aware of his shortcomings is more likely to be reflective and willing to express doubts and private thoughts. This kind of openness is facilitated, of course, by the ability of the counselor to listen actively and elicit trust. The combination of a nondefensive leader, comfortable with openness, and a sensitive, skilled counselor will lead to an effective helping relationship

Sometimes even self-confident leaders sabotage effective help by acting too quickly on decisions that merit counsel. Except in crises, decisions rarely have to be made immediately. At the new leader's managerial level, and on all but the most strategic issues, there is seldom a higher authority demanding action. When decisions are made too quickly, it is usually because the leader wants to get them behind him, lacks sufficient information to put a decision in context, or wants to exert authority and demonstrate decisiveness. On issues with far-reaching implications that demand careful reflection, quick action is often reckless. If the leader has the right advice-and-counsel network in place, he is more likely to pace his decision making appropriately.

Leaders also subvert the effectiveness of help from advisors or counselors by not listening carefully enough. Those who make the best use of help tend to have a deliberate decision-making style. They care most about making the right choice, and sacrifice speed for a higher-quality decision when they have the luxury to do so. It is the advisor's or counselor's responsibility to shape the help he provides to the leader's style, but the leader must take responsibility for using available help to its full potential.

The old maxim that two heads are better than one is nowhere more apt than it is for a new leader confronted with much to do and potentially great rewards for doing it well.

While advice and counsel are useful for all leaders, for the new leader they can make the difference between success and failure.

Because of the intensity and focus necessary to produce early wins, create a lasting foundation, and establish a level of credibility that will last over time (and to do so in a matter of months), the new leader is likely to benefit greatly from help that is tailored to his unique style and situation. At a time when much is uncertain and the consequences of mistakes are great, a balanced network of the right advisors and counselors can provide the edge the new leader needs to achieve his ultimate objective.

CONCLUSION

In concluding, we want to step back and summarize our key findings and their implications for how new leaders manage their transitions. We end with some questions to guide future research on leadership transitions and top management succession.

IMPLICATIONS FOR NEW LEADERS

Our experience and research are summed up in the following key propositions and associated prescriptions:

1. The transition period marks the beginning of an era of change that will permanently affect both the company's performance and its culture. *New leaders must actively plan their first era, undertaking a process of overlapping learning and planning.*

2. The transition period begins before entry. *New leaders must leverage the valuable time prior to entry, using it to prepare, learn, and plan.*

3. The actions that new leaders take during the transition period to generate support for their change agenda will determine their ultimate success or failure. *New leaders must quickly create momentum for change by tailoring their approaches to fit the technical, political, and cultural situations they enter.*

4. Momentum is created by securing early wins and building personal credibility while laying a foundation for sustained improvement. *New leaders must find a center of gravity around which to concentrate their efforts for early motivating successes. They must then establish A-item priorities, and relentlessly pursue early successes as a way to achieve them, while seeking the commitment and support of bosses, subordinates, and peers and taking initial steps to change the culture.*

5. New leaders' abilities to perform these tasks rest on mastering the enabling technologies of learning, visioning, and coalition building. *New leaders must quickly get oriented, develop a compelling personal vision of the organization's future, and begin to build supportive coalitions, working to establish virtuous circles while avoiding vicious ones.*

6. New leaders who fail to manage themselves can end up on a ragged emotional edge. *To stay on the rested edge, new leaders must learn to manage their emotions under pressure. They must also identify their own stylistic preferences and analyze how to make those preferences work most effectively.*

7. The greatest hazard of all is isolation. *New leaders need perspective on their new situations. One indispensable source of perspective is a network of advisors and counselors who offer an appropriate mix of technical, political, and personal help.*

IMPLICATIONS FOR FUTURE RESEARCH

We hope that our work will encourage future research on leadership transitions and succession processes, a topic we believe to be of immense importance. Good work has been done on change management, on succession, and on personal transitions, but surprisingly little is known about their combined effects even though these three transformative activities seldom occur in isolation. Leadership transitions and personal transitions are inextricably linked; likewise, organizational change and leadership succession often go hand in hand. To be useful, studies of leadership must begin and end with a clear focus on the phenomenon of leadership in situ. Subdividing leadership into distinct processes may be useful for the sake of conceptual clarity, but the distinctions are often arbitrary and may conceal more than they reveal.

Let us propose some research questions worthy of additional study:

- **Trends in top management succession.** The selection of new leaders for top management positions remains largely unstudied. Some attention has been given to CEOs who come in from the outside, but there has not been enough work on promotion and succession within the top management of corporations, or on the dynamics of coming in as a number two in line for succession to the number-one spot. How often do people enter top management teams from the outside, and how do outsiders fare compared to insiders? When does a person cease to be an outsider and become an insider? Does having made that transition facilitate succession to the top spot?

- **The roles of the CEO and the Board.** Leadership succession is jointly influenced by the CEO and the Board of Directors. Those relationships have not been adequately studied. What differentiates organizations that manage succession successfully from those that fail? Who has more influence on success or failure, the CEO or the Board—and who within the Board? How can CEOs be most helpful in transitions? What role should Boards play? How should the Board's performance in a leadership transition be measured? By whom? What is the impact of particular governance structures and systems to deal with this issue? Are there any general principles that apply, or in the end does it come down to the people involved?

- **The dynamics of successor syndrome.** Relationships between new leaders and those they hope to succeed seem destined to be problematic. The processes of taking charge and letting go inevitably conflict as incoming leaders seek to put their stamp on the organization and outgoing leaders seek to cement and preserve their legacies. Such tensions, though as old as time itself, have not been sufficiently studied. How can the new leader better manage the successor's dilemma: proving herself worthy to lead the organization without threatening the current CEO? How can the current leader preserve his legacy and dignity while still letting go, as he inevitably must? What can insiders do to smooth this process? What role should the Board play? What role do external counselors play in this process?

- **The role that human resource departments should play.** A new leader is often initially recruited by the senior HR person, or by an executive-search professional whom the HR director identifies. The first person the prospective new leader meets during recruiting is typically the head of HR. In our experience, however, and in the opinions of many executives who helped shape this book, human resource departments are rarely up to the task of helping with leadership transitions. We did find notable exceptions—instances in which HR heads played a central role in facilitating a successful transition, and especially in helping the new leader understand the organization's power dynamics. What role can HR play in leadership transitions? What differentiates HR people who are helpful from those who are not? What knowledge, skills, and behaviors does a HR person need to handle the vagaries of leadership transitions? What about the conflicts of interest and divided loyalties that can arise when the new leader will replace the person to whom the HR person currently reports? And if Boards of Directors are ultimately accountable for the success or failure of transitions, how should they evaluate HR's performance?

- **The art of advice giving and taking.** Finally, the central role of advice in leadership effectiveness emerged again and again throughout our study, but the relationship between leader and advisor remains something of an enigma. What makes for an effective leader–advisor relationship? How should a new leader go about building help networks? How are such networks best used? What is the difference in effectiveness between outside advisors and inside advisors? Should a leader's advisors and counselors work separately or together and, if the latter, how? In these and other ways, research can help new leaders get it right from the start.

Notes

Preface

1. Analysis of annual *Forbes* surveys of 800 leading U.S. companies ranked by assets.

Introduction

1. Information was gathered by comparing the SEC filings for year-end 1992, 1993, and 1997. Companies had to meet the following criteria: (1) No change occurred between 1992 and 1993 in the identity of the "number one" person in the company, whether Chairman/CEO or President/CEO. (2) A change did occur in the identity of the person occupying either the President or President/COO position or the CFO position. (3) The company was still in existence in 1997. Out of approximately 10,000 records searched, 141 companies met these criteria. Of the 141 data points, 94 represented the position of President or President/COO, and 47 the position of CFO.
2. We are continuing our analysis of (1) where the outsiders came from, (2) what happened to those who left their companies within the four-year period, and (3) firm performance during this period. Our intent is to explore possible relationships between prior experience and suc-

cess, and to find out whether people left for better jobs. Increased turnover on the part of outsiders may simply reflect a greater propensity to move.

3. See J. J. Gabarro, *The Dynamics of Taking Charge* (Boston: Harvard Business School Press, 1987), 15–34. Gabarro conducted detailed field studies of 17 successions involving general managers and functional managers.

4. Useful works on leadership transitions include J. J. Gabarro, *The Dynamics of Taking Charge* (Boston: Harvard Business School Press, 1987); T. Hsieh and S. Bear, "Managing CEO Transitions," *McKinsey Quarterly* no. 2 (1994); L. A. Hill, *On Becoming a Manager* (Boston: Harvard Business School Press, 1992). A good summary of the earliest work on organizational change (circa 1920 onward) is provided in Chapter 2 of N. M. Tichy, *Managing Strategic Change: Technical, Political, and Cultural Dynamics* (New York: John Wiley & Sons, 1983). Important later works on change management include R. Beckhard and R. T. Harris, *Organizational Transitions: Managing Complex Change* (Reading, MA: Addison-Wesley, 1997); C. Argyris and D. A. Schön, *Organizational Learning: A Theory of Action Perspective* (Reading, MA: Addison-Wesley, 1978); M. Beer, *Organizational Change and Development: A Systems View* (Santa Monica, CA: Goodyear, 1980); R. Kanter, *The Change Masters* (New York: Simon and Schuster, 1983); and N. M. Tichy and M. A. Devanna, *The Transformational Leader* (New York: John Wiley & Sons, 1986). More recent useful work includes J. Kotter, *Leading Change* (Boston: Harvard Business School Press, 1996); and D. C. Hambrick, D. A. Nadler, and M. L. Tushman, *Navigating Change* (Boston: Harvard Business School Press, 1998). Important works on CEO succession include R. F. Vancil, *Passing the Baton: Managing the Process of CEO Succession* (Boston: Harvard Business School Press, 1987); J. A. Sonnenfeld, *The Hero's Farewell: What Happens When CEOs Retire* (New York: Oxford University Press, 1988); W. Bennis, *On Becoming a Leader* (Reading, MA: Addison-Wesley, 1994); and R. Berenbeim, *Corporate Boards: CEO Selection, Evaluation and Succession* (New York: Conference Board report no. 1103-95-RR).

5. The term "political management" appears to have been coined by Philip Heymann. See P. B. Heymann, *The Politics of Public Management* (New Haven: Yale University Press, 1987). The political dimension of management has predictably received more attention in the public sector. For a thorough exploration of the techniques of political management, see M. H. Moore, *Creating Public Value: Strategic*

Management in Government (Cambridge, MA: Harvard University Press, 1995), chaps. 4–5. In Moore's words, "To achieve their operational objectives, public managers must often engage actors beyond the scope of their direct authority. Generally speaking, managers need these external actors for one (or both) of the following reasons: they need their permission to use public resources in pursuit of a given enterprise; or they need their operational assistance to help produce the results for which they are responsible" (p. 113).

Chapter 1: The Challenge

1. Gabarro identifies three core challenges: (1) learning, assessment, and diagnosis; (2) working out shared expectations; and (3) changing the organization to improve performance. J. J. Gabarro, *The Dynamics of Taking Charge* (Boston: Harvard Business School Press, 1987), 71. Hsieh and Bear identify the core challenges as (1) starting where you want to end up; (2) getting clear on the lay of the land; (3) selecting which expectations to change, honor, and defend; (4) getting the real team together; (5) focusing on a few themes; and (6) balancing the short term and the long term. See T. Hsieh and S. Bear, "Managing CEO Transitions," *McKinsey Quarterly* no. 2 (1994).
2. The technical/political/cultural distinction originated in the work of Tichy. The framework appears in many of his publications, but its most comprehensive theoretical statement is in N. M. Tichy, *Managing Strategic Change: Technical, Political, and Cultural Dynamics* (New York: John Wiley & Sons, 1983).
3. See G. Egan, *Working the Shadow Side: A Guide to Positive Behind-the-Scenes Management* (San Francisco: Jossey-Bass, 1994). The shadow organization is more commonly called the *informal organization;* informal organizations consist of networks of influence and information flow that are emergent rather than prescribed. Chester Barnard was among the first to elaborate on the distinction between formal and informal organizations. See C. I. Barnard, *The Functions of the Executive* (Cambridge, MA: Harvard University Press, 1938), chap. 9. Barnard was strongly influenced by the research of Roethlisberger, especially the Hawthorne experiments, which explored the impact of informal relationship networks on organizational behavior. See F. J. Roethlisberger and W. J. Dickson, *Management and the Worker* (Cambridge, MA: Harvard University Press, 1939). Barnard also cites Mary Parker Follett for "her great insight into the dynamic elements of organizations." See H. C. Metcalf and L. Urwick, eds.,

Dynamic Administration: The Collected Papers of Mary Parker Follett (New York: Harper, 1940). For a classic account of the impact of informal relationships, see E. Trist and K. W. Bamforth, "Some Social and Psychological Consequences of the Longwall Method of Coal-Getting," *Human Relations* 4 (1951): 3–38. For interesting discussions of emergent social networks in organizations, see Tichy, *Managing Strategic Change,* chap. 3, and J. Pfeffer, *Managing with Power: Politics and Influence in Organizations* (Boston, MA: Harvard Business School Press, 1992), chap. 3. For a comprehensive theoretical treatment, see N. Nohria and R. G. Eccles, eds., *Networks and Organizations: Structure, Form, and Action* (Boston, MA: Harvard Business School Press, 1992).

4. As Gabarro observed of managers who failed: "Their assessments of their new situations tended to be more narrowly focused than those who succeeded, especially during the important Taking Hold stage, so they failed to address important organizational priorities." J. J. Gabarro, *The Dynamics of Taking Charge* (Boston: Harvard Business School Press, 1987), 72.

5. P. G. Smith and D. G. Reinertsen, *Developing Products in Half the Time* (New York: Van Nostrand Reinhold, 1991).

6. Developing the concept of *design hierarchies,* Kim Clark asserts that a few fundamental early design choices shape the core characteristics of a product, giving rise to subsequent layers of decisions as the design gets elaborated. If these pivotal early decisions are not "right," much of the subsequent work of elaboration may have to be redone. See K. B. Clark, "The Interaction of Design Hierarchies and Market Concepts in Technological Innovation," *Research Policy* 14 (1985): 235–251. See also F. W. Gluck and R. N. Foster, "Managing Technological Change: A Box of Cigars for Brad," *Harvard Business Review* (September–October 1975): 139–150.

7. In physics, *inertia* is the property of matter that causes objects to resist changes in their direction or speed. Force must therefore be applied to make such a change. *Momentum* is the fundamental quantity characterizing the motion of any object; it is the product of the mass of a body multiplied by its velocity. The larger the mass, therefore, the greater the force that must be applied to get it to change direction or speed. In our terms, organizations tend to behave like very large masses, and hence it is difficult to change their direction and pace. Leaders build momentum by creating forces that overcome inertia to move the organization in desired directions. Once sufficient momentum is built up, it becomes difficult to reverse the process of change.

See R. M. Eisberg and L. S. Lerner, *Physics: Foundations and Applications* (New York: McGraw-Hill, 1981), 108–113 and 126–137.

8. For an early discussion of the role of dominant coalitions in the allocation of resources and maintenance of control in organizations, see J. G. March, "The Business Firm as a Political Coalition," *Journal of Politics* 24 (1962): 662–678. More recently, Kotter focused on the process of coalition building in J. Kotter, *Leading Change* (Boston: Harvard Business School Press, 1996). See also J. Pfeffer, *Managing with Power: Politics and Influence in Organizations* (Boston, MA: Harvard Business School Press, 1992).

Chapter 2: Securing Early Wins

1. The term *center of gravity,* drawn from physics, refers to the point where the weight of an object is concentrated. If supported at this point, the object will remain in equilibrium in any position. If a force is applied at its center of gravity, the object can be moved without twisting or rotation. We use the term in a different but related sense: the center of gravity is the point at which the new leader can concentrate energy to make the organization move in desired directions. Our usage incorporates the idea that it is easier to generate movement by applying force at some places than at others. See R. M. Eisberg and L. S. Lerner, *Physics: Foundations and Applications* (New York: McGraw-Hill, 1981), 376.

2. Organizational theorist James Brian Quinn introduced the concept of "logical incrementalism" in strategy formulation. He asserted that rational-analytical approaches to strategy formulation, in which grand strategies are formulated and then implemented, generate faulty descriptive models because of inherent limitations on knowledge: "Strategy deals with the unknowable, not the uncertain. It involves forces of such great number, strength, and combinatory power that one cannot predict events in a probabilistic sense. Hence logic dictates that one proceed flexibly and experimentally from broad concepts toward specific commitments, making the latter concrete as late as possible in order to narrow the bands of uncertainty and to benefit from the best available information. This is the process of 'logical incrementalism.' " See J. B. Quinn, "Strategic Change: Logical Incrementalism," in *The Strategy Process: Concepts, Contexts, and Cases,* ed. H. Mintzberg and J. B. Quinn (Englewood Cliffs, N.J.: Prentice-Hall, 1998), 96–104. The relationship between learning and planning is further developed in H. Mintzberg, *The Rise and Fall of*

Strategic Planning: Reconceiving Roles for Planning, Plans, Planners (New York: Free Press, 1994).

3. As Eisenhower put it: "There is a vast difference between a definite plan of battle or campaign and the hoped-for eventual results of the operation. In committing troops to battle there are certain minimum objectives to be attained, else the operation is a failure. Beyond this lies the area of reasonable expectation, while still further beyond lies the realm of hope. . . . A battle plan normally attempts to provide guidance even into this final area, so that no opportunity for extensive exploitation may be lost through ignorance on the part of the troops concerning the intent of the commander. These phases of a plan do not comprise rigid instructions, they are merely guideposts. A sound battle plan provides flexibility in both space and time to meet the constantly changing factors. . . . Rigidity inevitably defeats itself, and the analysts who point to a changed detail as evidence of a plan's weakness are completely unaware of the characteristics of the battlefield." D. D. Eisenhower, *Crusade in Europe* (New York: Doubleday, 1948), 256.

4. Richard Holbrooke, interview by Susan Rosegrant, in "Getting to Dayton: Negotiating an End to the War in Bosnia," ed. S. Rosegrant with Michael Watkins, Kennedy School of Government, Harvard University, C125-96-1356.

Chapter 3: Laying a Foundation

1. Robert Simons has explored how newly appointed managers use formal control systems as levers of strategic change and renewal. See R. Simons, "How New Top Managers Use Control Systems as Levers of Strategic Renewal," *Strategic Management Journal* 15, no. 3 (1994): 169–189, and R. L. Simons, "Control in an Age of Empowerment," *Harvard Business Review* (March–April 1995): 80–88.

2. Kaplan and Norton developed a "balanced-scorecard" performance-measurement system that allows executives to view a company from several perspectives. The scorecard supplements financial measures with operational measures of customer satisfaction, internal processes, and the organization's ability to learn and improve. See R. S. Kaplan and D. P. Norton, "Balanced Scorecard: Measures That Drive Performance," *Harvard Business Review* (January–February 1992): 71–79. For approaches to implementation, see R. S. Kaplan and D. P. Norton, "Putting the Balanced Scorecard to Work," *Harvard Business Review* (September–October 1993): 134–142.

3. For a comprehensive look at best-practice benchmarking, see R. C. Camp, *Benchmarking: The Search for Industry Best Practices that Lead to Superior Performance* (Milwaukee, WI: Quality Press, 1989), and C. E. Bogan and M. J. English, *Benchmarking for Best Practices: Winning through Innovative Adaptation* (New York: McGraw-Hill, 1994).

Chapter 4: Building Credibility

1. Examining patterns associated with failure, Gabarro observed that new leaders who failed were "more often industry outsiders whose functional experience may not have been a good fit and also more often involved in problems with two or more subordinates, two or more peers or their superiors." J. J. Gabarro, *The Dynamics of Taking Charge* (Boston: Harvard Business School Press, 1987), 62.
2. For a useful discussion of approaches to "managing one's boss," see J. P. Kotter, *Power and Influence* (New York: Free Press), chap. 6; and J. J. Gabarro, and J. P. Kotter, "Managing Your Boss," *Harvard Business Review* (May–June 1993): Reprint 93306.
3. See Kotter, *Power and Influence,* chap. 4.
4. This is one of four core principles of mutual-gains negotiation put forward by Roger Fisher and William Ury. The others are: focus on interests, not positions; invent options for mutual gain; and insist on using objective criteria. See R. Fisher and W. Ury with B. Patton, ed. *Getting to Yes: Negotiating Agreement without Giving In,* 2d ed. (New York: Penguin, 1991).
5. For a discussion of human sense-making and its implications for behavior in organizations, see K. E. Weick, *Sensemaking in Organizations* (Thousand Oaks, CA: Sage Publications, 1995).
6. For an in-depth exploration of persuasion strategies and opinion formation, see P. G. Zimbardo and M. R. Lieppe, *The Psychology of Attitude Change and Social Influence* (New York: McGraw-Hill, 1991). For an interesting look at how public opinion gets formed, see M. A. Milburn, *Persuasion and Politics: The Social Psychology of Public Opinion* (Pacific Grove, CA: Brooks/Cole, 1991).
7. As Ron Heifetz notes, "Leadership operates within particular worlds and requires an experimental mindset—the willingness to work by trial and error—where the community's reactions at each stage provide the basis for planning future actions. Research about each particular context is crucially important, but no analysis or catalogue can substitute for a leader's improvisational skills. Thus, a leader stays

alive not by 'playing it safe' but by taking deliberate risks based on his ongoing assessment of the territory, knowing that corrective action will almost always be necessary." R. A. Heifetz, *Leadership without Easy Answers* (Cambridge, MA: Belknap Press of Harvard University Press, 1994), 243.

Chapter 5: Getting Oriented

1. Noting that "strategies may result from human actions but not human designs," Henry Mintzberg distinguished between *deliberate strategy,* which pursues intentions, and *emergent strategy*, which develops despite or in the absence of intentions. See H. Mintzberg, "Five P's for Strategy," *California Management Review* 30, no. 1 (Fall 1987): 11–24.
2. For an excellent overview of the development approaches to business strategy, see P. Ghemawat, *Competition and Business Strategy in Perspective,* Note 9-798-010 (Boston: Harvard Business School, 1997). See also M. E. Porter, *Competitive Strategy: Techniques for Analyzing Industries and Competitors* (New York: Free Press, 1980); M. E. Porter, *Competitive Advantage: Creating and Sustaining Superior Performance* (New York: Free Press, 1985); P. Ghemawat, *Commitment: The Dynamic of Strategy* (New York: Free Press, 1991); G. Hamel and C. K. Prahalad, *Competing for the Future* (Boston: Harvard Business School Press, 1994); and A. M. Brandenberger and B. Nalebuff, *Co-opetition* (New York: Doubleday, 1996).
3. This schema draws on the technical/political/cultural framework developed by Noel Tichy. See N. M. Tichy, *Managing Strategic Change: Technical, Political, and Cultural Dynamics* (New York: John Wiley & Sons, 1983).
4. Edgar Schein's useful framework for analyzing culture looks at artifacts, norms, and assumptions. *Artifacts* are the visible signs that differentiate one culture from another, including such symbols as national flags, anthems, and styles of dress. *Norms* are shared rules that guide "right behavior," such as modes of greeting and eating, and appropriate conduct for people at different levels in a social hierarchy. *Assumptions* are the deep and often unspoken beliefs that pervade and underpin social systems. Schein points out that the three sets of cultural signifiers differ "in the degree to which the cultural phenomenon is visible to the observer . . . [which can] range from the very tangible overt manifestations that one can see and feel to the deeply embedded, unconscious basic assumptions . . . [which are] the essence of culture." See E. H. Schein, *Organizational Culture and*

Leadership, 2d ed. (San Francisco: Jossey-Bass, 1992), 17. See also M. T. Trice and J. M. Beyer, *The Cultures of Work Organizations* (Englewood Cliffs, NJ: Prentice-Hall, 1993).

Part II: Enabling Technologies

1. For an interesting exploration of the role of feedback loops and systems thinking in organizations, see P. M. Senge, *The Fifth Discipline: The Art and Practice of the Learning Organization* (New York: Doubleday, 1990), chaps. 4 and 5.

Chapter 6: Learning

1. In his highly entertaining and informative essay on sources of innovation in naval artillery, Elting Morison notes that "Fortune . . . indeed favors the prepared mind, but even fortune and the prepared mind need a favorable environment before they can conspire to produce sudden change. No intelligence can proceed very far above the threshold of existing data." See E. Morison, *Men, Machines, and Modern Times* (Cambridge, MA: MIT Press, 1966).
2. For an informative discussion of the impact of selective perception and self-fulfilling prophecies on interpersonal relationships and intergroup conflict, see J. Z. Rubin, D. G. Pruitt, and S. H. Kim, *Social Conflict: Escalation, Stalemate, and Settlement* (New York: McGraw-Hill, 1994).
3. Carl Rogers and Richard Farson put it as follows: "The kind of listening we have in mind is called 'active listening.' It is called 'active' because the listener has a very definitive responsibility. He does not passively absorb words which are spoken to him. He actively tries to grasp the facts and the feelings in what he hears, and he tries, by his listening, to help the speaker work out his own problems." See C. R. Rogers and R. E. Farson, "Active Listening," in *The Organizational Behavior Reader,* 5th ed., ed. D. A. Kolb, I. R. Rubin, and J. O. Osland (Englewood Cliffs, NJ: Prentice-Hall, 1991), 187–198. See also C. Rogers and F. J. Roethlisberger, "Barriers and Gateways to Communication," *Harvard Business Review* (November–December 1991): 105–111.
4. For a fascinating discussion of perceptual processes and management, see S. S. Zalkind and T. W. Costello, "Perception: Implications for Administration" in *The Organizational Behavior Reader,* 5th ed., ed. D. A. Kolb, I. R. Rubin, and J. O. Osland (Englewood Cliffs, NJ: Prentice-Hall, 1991), 234–245.

5. For studies of managerial learning modes that highlight the importance of unstructured learning, see G. Burgoyne and R. Stuart, "The Nature, Use and Acquisition of Managerial Skills and Other Attributes," *Personnel Review* 5, no. 4 (1976): 19–29; and G. Burgoyne and V. E. Hodgson, "Natural Learning and Managerial Action: A Phenomenological Study in the Field Setting," *Journal of Management Studies* 20, no. 3 (1983): 387–399.

6. More formally, such people are "boundary spanners." For a discussion of boundary-spanning roles, see J. Thompson, *Organizations in Action* (New York: McGraw-Hill, 1967). Also see the work of Thomas Allen on "gatekeepers" in T. J. Allen, "Communication Networks in R&D Labs," *R&D Management* 1 (1971): 14–21.

7. For a thorough discussion of lateral relationships in organizations, see J. Galbraith, *Designing Complex Organizations* (Reading, MA: Addison Wesley, 1973), chap. 5.

8. For approaches to conducting focus-group interviews, see J. F. Templeton, *The Focus Group: A Strategic Guide to Organizing, Conducting and Analyzing the Focus Group Interview* (Chicago, Probu, 1994).

9. See D. M. Upton and S. E. Macadam, "Why (and How) to Take a Plant Tour," *Harvard Business Review* (May–June 1997): 97–106.

10. Polanyi (1951) made the distinction between tacit and explicit knowledge and developed the notion of interpretive frameworks for making sense of experience. See M. Polanyi, *Personal Knowledge: Toward a Post-Critical Philosophy* (Chicago: University of Chicago Press, 1958). In developing their behavioral theory of the firm, Cyert and March developed a model of the organization as an information-processing system and originated the concept of organizational learning. See R. Cyert and J. G. March, *A Behavioral Model of the Firm* (Englewood Cliffs, NJ: Prentice-Hall, 1963), 116. Wilensky focused on problem formulation, pointing out that managers must ask the right questions and gather the right information in order to promote learning. See H. L. Wilensky, *Organizational Intelligence: Knowledge and Policy in Government and Industry* (New York: Basic Books, 1967). Argyris and Schön, exploring how organizational learning systems promote or impede efforts to identify and solve problems, distinguished between single-loop and double-loop learning. See C. Argyris and D. A. Schön, *Organizational Learning: A Theory of Action Perspective* (Reading, MA: Addison-Wesley, 1978). Hedberg's model of organizational learning emphasizes the importance of unlearning, or shedding outmoded ways of formulating and solving problems. See B. L. T. Hedberg, "How Organizations Learn and Unlearn" in *Hand-*

book of *Organizational Design,* ed. P. C. Nystrom and W. H. Starbuck (New York: Oxford University Press, 1981). Daft and Weick argue that organizations are interpretation systems and focus attention on cycles of scanning, interpretation, and learning. See R. Daft and K. Weick, "Toward a Model of Organizations as Interpretation Systems," *Academy of Management Review* 9, no. 2 (1984): 284–295. Walsh and Ungson developed a model of organizational memory consisting of three processes: acquisition, retention, and retrieval. See J. P. Walsh and G. R. Ungson, "Organizational Memory," *Academy of Management Review* 16, no. 1 (1991): 57–91. Recent useful works in this tradition include P. M. Senge, *The Fifth Discipline: The Art and Practice of the Learning Organization* (New York: Doubleday, 1990); D. Garvin, "Building a Learning Organization," *Harvard Business Review* (July–August 1993): Reprint 93402; and G. P. Huber, "Organizational Learning: A Guide for Executives in Technology-Critical Organizations," *International Journal of Technology Management* 11, nos. 7 and 8 (1996): 821–832.

11. For a discussion of productive ways to structure individual and group problem solving, see R. L. Ackoff, *The Art of Problem-Solving* (New York: John Wiley & Sons, 1978). Useful approaches to structuring decisions are explored in J. Hammond, R. Keeney, and H. Raiffa, *Smart Choices* (Boston, MA: Harvard Business School Press, 1998).

12. "In nearly all problem-solving," Henderson notes, "there is a universe of alternative choices, most of which must be discarded without more than cursory attention. . . . [Hence, some] frame of reference is needed . . . to screen the relevance of the data, methodology and implicit value judgments. . . . [The most useful] frame of reference is the concept. Conceptual thinking is the skeleton or the framework on which all other choices are sorted out." Cited in P. Ghemawat, *Competition and Business Strategy in Perspective,* Note 9-798-010 (Boston, MA: Harvard Business School, 1997).

13. See M. E. Porter, "How Competitive Forces Shape Strategy," *Harvard Business Review* (March–April 1979): 137–145.

14. For an introduction to TQ concepts and a comprehensive set of references, see D. Ciampa, *Total Quality: A Users' Guide for Implementation* (Reading, MA: Addison-Wesley, 1991).

Chapter 7: Visioning

1. For an introduction to the process of visioning, see P. M. Senge, *The Fifth Discipline: The Art and Practice of the Learning Organization*

(New York: Doubleday, 1990), chap. 11. For examples of strategic visions, see G. Hamel and C. K. Prahalad, "Strategic Intent," *Harvard Business Review* (May–June 1989): 63–76.

2. According to Edgar Schein, "Visions do not have to be very clear or complete. They have to provide a path and a process of learning to assure the members of the organization that constructive change is possible." See E. H. Schein, *Organizational Culture and Leadership* (San Francisco: Jossey-Bass, 1992), 333.

3. P. M. Senge, *The Fifth Discipline,* 148–149.

4. This comes from an unpublished paper written by David Berlew when he was running Situation Management Systems, a consulting organization in Plymouth, MA.

5. D. C. McClelland, *Human Motivation* (Glenview, IL.: Scott, Foresman, 1985). For interesting perspectives on human motivation, see chapters by D. A. Nadler and E. E. Lawler, A. H. Maslow, B. M. Shaw, and S. Kerr in *Readings in Managerial Psychology,* 4th ed., ed. H. J. Leavitt, L. R. Pondy, and D. M. Boje (Chicago: University of Chicago Press, 1989). For models linking task design with motivation, see chapters by R. E. Walton and J. R. Hackman, G. Oldman, R. Janson, and K. Purdy in *The Organizational Behavior Reader,* 5th ed., ed. D. A. Kolb, I. R. Rubin, and J. O. Osland (Englewood Cliffs, NJ: Prentice-Hall, 1991).

6. Kotter defines *alignment* as "getting people lined up behind a vision and a set of strategies so as to help produce the change needed to cope with a changing environment." See J. Kotter, *A Force for Change* (New York: Free Press, 1990).

7. H. Gardner, *Leading Minds: An Anatomy of Leadership* (New York: Basic Books, 1995), 9. More generally, language is a powerful tool that leaders use to shape perceptions. See L. R. Pondy, "Leadership Is a Language Game" in *Readings in Managerial Psychology,* 4th ed., ed. H. J. Leavitt, L. R. Pondy, and D. M. Boje (Chicago: University of Chicago Press, 1989), 224–233. For more comprehensive approaches to "framing" problems and decisions, see E. Goffman, *Frame Analysis: An Essay on the Organization of Experience* (Cambridge, MA: Harvard University Press, 1974); G. T. Fairhurst and R. A. Sarr, *The Art of Framing: Managing the Language of Leadership* (San Francisco: Jossey-Bass, 1996), and J. A. Conger, "The Necessary Art of Persuasion," *Harvard Business Review* (May–June 1998): 84–95.

8. Myths are essential to the process of sense making in organizations. They create shared meaning that helps to coordinate behavior in the

face of uncertainty. See D. M. Boje, D. B. Fedor, and K. M. Rowland, "Myth Making: A Qualitative Step in OD Interventions," in *Readings in Managerial Psychology*, 4th ed., ed. H. J. Leavitt, L. R. Pondy, and D. M. Boje (Chicago: University of Chicago Press, 1989), 608–621.

9. For an accessible summary of research on communication, see P. G. Zimbardo and M. R. Lieppe, *The Psychology of Attitude Change and Social Influence* (New York: McGraw-Hill, 1991).

10. O. Harris, "A Primer for Polemicists," *Commentary* 78, no. 3 (September 1984).

11. The literature on propaganda calls this phenomenon *source credibility*. Jowett and O'Donnell note that "Source credibility is one of the contributing factors that seems to influence change. People have a tendency to look up to authority figures for knowledge and direction. Expert opinion is effective in establishing the legitimacy of change and is tied to information control. Once a source is accepted on one issue, another issue may be established as well on the basis of prior acceptance of the source." G. S. Jowett and V. O'Donnell, *Propaganda and Persuasion*, 2d ed. (Newbury Park, CA: Sage, 1992), 222.

Chapter 8: Coalition Building

1. Heifetz conceptualized this difference in terms of technical change and adaptive change. See R. A. Heifetz, *Leadership without Easy Answers* (Cambridge, MA: Harvard Univeristy Press, 1994.)

2. For a discussion of approaches to coalition building, see D. Lax and J. Sebenius, "Thinking Coalitionally," in *Negotiation Analysis,* ed. P. Young (Ann Arbor: University of Michigan Press, 1991).

3. Alderfer (1987) distinguished between organizational groups and identity groups in organizations. See C. P. Alderfer, "An Intergroup Perspective on Group Dynamics," in *Handbook of Organizational Behavior,* ed. J. W. Lorsch (Englewood Cliffs, NJ: Prentice-Hall, 1987), 190–222. He defines groups in terms of (1) boundaries, both physical and psychological, that determine who is and is not a group member; (2) power differences, or differences in the types of resources groups can obtain and use; (3) affective patterns among members of groups; and (4) cognitive formations, including distinct in-group languages. Identity groups are groups that individuals belong to from birth, such as ethnic groups and families; membership in organizational groups results from distinct choices on the part of the person and the organization. Examples of the latter include task groups and functions. For an early discussion of factors contributing to group co-

hesion and intergroup conflict, see M. Sherif and C. W. Sherif, "In-Group and Intergroup Relations: Experimental Analyses," in *The Organizational Behavior Reader*, 5th ed., ed. D. A. Kolb, I. R. Rubin, and J. O. Osland (Englewood Cliffs, NJ: Prentice-Hall, 1991), 335–339.

4. See D. Lax and J. Sebenius, "Thinking Coalitionally," in *Negotiation Analysis*, ed. P. Young (Ann Arbor: University of Michigan Press, 1991).

5. See "Authority: Directed Deference," in R. B. Cialdini, *Influence: The Psychology of Persuasion* (New York: Quill, 1993). This book is an excellent introduction to the psychology of interpersonal persuasion, exploring key processes such as consistency and commitment. Lax and Sebenius (1991) term these "patterns of deference."

6. D. Krackhardt and J. R. Hanson, "Informal Networks: The Company behind the Chart," *Harvard Business Review* (July–August 1993): 104–111.

7. In their studies of the 1940 presidential election, Lazarfeld and his associates observed that voters were influenced both directly by information that they were exposed to and by the people who passed on the information or to whom they looked for guidance about "right thinking." The result was a "multistep-flow" model of opinion formation. See P. Lazarfeld, L. Bereson, and H. Gaudet, *The People's Choice: How the Voter Makes Up His Mind in a Presidential Campaign* (New York: Duell, Sloan, & Pearce, 1948). See also M. A. Milburn, *Persuasion and Politics: The Social Psychology of Public Opinion* (Pacific Grove, CA: Brooks/Cole, 1991), chap. 8.

8. A seminal early discussion of sources of power, including information, expertise, and social influence, is J. R. French and B. Raven, "The Bases of Social Power," in *Group Dynamics: Research and Theory*, ed. D. Cartwright and A. Zander (New York: Harper & Row, 1960). See also Kanter, who notes, "The enterprise required of innovating managers and professionals, then, is not the creative spark of genius that invents a new idea, but rather the skill with which they move outside the formal bonds of their job, maneuvering through and around the organization in sometimes risky, unique, and novel ways. . . . Organizational genius is 10 percent inspiration and 90 percent acquisition—acquisition of power to move beyond a formal job charter and to influence others. . . . Organizational power derives from supplies of three 'basic commodities' that can be invested in action: *information* (data, technical knowledge, political intelligence, expertise); *resources* (funds, materials, space, staff,

time); and *support* (endorsement, backing, approval, legitimacy)."
R. Kanter, *The Change Masters* (New York: Simon and Schuster,
1983), 216. For a comprehensive treatment of sources of power in
organizations, see J. Pfeffer, *Managing with Power: Politics and Influence in Organizations* (Boston, MA: Harvard Business School
Press, 1992), chaps. 4–9.

9. For an early discussion of problem-solving ability as a source of
power, see G. R. Salancik and J. Pfeffer, "Who Gets Power—And
How They Hold onto It: A Strategic-Contingency Model of Power,"
Organizational Dynamics (Winter 1977).

10. For a discussion of approaches to diagnosing power structures in organizations, see J. Pfeffer, *Managing with Power: Politics and Influence in Organizations* (Boston, MA: Harvard Business School Press,
1992), chap. 3.

11. For discussions of reasons why people resist change, and approaches
to dealing with them, see P. Lawrence, "How to Deal with Resistance
to Change," *Harvard Business Review* (January–February 1969):
Reprint 69107; R. M. Kanter, "Managing the Human Side of
Change," in *The Organizational Behavior Reader*, 5th ed., ed. D. A.
Kolb, I. R. Rubin, and J. O. Osland (Englewood Cliffs, NJ: Prentice-
Hall, 1991), 662–673; and J. P. Kotter and L. A. Schlesinger, "Choosing Strategies for Change," *Harvard Business Review* (March–April
1979): Reprint 79202.

12. For a discussion of the psychological contract that underpins organizations, see E. H. Schein, *Organizational Psychology*, 2d ed. (Englewood Cliffs, NJ: Prentice-Hall, 1970). See also P. Strebel, "Why Do
Employees Resist Change?" *Harvard Business Review* (May–June
1997): Reprint 96310. Strebel distinguishes formal, psychological,
and social dimensions of what he calls "personal compacts" between
employees and employers. The formal dimension encompasses basic
task definitions and performance requirements. The psychological dimension addresses implicit aspects of the relationship, such as expectations concerning loyalty. The social dimension consists of the
company's values and its relationships to key outside stakeholders,
such as local communities.

13. See "Reciprocity: The Old Give and Take . . . and Take," in R. B.
Cialdini, *Influence: The Psychology of Persuasion* (New York: Quill,
1993).

14. For a discussion of social influences on individual choice, see P. G.
Zimbardo and M. R. Lieppe, *The Psychology of Influence and Attitude Change* (New York: McGraw-Hill, 1991).

15. Ron Heifetz developed an analogy between managing change and applying heat to a pressure cooker. The key is to avoid having the pot blow up by keeping things at a steady simmer. See R. A. Heifetz, *Leadership without Easy Answers* (Cambridge, MA: Belknap Press of Harvard University Press, 1994), 128.

Part III: Managing Oneself

1. See R. A. Heifetz, *Leadership without Easy Answers* (Cambridge, MA: Belknap Press of Harvard University Press, 1994), especially Part IV: Staying Alive. See also A. Zaleznik, *Human Dilemmas of Leadership* (New York: Harper & Row, 1966), and A. Zaleznik and M. F. R. Kets de Vries, *Power and the Corporate Mind* (Boston: Houghton Mifflin, 1975).

Chapter 9: Self-Awareness and Style

1. In their work on stress and job change, Feldman and Brett describe this approach to self-management: "If increased uncertainty and job change are key variables that create stress in new jobs, then increased predictability and control are the key goals of coping strategies. When people feel they have little hope of reducing uncertainty or reasserting control, they are much more likely to develop feelings of helplessness and depression. . . . Most [people] also want to be able to reestablish routines that are predictable, regain their confidence about performing well on their new jobs, and reaffirm their sense of personal control in the work setting." D. C. Feldman and J. M. Brett. "Coping with New Jobs: A Comparative Study of New Hires and Job Changers," *Academy of Management Journal* 26, no. 2 (1983): 258–272.

2. For a framework for self-diagnosis, see P. Brouwer, "The Power to See Ourselves," *Harvard Business Review* (November–December 1964): 156–165. As Schein put it: "The most important thing for managers or consultants to understand is what goes on inside their own heads. If they cannot observe and assess their own feelings, biases, perceptual distortions, and impulses, they cannot tell whether their interventions are based on perceptions or reality, of what would really be helpful, or only on their own needs to express or defend themselves." See E. H. Schein, *Process Consultation: Lessons for Managers and Consultants,* vol. II (Reading MA: Addison-Wesley, 1987), 63.

3. For an interesting discussion of emotional blocks to action, see J. L. Adams, "Emotional Blocks," in *Readings in Managerial Psychology,* 4th ed., ed. H. J. Leavitt, L. R. Pondy, and D. M. Boje (Chicago: University of Chicago Press, 1989), 107–116.

4. Ross and Ward term this the *fundamental attribution error.* See L. Ross and R. E. Nisbett, *The Person and the Situation: Perspectives of Social Psychology* (New York: McGraw Hill, 1991), 87–88.

5. According to Plutarch, this saying was inscribed at the shrine of the oracle at Delphi.

6. J. J. Gabarro, *The Dynamics of Taking Charge* (Boston: Harvard Business School Press, 1987), 39–48.

7. Chris Argyris, "Teaching Smart People How to Learn," *Harvard Business Review* (May–June 1991): 99–109.

8. This distinction originated with Kolb and Fry, who developed an experiential learning model linked to stages of cognitive development. Learning is treated as a cycle consisting of four stages: concrete experience, reflective observation, abstract conceptualization, and active experimentation. To be maximally effective, people need all four capabilities. Kolb and Fry posit that these capabilities represent preferences or styles on two scales: the concrete experience–abstract conceptualization scale and the active experimentation–reflective observation scale. Based on this construct, they developed a matrix of learning styles: *converger* (preferring abstract conceptualization and active experimentation), *diverger* (concrete experience and reflective observation), *assimilator* (abstract conceptualization and reflective observation), and *accommodator* (concrete experience and active experimentation.) Our simplified version of this framework focuses on whether one prefers to be experiential (combining concrete experience and reflective observation) or conceptual (combining abstract conceptualization and active experimentation). See D. Kolb and R. Fry, "Toward an Applied Theory of Experiential Learning," in *Theories of Group Process,* ed. C. C. Cooper (New York: John Wiley & Sons, 1975); and D. M. Wolfe and D. A. Kolb, "Career Development, Personal Growth and Experiential Learning" in *The Organizational Behavior Reader,* 5th ed., ed. D. A. Kolb, I. R. Rubin, and J. O. Osland (Englewood Cliffs, NJ: Prentice-Hall, 1991), 145–176. Kolb created a diagnostic questionnaire for assessing learning styles; see D. A. Kolb, *The Learning Style Inventory: Technical Manual* (Boston, MA: McBer & Co., 1976).

9. These categories were proposed by Alex George. See A. L. George, *Presidential Decision-Making in Foreign Policy: The Effective Use of*

Information and Advice (Boulder, CO: Westview Press, 1980), chap. 8.

10. Vroom and Yetton created a mechanism for determining which decision style suits a particular situation, depending on the quality, speed, and acceptance it requires. See V. Vroom and P. W. Yetton, *Leadership and Decision-Making* (Pittsburgh: University of Pittsburgh Press, 1973). For a very good hands-on guide to managing team decision making and problem solving, see T. A. Kayser, *Building Team Power: How to Unleash the Collaborative Genius of Work Teams* (Burr Ridge, IL: Irwin, 1994).

11. For an interesting discussion of motivational style, see D. C. McClelland and D. H. Burnham, "Power Is the Great Motivator," *Harvard Business Review* (January–February 1995): 126–139.

Chapter 10: Advice and Counsel

1. R. A. Heifetz, *Leadership without Easy Answers* (Cambridge, MA: Belknap Press of Harvard University Press, 1994), 251.

2. The theoretical basis and inspiration for much of what follows is in Alan Rush, "Advice and Counsel in Management." (Ph.D. diss., Graduate School of Business, Stanford University, 1981).

3. Research has examined the characteristics of helping relationships. See C. Rogers, *On Becoming a Person* (Cambridge, MA: Riverside Press, 1961), and D. Kolb and R. E. Boyatzis, "On the Dynamics of the Helping Relationship," *Readings in Managerial Psychology,* 4th ed., in ed. H. J. Leavitt, L. R. Pondy, and D. M. Boje (Chicago: University of Chicago Press, 1989), 234–252. Some work has also been done on choosing and working with a consultant; see, for example, R. R. Blake and J. G. Mouton, *Consultation: A Handbook for Individuals and Organization Development,* 2d ed. (Reading MA: Addison-Wesley, 1989). There is, of course, a vast literature on therapeutic relationships, and substantial work has been done on presidential decision making and the role of advice. See, for example, A. L. George, *Presidential Decision-Making in Foreign Policy: The Effective Use of Information and Advice* (Boulder, CO: Westview Press, 1980).

4. N. Machiavelli, *The Prince* (New York: Penguin Books, 1961), 126.

5. *Herodotus,* trans. by K. Cavander (Greenwich, CT: Premier Books, 1962), 27–28.

6. P. Ward, "On the King's Taking Counsel." Paper prepared for the National Council on Religion in Higher Education, 1958.

7. F. Bacon, *Essays* (New York: Hurst & Co., 1983).

8. R. Burke, "Dole, Ignoring His Advisors, Lashes Out," *The New York Times,* 12 June 1996.

9. C. M. Clifford and R. C. Holbrooke, *Counsel to the President: A Memoir* (New York: Random House, 1991), 423.

10. Ibid., 424.

11. For a brilliant account of presidential decision making during this crucial period, see E. R. May and P. D. Zelikow, eds., *The Kennedy Tapes: Inside the White House during the Cuban Missile Crisis* (Cambridge, MA: Harvard Univeristy Press, 1997).

12. Clifford and Holbrooke, *Counsel to the President,* 81.

13. For more on President and Mrs. Truman's relationship and her role as counselor, see D. McCullough, *Truman* (New York: Simon & Schuster, 1992).

14. Describing the key lessons of Vietnam, Robert McNamara writes, "Our misjudgments of friend and foe alike reflected our profound ignorance of the history, culture, and politics of the people of the area, and the personalities and habits of their leaders. We might have made similar misjudgments regarding the Soviets during our frequent confrontations . . . had we not had the advice of [senior diplomats who] had spent decades studying the Soviet Union, its people and its leaders, why they behaved as they did, and how they would react to our actions. Their advice proved invaluable in shaping our judgments and decisions. No Southeast Asian counterparts existed for senior officials to consult when making decisions on Vietnam." R. McNamara, *In Retrospect* (New York: Times Books, 1995), 322.

15. See George, *Presidential Decision-Making in Foreign Policy,* chap. 3.

16. For Clark Clifford's account of his role as presidential counselor, see Clifford and Holbrooke, *Counsel to the President.*

17. Machiavelli, *Prince,* 124.

Recommended Reading

Articles

Argyris, C. "Teaching Smart People How to Learn." *Harvard Business Review* (May–June 1991): 99–109. (Reprint 91301.)

Brouwer, P. J. "The Power to See Ourselves." *Harvard Business Review* (November–December 1964): 156–165. (Reprint 64602.)

Ciampa, D. "Managers as Change Agents." In *Strategic Manufacturing: Dynamic New Directors for the 1990s,* edited by P. Moody. Homewood, IL: Dow Jones-Irwin, 1990.

Ciampa, D. "Common Vision Leadership." In *Total Quality: A Users' Guide for Implementation,* edited by D. Ciampa. Reading, MA: Addison-Wesley, 1991.

Harris, O. "A Primer for Polemicists." *Commentary* 78, no. 3 (September 1984).

Hsieh, T., and S. Bear. "Managing CEO Transitions." *McKinsey Quarterly* 2 (1994).

Kim, W. C., and R. Mauborgne. "Fair Process: Managing in the Knowledge Economy." *Harvard Business Review* (July–August 1997): 65–75. (Reprint 97405.)

Rogers, C., and F. J. Roethlisberger. "Barriers and Gateways to Communication." *Harvard Business Review* (July–August 1952), reissued November–December 1991: 105–111. (Reprint 91610.)

Sherman, S. "How Tomorrow's Best Leaders Are Learning Their Stuff." *Fortune,* 27 November 1995.

Upton, D. M., and S. E. Macadam. "Why (and How) to Take a Plant Tour." *Harvard Business Review* (May–June 1997): 97–106. (Reprint 97310.)

Waldroop J., and T. Bulter, "The Executive as Coach." *Harvard Business Review* (November–December 1996): 111–117. (Reprint 96611.)

"A President Who Wasn't Afraid to Lead." *The Wall Street Journal,* 11 August 1997.

Books

Cialdini, R. B. *Influence: The Psychology of Persuasion.* New York: William Morrow, 1984.

Drucker, P. *Managing in a Time of Great Change.* New York: Truman Talley Books/Dutton, 1995.

Finkelstein, S., and D. Hambrick. *Strategic Leadership: Top Executives and Their Effects on Organizations.* Minneapolis/St. Paul: West Publishing, 1996.

Gabarro, J. J. *The Dynamics of Taking Charge.* Boston: Harvard Business School Press, 1987.

Hass, H. *The Leader Within: An Empowering Path of Self-Discovery.* New York: HarperBusiness, 1992.

Heifetz, R. A. *Leadership without Easy Answers.* Cambridge, MA: Belknap Press of Harvard University Press, 1994.

Jay, A. *Management and Machiavelli: An Inquiry into the Politics of Corporate Life.* New York: Holt, Rinehart and Winston, 1967.

Kaplan, R. E. *Beyond Ambition: How Driven Managers Can Lead Better and Live Better.* San Francisco: Jossey-Bass, 1991.

Schein, E. H. *Organizational Culture and Leadership,* 2d ed. San Francisco: Jossey-Bass, 1992.

Senge, P. M. *The Fifth Discipline: The Art and Practice of the Learning Organization.* New York: Doubleday, 1990.

Sonnenfeld, J. A. *The Hero's Farewell: What Happens When CEOs Retire.* New York: Oxford University Press, 1988.

Steiner, G. *The New CEO.* New York: Macmillan, 1983.

Tichy, N. M., and M. A. Devanna. *The Transformational Leader.* New York: John Wiley & Sons, 1986.

Ury, W. *Getting Past No: Negotiating Your Way from Confrontations to Cooperation*. New York: Bantam Books, 1991.

Watson, T. *Father, Son & Co.: My Life at IBM and Beyond*. New York: Bantam Books, 1990.

Zaleznick, A. *Learning Leadership: Cases and Commentaries on Abuses of Power in Organizations*. Chicago: Bonus Books, 1998.

Index

About the Authors

Dan Ciampa is an advisor and a counselor to leaders (particularly during their transitions) who must improve overall organizational performance and also change the corporate culture to sustain it. At Rath & Strong, Inc., from 1972 to 1996, he consulted on leadership challenges and operations improvement with leading manufacturing, consumer packaged goods, financial services, and pharmaceutical companies. He led the first successful integration of organization development and technical problem solving, participated in the introduction to the United States of total quality management and lean manufacturing, and chaired cross-industry collaboration groups such as the Automation Forum. From 1984 to 1996, he served as Rath & Strong's Chairman & CEO. Ciampa currently serves on the boards of NAC Reinsurance Corporation, Delta Rubber Company, Union College, National Public Radio Foundation, the American Health Foundation, the Health Priorities Project of the Progressive Policy Institute, and the Heart Leadership Program at Duke University. He is the author of two previous books and numerous articles.

Michael Watkins is an associate professor of business administration at the Harvard Business School, where he is a member of
the Negotiation and Decision Making faculty group. His research
and consulting focus on negotiation and persuasion, exploring
how leaders build coalitions to transform their organizations and
to shape the external environment. In addition to his work on taking charge, he teaches corporate diplomacy, a course about how
top managers negotiate joint ventures and alliances, manage the
press, work with analysts, and influence government. In addition,
he is a faculty member of the Program on Negotiation at Harvard
Law School, where he teaches negotiation in the Senior Executive
Program. Prior to joining the Harvard Business School, Watkins
was an associate professor of public policy at Harvard's Kennedy
School of Government, where he taught negotiation and persuasion and did research on international diplomacy and the management of organizational change. He is the author or co-author of
numerous articles and case studies on complex negotiations within
and among businesses and governments.